Joan
with much love
and my prayers that,
will bless and comfor
with His love and p
                    Alan Gaius

HEALING WOUNDS
in the FIELD HOSPITAL
of the CHURCH

This collection of the papers shared at the symposium in Oscott College during 2015 offers the reader an invaluable insight into the gift of healing that God has entrusted to the Church. Each chapter, offering a different aspect of the healing ministry, reflects on lived experiences of the contributor that witness to the power of God to renew and transform people's lives in the world today.

I am most grateful to Professor Alan Guile and Fr Jim McManus CSsR for assembling this timely and welcome contribution to a wider understanding of the healing ministry. I know it will benefit priests, deacons and lay faithful in their pastoral outreach to others.

Most Rev Bernard Longley, Archbishop of Birmingham

Shakespeare's Hamlet was deeply troubled by 'the slings and arrows of outrageous fortune'. We all have our share of these hidden wounds. This collection of essays by practitioners of Christian healing, demonstrates how prayer and sacraments have brought renewal of body and soul to a vast variety of sufferers. Written primarily from a Roman Catholic viewpoint, it is generously ecumenical in spirit. I echo its passionate plea for the advancement of the healing ministry across the Church.

Most Rev John Sentamu, Archbishop of York

This book covers Deliverance and Healing of childhood abuse, addictions and ailments resulting from our broken society with sensitivity. It emphasises the need for training: Priests to recognise the gifts of lay people and use them; Lay sick-visitors and Eucharistic ministers to pray, discern and listen so as to become an invaluable resource in the healing ministry of the church. You may like some things clarified and others expanded but the book covers a most important area of ministry and evangelisation.

Rt Rev Seamus Cunningham, Bishop of Hexham and Newcastle

Alan Guile and others offer rich fare in terms of the ministry of healing and venture into areas largely untouched, and even unrecognised, as being within its scope. As well as his own extensive involvement and close co-operation with bishops and clergy he has drawn on the experience and skills of those who have worked in specific areas of this ministry.

Rt Rev Alan Hopes, Bishop of East Anglia

The Gospels relate many encounters between Our Blessed Lord and those individuals who come to Him for healing. A common characteristic of the Divine Physician's ministry is to heal those wounds which rob individuals of peace: '*Your faith has saved you. Go, in peace*'. I commend to you, *Healing Wounds in the Field Hospital of the Church*, which brings to the fore the multifaceted nature of the Church's healing ministry and the gift of peace it brings to people's lives.

Rt Rev Marcus Stock, Bishop of Leeds

So many people are hurting, feeling damaged and rejected; so many know that they have caused hurt, damaged and rejected others; so many wonder where to turn for help, advice and healing. The healing power of Christ can reconcile, make whole and gather into one all those who are willing to receive the gifts of His Spirit. It is so good that these issues are discussed and brought to light and I am grateful that this publication leads us yet one more step along the road to the wholeness that Christ brings.

Rt Rev Terence Drainey, Bishop of Middlesbrough

This book is a valuable resource to help the healing of people who have been damaged by life's circumstances. The contributors to this collection of essays are experts who bring together knowledge and praxis in ways that have enabled people to find peace through the power of God's grace and the support of others. It will help many people and serve Pope Francis' invitation that the Church should be like a field-hospital to help people find again the joy of Christ's love.

The Rt Revd John Sherrington, Auxiliary Bishop of Westminster

That Jesus in his own lifetime was regarded as a healer, by friend and foe alike, is amongst the best attested facts we know about him. The restoration of health—in Latin, *salus*, from which we get 'salvation'— might well be taken as the single most appropriate category in which to understand the entire work of Jesus, ranging across spiritual bondage, physical and psychological illness, and social and cultural marginalisation. However, for all this centrality of Christ's ministry of healing in our tradition, we hear relatively little about it as a core activity within the Catholic Church. This volume of pastorally-rooted essays helpfully seeks to redress the balance. Drawing, in some cases, on more than 40 years relevant experience of a wide-range of pastoral contexts and needs, the editors provide a resource-book in service of Pope Francis's appeal for the Church to be like a 'field hospital' ministering to the wounds of the world where they are to be found.

Professor Paul D Murray,
Professor of Systematic Theology and Director of the Centre for Catholic Studies, Durham University

Fr Jim McManus CSsR and Professor Alan Guile's new book illuminates and honours the stories of those in the Church for whom the healing ministry is both a lived experience and daily practice. Each chapter offers a most telling and profound way of describing, through a series of personal testimonies, how the concept of 'New Evangelisation' is practised and experienced in different settings and contexts, and with those in churches and communities. The 'practise' of evangelisation and healing is revealed. The testimonies give voice to the words: 'whatever good we do, it is Christ who does it by us'.

As each chapter unfolds, the sense of the healing ministries in action belongs to the many, all followers of Christ, while honouring the 'special' place of the priest. Through witness, we are invited to relive the Church's practice and belief in the power of 'prayer of petition'. Prayer is evidenced by each practitioner as more than simply articulating 'hope', but rather an invitation for the Holy Spirit's intervention. Put simply, 'the witness of those Christians, whose lives are filled with the hope of Christ, opens the hearts and minds of those around them to Christ.'

This book provides a voice for those in the healing ministries to evidence through practice the powerful good they can offer the Church. Whilst each chapter presents a profound set of different experiences of 'practising' healing, the book overall provides a foundation on which to research and develop further a critical understanding and knowledge of New Evangelisation in practice. In this way, we can learn from, as well as provide skilled support and development for, those working in the 'field hospital'. The book recognises the unfailing commitment and dedication of those practitioners contributing to the Church's healing mission; for, as one writer states: 'Those who are seeking God's guidance and help and those who are supported in prayer, heal more quickly and more completely.'

Professor Elizabeth L Leo, School of Education, Durham University

HEALING WOUNDS
in the FIELD HOSPITAL
of the CHURCH

Edited by
Alan Guile
and
Fr Jim McManus CSsR

GRACEWING

First published in England in 2017
by
Gracewing
2 Southern Avenue
Leominster
Herefordshire HR6 0QF
United Kingdom
www.gracewing.co.uk

ISBN 978 085244 918 9

Imprimi potest: Very Rev. Ronald J. McAinsh, CSsR, Provincial Superior,
London Province, Congregation of the Most Holy Redeemer.

Typeset by Gracewing

Cover design by Bernardita Peña Hurtado, back cover image by Judy McLain

CONTENTS

Contents

Contents

19: THE HEALING ROLE OF PEER SUPPORT AND FORGIVENESS FOLLOWING A HOMICIDE Barry Mizen..283

20: HEALING AND PARISH LIFE Kathryn Turner..................293

PREFACE

One of the key concerns in the witness and the writings of Pope Francis is the way in which the Church ministers to individuals, particularly those in need of healing and forgiveness. The Year of Mercy was all about that and it was intended to shape the way in which the Church perceives and responds to the various kinds of trouble that are part of the human condition. The Doctrinal Commission of the International Catholic Charismatic Renewal Services (ICCRS) will shortly be publishing an important document on Deliverance Ministry which is a sensitive but very important dimension of this ministry as, of course, it was of the ministry of Jesus Christ. But that is just one of the many aspects of the Church's outreach to human need and human suffering that are dealt with in this volume. Some dimensions of this ministry are much more integral to the ministry of the Church in the developing nations than they are in Europe. For Catholics who come to Britain from Africa and Asia this can be one of the ways in which the Church here can seem very different.

This book opens up this whole dimension of the Church's ministry. I hope it will be a useful resource and I also hope it will stimulate thought and reflection on the role and profile of the Catholic Church in the world of today.

✠ Archbishop Kevin McDonald,
Liaison Bishop for the Catholic Charismatic Renewal in England and Wales

FOREWORD

In an interview in 2013, Pope Francis referred to the Church as 'a field hospital after a battle'. Pope Francis' vision of the Church is a clear recognition and acknowledgement that people within the Church often have wounds, even though we cannot see them. These wounds sometimes have an effect that hampers a full, free and joyful relationship with God in the Church. It is Pope Francis' hope that those in such need will find the healing they require with the 'medicine of mercy' in the Church. It is this vision of the Church of Pope Francis that was the inspiration for a Symposium that took place in St Mary's College, Oscott in April 2015. The content of the Symposium is to be found in this collection of all the papers that were considered during those days.

The book brings together a breadth of experience and depth of pastoral approach of lay people and priests who are at present ministering to people in a variety of different and often difficult and painful situations.

I recently gave my first Parish Mission since I became a bishop. For a number of years now the opening service of the Redemptorist mission has been a Healing Service. It was the best attended of the Mission Week, as it often is. This is indicative, I think, of the recognition of a real need of those attending the mission for healing in some aspect of their lives, and the belief that the Church is the place where that healing can be found through the ministry of prayer for healing and the sacraments. My experience of participating in the Healing Service, once again in the context of Parish Mission, has been a reminder to me why, perhaps, as one of the contributors remarks, 'There is an urgent pastoral need to provide all priests and lay ministers with the opportunity to learn more about the healing ministry'. This book provides such an opportunity.

The book is timely, therefore, and I am sure it will give both greater confidence to those priests and lay people who are already engaged in the healing ministry in any way in our parishes, schools, colleges, universities and prisons, and encourage others to 'put out into the deep'.

I highly recommend this book.

✠ Ralph Heskett CSsR
Bishop of Hallam

SCOPE AND THEME

Chapter 1

The book opens with an overview of liturgical prayers in the Church for the healing of the whole person, by a priest who has taught and ministered to many people and published books on healing for over forty years. He calls upon seminaries to prepare future priests well for their ministry of healing, noting that at present most of them do not introduce their students to this ministry. He applauds Oscott College for having begun to provide its students with various opportunities to familiarise themselves with some aspects. He reminds the Church that healing, particularly inner healing, in accord with calls of Pope Francis, should be seen as a normal ministry of any parish.

Chapter 2

This theme is continued and amplified in chapter 2, written by a layman who also has worked in the inner healing ministry for over forty years, for most of which he has been available at any time of the week. This ministry is shown to be an essential part of the mission given by Christ in the Scriptures, and closely connected to The New Evangelisation. Some of over 550 people who have come to his home travelled very long distances, even hundreds of miles, because there was no known and reliable ministry in their locality. The three underlying areas of roots before the age of about seven, which need to be healed by Christ in prayer are discussed. In order for more lay people to become called and ready for this ministry, there needs to be more awareness and openness in priests and bishops.

Chapter 3

The same author examines many aspects of this last point in the previous chapter. There are many factors which play a part in people who are hurting being unable to get all of the help which they need from their priests. This leads on to discussion of aspects which if possible should be considered for inclusion in the seminaries. Much of this ministry will always fall on the laity, partly because of the heavy loads of the priests, but the latter need to discern, recognise and foster the giftedness and calling in some in their congregation. This is all part of the challenge towards deeper spirituality in growing relationship with Christ for each individual, and there is a great need to encourage this within small Christ—centred groups within a parish. The lack of teaching about spiritual warfare and of warnings of dangers such as occult practices and of proclaiming the authority of Christ over all sources of evil is deplored.

Chapter 4

This chapter, written by a very experienced diocesan exorcist picks up this latter area of inner healing, namely the freeing of people from evil spirits. He makes a strong case for more attention to be given to this ministry, partly because some bishops and priests do not see the need for it at all. He appeals to bishops to be more open to the need for deliverance and exorcism as recent Popes have stressed. He writes of how some bishops, priests, theologians and other scholars argue that those delivered of evil spirits by Christ had some mental illness. As a result priests may cause severe, even horrendous suffering by advising someone to visit their doctor, when in fact they need prayer for deliverance. Again the need emerges for teaching and training in seminaries to cover vital aspects required for priesthood.

Chapter 5

This chapter is written by the Rector of Oscott College who first suggested that a symposium might be held there. He discusses four strands of formation:

- Intellectual—aiming at the renewing of mind (Rm 12:2)
- Spiritual—deepening personal relationship with God through prayer
- Pastoral—developing gifts and skills
- Human—personal growth to become the person created by God

All of these contribute to the journey of inner healing which must take place if a man is to respond to the demands of seminary training. Developments in recent years at Oscott College include teaching on healing and deliverance, and providing opportunities for prayer for healing, including students praying with other students for inner healing.

Chapter 6

Before going on to consider areas and conditions in life which need healing, an important question is posed (which can have wider significance than in healing alone), It is this—'Is the Church, only too frequently, unconsciously failing to get the right balance between dependence upon those human resources which God allows and enables us to develop and direct dependence upon the loving merciful power of God?' Reference to this has already been noted in chapter 4 with regard to mental health treatment or prayer for deliverance. Can there be traces of this in seminary training when pressure for theological and philosophical studies squeeze out pastoral aspects and experience of our ultimate but also immediate reliance on God? Does the Church, too often encourage those, whether priests, sisters or laity, who are in some form of distress to turn primarily (or even almost entirely) to those with professional qualifications?

Chapter 7

Having established a general foundation in the first six chapters, attention now turns to areas which may need healing, beginning with harmful bonds and patterns from past generations which can start to exert influences once one is conceived and then on to other aspects occurring through life until one dies. A book published in 1982 by a psychiatrist brought out the vital role of prayer at a Mass, celebrated particularly for all past, present and future family members, so as to free them from damaged patterns of behaviour and experiences in earlier generations. This led two priests to write books recommending that this means of healing should be more available. Sadly very few priests have responded and celebrated Mass with this intention in the years since then. When such a Mass is advertised in the parish of the author, the congregation rises from under 30 to 60—110, with some travelling long distances. It is recommended that a serious study should be commissioned by bishops, so that priests and seminarians as well as lay people can recognise and benefit from the great blessings which God can give to families.

Chapter 8

The need for prayers for Christ to heal the child at conception, in the womb and at birth, which includes any threat to its life by consideration of abortion is discussed in Chapter 2. Chapter 8 has been written by a lady who for decades has worked with women struggling with the decision about whether or not to have an abortion, or who years later are trying to deal with deep distress that they agreed to it, and who may be experiencing physical, psychological and emotional consequences. She has long been at the forefront of listening to and praying with these suffering women, but has also been listening to and teaching young people, so that this is a detailed examination of the issues, written by an acknowledged expert practitioner. Although abortion is arguably the most common medical procedure in the world, most of the public know little or nothing of the realities and how great the impact can be on mothers, fathers, grandparents and society in general.

Chapter 9

Chapter 2 explained the need to pray for Christ to heal all root causes of hurt in babyhood and childhood up to age seven or eight. Chapter 9 begins with a *cri de coeur* for there to be people who will give sufficient time to listen to children who are suffering deep emotional pain, and then to pray with them for Christ to heal all roots of hurt, loss, rejection and so on. This can help them to develop a personal relationship with Christ and to receive growing trust that He loves them and can bring healing and peace through their later life. If this can be done whilst they are still children, their subsequent life and choices and relationships can be much more likely to be positive and happy. This heartfelt cry was written years ago by a lady whose testimony in chapter 13 tells of childhood sexual abuse by several people and of three abortions before she was twenty. Chapter 9 looks at some of the ways in which it has been found possible to overcome the difficulties of finding safe and sensitive ways to help children to share their painful feelings with other children who suffer similarly, and be ready to receive inner healing prayer ministry.

Chapter 10

The need to help others to receive healing in and through marriage is discussed by a couple whose own journey of being healed and becoming 'wounded healers' began at a Marriage Encounter weekend almost forty years ago. They learned how their married love is important to the Church in its mission of seeking out lost souls, and they began to help other couples to learn and experience this privilege. This led them to turn part of their offices and later they own home into a Christian centre, where couples could come and even stay for a weekend, in order to review and refresh their own marriages. An appendix to this chapter connects with what appears in chapter 2 concerning bitter root judgements and bitter root expectancy, and explains how these frequently play a very significant role in stresses within marriage and so need prayer for healing.

Chapter 11

Sadly some marriages come to a premature end through death, separation or divorce. Chapter 11 describes how one particular approach which has been developed within the Church has brought together men and women who have lost a spouse in one of these ways. As they meet and gain trust and courage to share their pain and they listen to the stories of each one, they grow in compassion for one another and their prayers can begin to bring deeper and deeper inner healing. This can happen during a series of evening meetings as they work through a structured programme, and then spend one or more weekends together in a retreat centre. This is then followed up by a variety of ways in which ongoing support and friendship are offered and developed. Personal testimonies are woven into the outline of this process which is given in this chapter.

Chapter 12

This is written by a lady who works in a hospice as a qualified counsellor and who considers the vital work of being with the dying and helping them and their family. She begins by sharing how her own experiences of a damaged childhood and broken family, led her as a child into a deepening relationship with and dependence upon Christ, which has formed the basis for the work which she now does. Even dying patients in whose lives God has previously had no place, may eventually want to talk about God, and may even ask for a chaplain, because as they come closer to death they somehow become ready to reach out to a God whom they didn't know. Her ministry also involves bereaved adults and the special needs of bereaved children. A testimony is included of a senior nurse who cared for the dying both in hospital and in a hospice, and who had moving experiences of praying with them.

Chapter 13

At this stage we move from general aspects of prayer from before conception through life to death, and begin to consider how Christ can heal some of the specific areas of damage which may occur during a lifetime. Sadly a very substantial number of the women who have been coming for prayer ministry to the home referred to in Chapter 2 have revealed that they are victims of sexual abuse, whereas the proportion of men is very small. Only a woman who has herself been desperately hurt in this way, can begin to understand the depths of pain and the long-lasting damage which other women have to live with. There is very great need of more people to be called by God to listen and to pray for Jesus to bring healing and the grace with which forgiveness is possible. Though this chapter was written by a man, help in the writing was given by a lady who was a victim and who contributed insights into how both the emotional life and the spiritual life can be gravely affected for many years until the healing power of Christ is invited in through ongoing prayer ministry which may take a long time. A first-hand a testimony of another victim is included.

Chapter 14

Some of those who experience childhood sexual abuse and other deep hurts may need prayer ministry for Christ to heal wounds hidden behind dissociative identity disorder (DID), formerly known as multiple personality disorder. Chapter 14 begins by outlining how some people may be so severely traumatised in childhood that they learn to escape internally by their minds splitting into separate parts (or 'alters', alternative personalities). The stories are summarised of four women, three of them taken from books in which they wrote these stories and one who wrote for the present work (see Appendix 1). The damage can be so deep that full healing may take as much as ten years of powerful prayer ministry attending regular sessions, perhaps residentially at times. However they can then be used by God in wonderful ways to bring healing to other sufferers.

Chapter 15

This tells of an unexpected call from God to reach out to suffering people, when the author and others in obedience to God began to go out to women involved in street-based prostitution, some of whom had been victims of sexual abuse in childhood. Those called to help them had to learn that however much they longed for the women to leave this way of life, they could only show love and care for them and wait for them to come to the decision for themselves. Sometimes they have had the joy of witnessing a wonderful change in someone's life as they invite God to come to their help. They persist in sowing seeds of God's love and care and praying for God's blessing in their certain faith that He knows and loves each one of the women.

Chapter 16

Like the previous chapter, this gives an inspiring example of how the Lord may surprise anyone He chooses by calling them into an area of healing into which they would never have dreamt of setting foot. In this case it was a totally unexpected and at first unwanted summons by God to go into prisons to lead a meditation group. The lives of women prisoners, some of whom were convicted murderers, changed wonderfully. This led to her being appointed as a chaplain to the whole prison, so that she now met and prayed with male prisoners as well as female ones. The plight of prisoners and many moving experiences gave her a deep longing to help ex-offenders. She established a charity to help them after release from prison and was nationally honoured for her work.

Chapter 17

This is written by a priest who obtained his bishop's permission to live for four months alongside the addicts in one of the 60 Cenacolo Communities, run entirely by themselves, established by Mother Elvira over the last 30 years. Though not himself an addict and known to be a priest, he was accepted by them as another person in need of healing and of knowing the love of Jesus on a new and more profound level which was not superficial, safe or comfortable. He writes that these most broken of God's children will evangelise the world in a most profound way, as he himself saw happen when they gave testimonies of God's love and healing to pilgrims when they went out on mission. He also writes 'this was the most honest and humble way of discovery and truthful healing of self and others that I have ever encountered in my life—surely a most profound way to train seminarians?'

Chapter 18

The previous chapter describes the ultimate healing power that God can bring through people living in community for long periods. This is not available for most people, but chapter 18 shows that substantial numbers seek to live within a community-type setting for a few days so that they can seek healing from God. Chapter 14 also brought out the need for residential ministry for one acute condition. There is no Catholic residential centre in the UK wholly devoted the healing ministry whereas there are a number of these centres, some very large, run by other Christians. Information given here shows that around 5,000 people a year make residential visits of some days duration to these latter centres, seeking prayer ministry for healing. There is need for a Catholic centre for healing both for ministry and to train people to listen and pray with others who are in need of healing of various kinds.

Chapter 19

This is written by a father whose 16-year-old son was murdered in 2008. He tells the story of that dreadful day and how he, his wife and their other children have handled that grief. He stresses the need for the healing power of peer support. Within two weeks of their own son's death, they had reached out to another family immediately after they in turn were bereaved. In this and all the other many ways in which their family are involved, including a foundation in the name of the son, talks in churches and schools and many other activities, they experience Christ walking with them and others who are in pain. He writes very movingly about the struggles of forgiveness.

Chapter 20

This is written by the Head of the Department of Spirituality of a diocese who begins with the recovery of more of the mission to heal given by Christ, through charismatic renewal and the renaming of the Sacrament of Extreme Unction. She examines blocks and fears which impede progress in understanding and experiencing more of Christ's power to heal. The need for support and the right kind of supervision is addressed. Extensive experiences in one diocese of Liturgies of Mercy during the Jubilee Year are described, including the Word of God, listening to and praying with others, anointing with the oil of gladness, the Sacrament of Reconciliation and the use of objects in a simple ritual. There are signs that the wider church is gradually reclaiming the gift of healing left to her by Christ, and which should become part of the normal work and outreach of parishes.

Appendix 1

Is the Church listening to the cries of the wounded? This gives the first-hand account of a lady, deeply hurt by sexual abuse in childhood and by a dysfunctional family, who began to ask for help from priests and others in the church well over thirty years ago. The kind of comments she received included 'you will get out of it—pray about it?'

Appendix 2

This is a first-hand account of a young man who became deeply involved with drugs and alcohol until he cried out to God and went first to the Cenacolo community in Florida and then to the one in Lourdes. There he went through the darkest period of his life until he opened up all his emotions to his father and became reconciled with him. Later he became reconciled with his mother.

INTRODUCTION

Pope Francis loves to compare the Church to a 'field hospital after battle'. He keeps insisting that the first duty of the Church is to heal the wounds that have been inflicted, by unkind words or unjust deeds, on her members. In response to his enthusiasm for the healing mission of the Church we invited a number of men and women to a Symposium on the Healing Ministry held in Oscott College, the seminary for the Archdiocese of Birmingham, from 29 April to 1 May 2015. In preparation for the Symposium we asked some of them and certain others to write papers on their understanding of the healing ministry and their experience of working in 'the field hospital' in their parishes or dioceses.

Our aim in holding the Symposium was to focus on the healing mission of the Church and on the many different ways in which members of the Church are seeking to bring the experience of healing to others. Twelve priests, twelve lay people and four religious Sisters participated in the Symposium. They shared their experience of praying with people in need of healing and they also shared their experience of the lack of an active healing ministry in many parishes. Fr Jim McManus CSsR wrote a report of the Symposium which was agreed by all the participants and published in the Pastoral Review. This report appears immediately following this Introduction.

Because the healing ministry is a pastoral ministry, and not a theological theory, we were not looking for theological experts. We invited participants who were involved in bringing the healing love of Christ to those to whom they ministered. We all learned from the experiences of each other of how the Lord brings His healing, in so many different ways, to His wounded brothers and sisters. We believe that you too will learn from their experience. That is why we are now publishing the papers which were written for the Symposium, together with three written later. It is our hope that the book will contribute to the integration of healing into normal parish life and outreach.

There is a multitude of ways in which humanity and society have become deeply damaged and corrupted. We do not claim that all the areas in which the human heart needs inner healing are covered in this book. But, because we believe that there is no limit to the power of God to meet every human need and bind up every broken heart, we think the specific ways in which the participants in our Symposium carry out their healing ministry may be helpful to you in reflecting on your own pastoral ministry. It is our hope that as you read through the chapters of this book you will discuss the great variety of approaches to the healing ministry with others and in this way spread the good news that God is in our midst and we can turn to Him at any time for His mercy and healing.

We gratefully acknowledge both the welcome given to the idea of this book by Canon David Oakley and his suggestion of preceding it with a symposium at Oscott College. We thank all those who attended it and those who wrote the chapters. We are particularly indebted to David Mackintosh who patiently spent many hours with one of us at the computer.

Alan Guile and Jim McManus CSsR

Oscott Symposium on the Healing Ministry

29 April—1 May 2015

Report

Fr Jim McManus CSsR

Pope Francis' image of the Church as 'a field hospital' provided the vision for our Symposium. This is a powerful image which communicates with people at great depth. But how can we share his vision when he says, 'I see clearly that the thing the church needs most today is the ability to heal wounds and to warm the hearts of the faithful; it needs nearness, proximity'.[1] His colourful expressions have made us all more aware that the healing ministry is an essential component of the Church's mission in the world. Thirty years ago the Holy See was already asking the whole Church to take the healing ministry more seriously. In its document on how to meet the challenges of so many Catholics leaving the Catholic Church to join Pentecostal Churches and Sects the Holy See said, 'Special attention must be given to the healing ministry through prayers, reconciliation, fellowship and care. Our pastoral concern should not be one-dimensional. It should extend not only to the spiritual, but also to the physical, psychological, social, cultural, economic, and political dimensions'.[2] This was a very helpful statement at the time. But now the Pope himself sees in the healing ministry the Church's first response to many of the pastoral needs of the faithful. As he says, 'It is useless to ask a seriously injured person if he has high cholesterol and about the level of his blood sugars! You have to heal his wounds. Then we can talk about everything else'.[3] This call of Pope Francis will encourage bishops, priests and lay ministers to see in the healing ministry the manifestation of God's love and care for His people.

The Symposium gratefully recognises that great healing, often under a different description, takes place in the ordinary day life of the parish. The liturgy is well celebrated, the sick and the housebound are visited by Eucharistic ministers, and priests called to celebrate the sacrament of

Anointing. In the celebration of Reconciliation many people are healed of what Blessed Paul VI, in his new Rite of Penance, called 'the wounds of sin' and experience a new inner freedom and peace. And, of course, in the celebration of the Sunday Mass people, often without mentioning it, 'unload all the worries onto the Lord who has care for them'. (1 P 5: 14).

Those who celebrate the liturgy in our parishes, therefore, should experience the healing power of the sacraments, especially of the Eucharist. As the Catechism of the Catholic Church teaches:

> The Eucharist is the 'source and summit of the Christian life. The other sacraments, and indeed all ecclesiastical ministries and works of the apostolate, are bound up with the Eucharist and are orientated to it. For in the blessed Eucharist is contained the whole spiritual good of the Church, namely Christ himself, our Pasch.[4]

During our discussions and sharing in the symposium we became even more aware that the ministry of prayer for healing, especially inner healing, could play a much more significant role in the pastoral ministry of the parish and in the consciousness of priests and people. The approach of the Jubilee of the Year of Mercy provides us with a providential opportunity to develop new approaches to this ministry in the life of our parishes and dioceses.

The Bishop's Pastoral Leadership

We are living in a *kairos* moment in the life of our Church. This should give our bishops great confidence that the Holy Spirit is endowing the faithful with the graces and charisms necessary for the new evangelisation. We felt as a symposium that priests and lay ministers urgently need the encouragement of their bishops to step out in faith and 'heal the wounds' that can fester in the lives of parishioners and witness to Christ's healing love for all people.

We are aware that some priests would benefit from pastoral study days on the healing ministry when they would have the opportunity to see how their ministry could be greatly enriched by praying with people who have become embittered because of 'the wounds' inflicted by the sins of others. In the penitential rite of the Mass we begin by saying 'you were sent to heal the contrite of heart, Lord have mercy'. This prayer acknowledges our need for both forgiveness and healing. Sometimes, however, we can ignore the healing dimension of the Lord's forgiveness and fail to foster in the people of God this awareness that our God not only forgives us but also heals us.

We were very aware from our own pastoral experience that if our Catholic people have no access to the healing ministry in their parishes they will seek healing wherever it is offered. Catholics leave the Church in large numbers to join Pentecostal type Churches. Other Catholics, in ignorance of the spiritual dangers, often seek healing at the poisonous well of New Age spiritualities and occult practices, to the detriment of their faith. The document, *Jesus Christ: The Bearer of the Water of Life* published by the Pontifical Council of Culture published in 2003 gives us good guidance on New Age thinking.

Not a One-Man Ministry

We recognize that the individual parish priest cannot bear the burden of the healing ministry by himself. We believe that pastoral teams of laymen and women who are open to the Holy Spirit and willing to serve in 'the field hospital of the Church', could be trained for the exercise of this ministry in many parishes without too much expense or resistance. The parish priest would be expected to do as the Vatican Council's Decree on Priests recommends:

> While trying the spirits if they be from God, priests must discover with faith, recognise with joy, and foster with diligence the many and varied charismatic gifts of the laity, whether they be of a humble or more exalted kind.[5]

We are very aware that the many hundreds of lay Eucharistic ministers who bring Holy Communion to the sick and the housebound exercise a significant healing ministry and that their ministry could be greatly enriched by further training in art of lovingly listening to how the sick are feeling and in praying with them about their specific anxieties and fears.

The Meaning of Words

We are aware too that the very word healing can create anxieties in some priests. While physical healing does occur through the celebration of the sacraments and through prayer, the greater healing is the inner healing that brings the person into a new and deeper personal relationship with Jesus Christ. As the Catechism says:

> Healing the wounds of sin, the Holy Spirit renews us interiorly
> through a spiritual transformation. He enlightens and strengthens
> us to live as 'children of the light' through all that is good and right
> and true.[6]

Healing is the restoration of wholeness. As the Church prays, 'O God, who restore human nature to yet greater dignity than at its beginnings...'[7] By accepting Christ personally as their Lord and Saviour and, through conforming their wills by Christ's grace, to God's will, the faithful grow in holiness and experience the gift of 'life in abundance' (Jn 10:10) Healing is not synonymous with curing. While curing is what happens to the diseased organ of the body, healing is the transformation of the whole person. Many prayers for healing result, not in the cure of the diseased organ of the body, but in the spiritual renewal of the whole person. We can therefore confidently pray for 'the healing of the dying', on their final journey into eternal life.

Healing and New Evangelisation

We discussed in detail the relationship between the healing ministry and evangelisation and we recognized that the Holy Spirit, by stirring up the charisms of healing in the Church in our time, is preparing the way for a more effective evangelisation. This emboldens us to go out 'to the fringes' and meet the people who may feel abandoned by both the Church and society. We have good news to share. As Pope St John Paul II said, 'God is opening before the Church the horizons of a humanity more fully prepared for the sowing of the Gospel. I sense that the moment has come to commit all of the Church's energies to a new evangelisation and to the mission *ad gentes*. No believer in Christ, no institution of the Church can avoid this supreme duty: to proclaim Christ to all people.[8] The knowledge that the Christ whom we proclaim heals the wounds and binds up the broken hearts of his brothers and sisters gives many evangelists today the courage to witness to him.

The Symposium sees in Pope Francis' frequent exhortations that the Church must heal the wounds in her people a clarion call to our Church to take the healing ministry more seriously and to dedicate both time and resources to training her priests and her many lay ministers to exercise this ministry with prudence and sensitivity.

Notes

1   Pope Francis, 'A Big Heart Open to God' interview with Fr Antonio Spadaro in *America Magazine*, 30 September 2013.

2   Sects or New Religious Movements – Pastoral Challenge in *l'Osservatore Romano*, 19 May 1986, English Edition, pp. 5–8.

3   Pope Francis, 'A Big Heart Open to God'.

4   *Catechism of the Catholic Church*, 1324.

5   Vatican II, *Presbyterum Ordinis*, 9.

6   *Catechism of the Catholic Church*, 1695.

7   Collect of Mass, Thursday of Week 4 of Eastertide, The Roman Missal (London: CTS, 2011), p. 452.

8   Pope St John Paul II, *Redemptoris Missio*, 3.

1

An Overview of the Ministry of Prayer for Healing in the Church Today

Jim McManus CSsR

Prayer for the healing of body, mind and spirit is an integral part of all our liturgical prayers. In this overview of the healing ministry in the Church, Jim McManus invites us to reflect on our sacramental prayers which testify to the Church's belief in God's will to heal his people. Fidelity to our sacraments requires the ministers of the Church, both clerical and lay, to become personally involved in a ministry of prayer for healing.

The Call of Pope Francis

Pope Francis spelled out very clearly his vision of the healing ministry of the Church when he said:

> I see clearly that the thing the Church needs most today is the ability to heal wounds and to warm the hearts of the faithful; it needs nearness, proximity. I see the Church as a field hospital after battle. It is useless to ask a seriously injured person if he has high cholesterol and about the level of his blood sugars! You have to heal his wounds. Then we can talk about everything else. Heal the wounds, heal the wounds... And you have to start from the ground up.[1]

In a homily in 2015 he said:

> There are many wounded people waiting in the aisles of the church for a minister of Christ to heal them. This requires healing the wounded hearts, opening doors, freeing people, and saying that God is good, forgives all, is our Father, is tender and always waiting for us.[2]

Any person, clerical or lay, applying for a job in Pope Francis' 'field hospital' would have to be ready and willing to get involved in the healing of the wounded. Pope Francis, with his colourful expressions, has made us all more aware that the healing ministry is an essential component of the Church's mission in the world. Thirty years ago the Holy See was already asking the whole Church to take this ministry more seriously. In its document on how to meet the challenges of so many Catholics leaving the Catholic Church to join Pentecostal Churches and Sects we read:

> Special attention must be given to the healing ministry through prayers, reconciliation, fellowship and care. Our pastoral concern should not be one-dimensional. It should extend not only to the spiritual, but also to the physical, psychological, social, cultural, economic, and political dimensions.[3]

This was a very helpful statement at the time. The fact that it is now the Pope and not some Office in the Holy See, who is calling for the healing ministry to be taken more seriously, will encourage many to respond in a more conscientious and creative way.

Where should we begin to develop the healing ministry in our parishes today? Pope Francis tells us: begin with those in the pews. In other words, with those who join in the celebration of the Eucharist or in other liturgical celebrations. Those who celebrate the liturgy in our parishes should experience the healing power of the sacraments, especially of the Eucharist. As the Catechism of the Catholic Church teaches:

> The Eucharist is the source and summit of the Christian life. The other sacraments, and indeed all ecclesiastical ministries and works of the apostolate, are bound up with the Eucharist and are orientated to it. For in the blessed Eucharist is contained the whole spiritual good of the Church, namely Christ himself, our Pasch.[4]

Attuning Our Minds to Our Voices

During Mass we say some wonderful prayers to God, prayers which express the truth about God and the truth about ourselves, and we ask for healing in body, mind and spirit. But before these prayers can form in us a habitual way of seeing ourselves in the light of these truths, we have to conform our minds to the words we are saying. The Vatican Council said:

> In order that the liturgy may be able to produce its full results it is necessary that the faithful come to it with proper dispositions, that their minds are attuned to their voices, that they cooperate with heavenly graces lest they receive in vain.[5]

The Faith of the Church

What does the Church believe about divine healing today? The simplest and most direct way to answer this question is to examine how the Church prays for healing in her prayers, especially in the liturgy of the Sacraments. There is an ancient theological Latin maxim which states, *lex orandi, lex credendi*, that can be translated as *the way the Church prays reveals what the Church believes.* If you want to find out what the Church believes about anything you will find that faith expressed in her liturgical prayer, in the prayers of the Mass and the other sacraments. The principle is this: if the Church prays for something in the liturgy she believes that her request is according to the mind of God, and that God will grant the request. Liturgical prayers, therefore, are an immediate source for studying the faith of the Church. In the light of this truth let us look more closely at some of the liturgical prayers that we say throughout the year.

Specific Prayers for Healing in the Eucharist

For the past fifteen hundred years, in the Roman Canon of the Mass, the priest has prayed:

> For them, we offer you this sacrifice of praise or they offer it for themselves and all who are dear to them: for the redemption of their souls, *in the hope of health and well-being*, and paying their homage to you, the eternal God, living and true.

Before receiving Holy Communion the priest prays silently,

> May the receiving of your Body and Blood, Lord Jesus Christ, not bring me to judgment and condemnation, but through your loving mercy be for me *protection in mind and body and a healing remedy.*

And just before receiving Holy Communion he holds the sacred host in his hands as he proclaims, 'Behold the lamb of God, behold him who takes away the sins of the world' to which the whole assembly responds, 'Lord I am not worthy that you should enter under my roof, but only say the word and *my soul shall be healed*'. The community is united in making this prayer of faith. My soul means my innermost self, my whole embodied self. As St John Paul II said, 'The body can never be reduced to mere matter: it is a spiritualised body, just as the spirit is so closely united to the body that it can described as an embodied spirit'.[6]

The Prayer of Faith

It is surely very significant that during the Mass the whole community cries out for health in body, mind and spirit just before they receive Our Lord in Holy Communion. The community is united in saying the prayer of faith. In the Ritual of Anointing of the Sick we are told,

> The community, asking God's help for the sick, makes the prayer of faith in response to God's word and in a spirit of trust. In the rites of the sick, it is the people of God who pray in faith.[7]

At Mass the people of God pray in faith and they ask for health.

Some post-communion prayers have very specific requests for healing. These beautiful prayers are the last prayers of the Mass and very often we don't pay close attention to them. The post-communion prayer generally consists of two parts. In the first part we thank God for the grace of the Holy Eucharist which we have just celebrated, and in the second part we ask that this Eucharist will affect some very specific area of our life.

On the Monday, the first week of Lent, this is how the Church gives thanks for the Eucharist and requests healing: 'We pray, O Lord, that, in receiving your Sacrament, we may experience **help in mind and body** so that kept safe in both we may glory in the fullness of heavenly healing'.

The request in this prayer is very daring. We pray to 'experience help in mind and body'. It is one thing to have a theoretical knowledge of God's love. It is quite another thing to experience God's healing love and to expect 'to glory in the fullness of heavenly healing'. To say this prayer with faith we must open our whole being to God and allow the healing love of God to fill us, removing all barriers. We open our minds and submit to the all holy God and allow the presence of God's healing Spirit to renew and transform our minds. We surrender all care and worry, all fear and doubt, and we invite God to renew us. But too often our pray is half-hearted. We want to be healed, but we don't want to trust; we want to be protected from anxiety, but we want to hold on to our worries; we want to forgive from the heart, but we also want to get our own back in some way.

Consider another post-communion prayer:

> We pray, O Lord God, that, as you have given these most sacred mysteries to be the safeguard of our salvation, so you may make them a healing remedy for us, both now and in time to come'.[8]

Notice the word 'now' in that prayer. The Church wants something to happen now, not tomorrow, nor next week, but now! It is now, in this hour, that we need to know the healing presence of God. Just before Christmas this is how the Church prayed: 'Lord, may participation in this divine mystery provide enduring protection for your people, so that, being subject to your glorious majesty in dedicated service, they may know *abundant health in mind and body*'.

Finally, consider the prayer in the Mass in honour of Our Blessed Lady:

> Grant, Lord God, that we, your servants, may rejoice in unfailing health of mind and body and through the glorious intercession of Blessed Mary ever-Virgin, may we be set free from present sorrow and come to enjoy eternal happiness'.[9]

That request for 'unfailing health of mind and body', through the intercession or Our Blessed Lady, should give us great confidence as we pray for healing at Mass.

All these prayers for healing within the Mass indicate how strongly the Church believes in God's healing love, and how she expects that healing power to be experienced in the Mass. Does our faith correspond to the faith of the Church? Do we believe as strongly in divine healing? Do we 'attune our minds to our voices' as we say these prayers?

With so many prayers for the healing of body, mind and spirit in the Mass, isn't it extraordinary, that for so long, we didn't allow these prayers to form in us an expectant faith in God's healing love. Nor did we allow this faith of the Church in God's will to grant us health in mind and body to inform our theology and our catechetical instruction on the Mass. Had we acted consistently on the ancient Latin maxim, *Lex orandi, lex credendi* we would have no difficulty in accepting the healing ministry in our time. But, sadly, we over-spiritualised the meaning of these prayers and thought that they were just referring to helping the soul get to heaven. While we always expected the forgiveness of sins, we didn't always expect the healing of the wounds of sin, the healing of body, mind and spirit.

The Catechism of the Catholic Church

The new Catechism of the Church stresses that the healing of the whole person is the will of Christ. We read: 'The Lord Jesus Christ, physician of souls and bodies, who forgave the sins of the paralytic and restored him to bodily health, has willed that his Church continue, in the power of the Holy

Spirit, his work of healing and salvation, even among her own members. This is the purpose of the two sacraments of healing: the sacrament of Penance and the sacrament of Anointing of the Sick.'[10] The Church's formal teaching on the healing ministry today states clearly that there are two sacraments of healing in the Church: Penance and Anointing.

Confession is a Sacrament of Healing

We always believed strongly that the sacrament of confession is for the forgiveness of our sins. But we didn't pay much attention to the healing effects of the sacrament. Carl Jung, the son of a Calvinist pastor and one of the founders of modern Psychiatry, was more aware of this healing effect than the theologians and confessors of the time. He wrote,

> The fact is there are relatively few neurotic Catholics, and yet they are living under the same conditions as we do. They are presumably suffering from the same social conditions and so on, and so one would expect a similar amount of neurosis. There must be something in the cult, in the actual religious practice, which explains that peculiar fact that there are fewer complexes, or that these complexes manifest themselves much less in Catholic than in other people. That something, besides confession, is really the cult itself. It is the Mass.[11]

What was Jung observing? Not the forgiveness of sins, but what the new rite of Reconciliation calls 'the healing of the wounds of sin'. We read in the new Rite:

> In order that this sacrament of healing may truly achieve its purpose among Christ's faithful, it must take root in their whole lives and lead them to more fervent service of God and neighbour...Just as the wound of sin is varied and multiple in the life of individuals and of a community, so the healing which penance provides is varied.[12]

We recognize two effects of sin: sin as an offence against God, causing an alienation between God and self; and the wound of sin, that is the inner hurt caused in a person by sin, sometimes by his or her own sin but also, and maybe more frequently, by the sinful action or words of others. The sin itself will be manifested in a cold, deliberate malicious act of one kind or another; the wound of sin will reveal itself through some kind of reaction. Just as a person in pain may cry out, so a person with the wound of sin may very well 'strike out', verbally or non-verbally.

For the sin itself we need God's forgiveness; for the wound of sin we need the Lord's healing. Both are signified in the words of Absolution: 'Through the ministry of the Church may God give you pardon and peace'. Pardon is for the sin; peace is for the healing of the wound of sin. This is the work of the Holy Spirit. As the Catholic Catechism says:

> Healing the wounds of sin, the Holy Spirit renews us interiorly through a spiritual transformation. He enlightens and strengthens us to live as 'children of the light' through all that is good and right and true'.[13]

That 'healing of the wound of sin' was what Carl Jung was noticing when he wrote 70 years ago that there were 'relatively few neurotic Catholics'. It was inner healing through a good confession.

Sacrament of the Anointing of the Sick

Since the Second Vatican Council the Church has revised the rite of the Anointing of the Sick and has placed a new emphasis on the healing power of the sacrament. In the New Rite we are told of the effects of the sacrament: 'This sacrament gives the grace of the Holy Spirit to those who are sick: by this grace the whole person is helped and saved, sustained by trust in God, and strengthened against the temptation of the Evil One and against anxiety over death'. This prayer after the anointing illustrates the faith of the Church in the healing power of the sacrament:

> Lord Jesus Christ, our Redeemer, by the grace of the Holy Spirit cure the weakness of your servant... Heal his/her sickness and forgive his/her sins; expel all afflictions of mind and body; mercifully restore her/him to full health, and enable him/her to resume his/her former duties, for you are Lord for ever and ever'.[14]

That is a confident prayer for the healing of the whole person, the prayer of faith. And, as we saw above, 'In the rites of the sick, it is the people of God who pray in faith.'[15]

The Renewal of the Healing Ministry in the Church Today

Where do we begin when we think about how best to renew the ministry of healing in the Church today? Pope Francis answered that question when he said, 'there are many wounded people waiting in the aisles of the church for a minister of Christ to heal them'.[16] We begin with the people who assemble in faith to celebrate the sacraments. We need two new pastoral initiatives:

1. A good catechetical programme, educating the faithful on the healing power of the sacraments.

2. A pastoral programme for ministers, both clerical and lay, to encourage them to begin to minister in the way Pope Francis expects, namely, 'You have to heal his wounds. Then we can talk about everything else.[17]

Catechetical Programme

We have seen, as we examined the prayers in the rites of the sacraments, that the healing of the whole person is central to the purpose of each celebration. It is true that we celebrate the sacraments to give glory to God, in the first place. But it is also true, in the words of St Irenaeus, that 'the glory of God is the person fully alive'. The prayers of the Mass and the other sacraments invite us to open up our whole being to the healing love of God so that we can enter into his peace and share that peace with others. We have to train ourselves, as the Second Vatican Council said, 'to attune our minds to our voices'.[18] We need to bring an 'expectant faith' to each celebration. In the prayers of the sacraments we are asking God for manifold blessings, for body, mind and spirit: we pray for health of body, peace of mind, faithfulness of spirit. We humbly expect to receive these blessings because Jesus says, 'ask and you will receive, seek and you will find, knock and the door will be opened to you'. (Mt, 7:7). We should not take this 'expectant faith' for granted. Rather, in the work of ministry we always ask the Lord to give us the word that will arouse this faith in those to whom we minister, As we minister to the faithful, then, we should be alive to the way in which inner wounds can prevent a person from hearing the word of God, responding with praise and thanksgiving to the gifts of God, and sharing their faith with others as the opportunity arises.

We can learn a lot from the recent experience of Anglican initiatives in promoting the healing ministry. The Anglican Church published a major report on the healing ministry in 2000 and entitled *A Time To Heal*.[19] This is a very comprehensive survey of the state of the healing ministry in the Anglican Church. They can report:

> We are glad to discover that almost every bishop has some involvement in the healing ministry, particularly anointing, laying

on of hands and intercessory prayer as well as taking part in the annual Chrism service during Holy Week. About half of the diocesan bishops currently chair their diocesan committees involved in or relating to this ministry, which is a clear signal of the importance they attach to its place in their dioceses…Some bishops encourage and are also involved in training conferences and annual diocesan healing days and services. A few bishops are also involved with healing organizations or a particular initiative, or hold a national post related to the healing ministry. Many diocesan advisors feel that the involvement and support of their bishops is a crucial factor in promoting this ministry within the diocese. It is also important that the media see that the bishops have a keen interest in it; this helps to show society that healing is a central part of the Church's mission.[20]

The Report, while acknowledging that in the past fifty years since the last official Report, some very significant developments have taken place within the Anglican approach to and acceptance of the healing ministry, also says 'it is clear from our research carried out recently that there is still much to be done to establish this ministry as part of normal everyday life within every parish'.[21] In a 2006 review of developments since the publication of A Time to Heal the authors were able to record, 'There is a widespread recognition that since the publication of A Time to Heal, there has been a considerable and very encouraging increase in interest and awareness of this ministry'.[22] Among the developments, it can report that 'The work of the House of Bishops' healing ministry steering group continues to provide valuable opportunities and initiatives to affirm, enable and develop the healing ministry throughout the Church of England and in closer ecumenical co-operation with our ecumenical partners.'[23]

Despite the renewal of our Liturgy, with those wonderful prayers for healing, and the emergence of lay ministry in the Catholic Church, there has been little, official support and encouragement for the healing ministry beyond the normal ministry to the sick in the sacrament of Anointing. Happily, thousands of devoted lay ministers are involved in the healing ministry of the Church by bringing Holy Communion to the sick and the elderly in their homes each week. This is a very significant manifestation of the healing ministry. The diocese or the parish should surely develop a training programme for these 'field hospital' workers, to affirm and encourage them and help them to develop their ministerial gifts. These committed men and women work every week in 'the field hospital' of the

Church and their ministry would be greatly enriched by simple training. They would be greatly supported and encouraged by the opportunity to meet together with their parish priest, and from time to time with their bishop, for a time of further training and reflection on their ministry.

Pastoral Programmes for Ministers, both Clerical and Lay

In the past fifty years our Liturgy has undergone a great renewal. We now have a much clearer awareness that the Liturgy is the community at prayer. It is not just the priest 'who says the Mass'. The whole community participate in the celebration of the Mass. For a fully conscious participation, as the Vatican Council said, 'our minds must be attuned to our voices'. As we pray for healing throughout the Mass we should mean what we say.

In 1989 I was giving a day on the healing ministry to the priests of a Nigerian diocese. The young priest whom the bishop asked to thank me at the end of the day began by saying, 'I am delighted to hear that the healing ministry has arrived at last. I finished my doctorate in theology in the Gregorian University in Rome two years ago and the healing ministry was never mentioned'.

It is surely ironic that Medical Schools may have been giving much more time to talking about the role of prayer in healing than Theological Schools. Dr Larry Dossey could write in 1999,

> Courses on the role of religious devotion and prayer in healing are currently being taught in approximately fifty US medical schools. This is a historic event, a stunning reversal of the exclusion of these factors from medical education for most of the twentieth century.[24]

Herbert Benson, professor of Medicine at Harvard University could write,

> My patients have taught me a great deal about the opportunities that emerge when artificial barriers are broken down, and how physical ailments inspire soul-searching and a revival of meaningful living, and about how the human spirit enlivens and transforms the body'.[25]

If 'the human spirit enlivens and transforms the body' our Seminaries should follow the example of those Medical Schools and in Dossey's words, include 'courses on the role of religious devotion and prayer for healing' in the training of future priests. When the Spiritual and Psychology Special Interest Group was formed in the Royal Institute of Psychiatry in Britain in 1999 just 120 psychiatrists joined it. Today the membership numbers over 3000. In the last twenty years, then, in the secular world of medicine and psychiatry, there has been a growing awareness that there is a vital place for faith, prayer and spirituality in the holistic care of patients. Hopefully our Seminaries will begin to take their cue from these exciting developments and prepare future priests well for their ministry of healing. It is sadly true that, despite the great renewal in theology and liturgy, most seminaries do not introduce their students to the healing ministry. While giving a retreat to priests in 2016 one parish priest told me that his recently ordained assistant wanted to learn about the healing ministry because it was never mentioned as he was going through his seminary.

Oscott College, the seminary of the archdiocese of Birmingham, deserves great credit in having begun to provide its students with various opportunities to familiarise themselves with different aspects of the healing ministry. Students in their final year have seminars on the deliverance ministry while the third year students have seminars on different aspects of the healing ministry. This is a development which, I am sure, the Symposium would want to applaud. Hopefully the other Seminaries will begin to take note and provide their students with similar learning opportunities.

There is now an urgent pastoral need to provide all priests and lay ministers with the opportunity to learn more about the healing ministry. When Pope Francis says, 'You have to heal his wounds. Then we can talk about everything else', he is probably quite aware that the very opposite frequently happens, namely, we talk about everything else and we don't heal the wounds. We cannot presume that every minister in the Church has the experience of ministering in prayer for the healing of the inner wounds that have been inflicted on people. Many of them never had the opportunity to learn about this ministry. Nor can we be satisfied, as a Church, to allow the healing ministry to become the preserve of the few gifted men and women who have special charisms of healing. While we always thank God for their ministries we have to remind ourselves that the healing ministry is a normal ministry of prayer that should be available within the Eucharistic community of the parish. As we have seen, whoever participates in the celebration of the Eucharist prays for healing. Praying for healing is not an extraordinary ministry but a normal Christian ministry that should be exercised within the parish community. We, as a Church, must accept Pope Francis' challenge to 'heal the wounds'. It is our responsibility to learn how best to do this.

Notes

1   Pope Francis, 'A Big Heart Open to God', interview with Antonio Spadaro in *America Magazine*, 30 September 2013.

2   Pope Francis, *Homily* (5 February 2015).

3   Sects or New Religious Movements—Pastoral Challenge in *l'Osservatore Romano*, 19 May 1986, English Edition, pp. 5–8.

4   *Catechism of the Catholic Church*, 1324.

5   Vatican II, *Sacrosanctum Concilium*, 11.

6   Pope St John Paul II, *Letter to Families* (1994), 19.

7   Pastoral Care of the Sick—Rite of Anointing and Viaticum (1983), 44.

8   Thursday of the First Week of Lent, The Roman Missal (London: CTS, 2011), p. 247.

9   Memorial Mass of Our Lady on Saturday, The Roman Missal (London: CTS, 2011), p. 1098.

10   *Catechism of the Catholic Church*, 1421.

11   C. G. Jung, *The Collected Works* (London: Routledge & Kegan Paul, 1977), vol. 18 para 613.

12   New Rite of Penance (1973), 7.

13   *Catechism of the Catholic Church*, 1695.

14   Pastoral Care of the Sick—Rite of Anointing and Viaticum (1983), 6.

15   *Ibid.*, 44.

16   Pope Francis, *Homily* (5 February 2015).

17   Pope Francis, 'A Big Heart Open to God'.

18   Vatican II, *Sacrosanctum Concilium*, 11.

19   House of Bishops of the General Synod of the Church of England, *A Time to Heal—A Contribution towards the Ministry of Healing* (London: Church House Publishing, 2000).

20   *Ibid.*, p. 41.

21   *Ibid.*, p. 37.

22   The Healing Ministry: Developments since the Publication of A Time to Heal', *General Synod Miscellaneous* 835, p. 11.

23   *Ibid.*

24   L. Dossey, *Reinventing Medicine: Beyond Mind-Body to a New Era of Healing* (San Francisco: Harper & Row, 1999), p. 199.

25   H. Benson, *Timeless Healing: The Power and Biology of Belief* (New York: Schribner, 1996), p. 195.

2

The New Evangelisation—Healing the Wounds of our Brokenness

Alan Guile

In the first chapter we saw how the Church, in her liturgical prayers, constantly prays for health of mind and body. In this chapter we will see the necessary relationship between evangelisation which is the primary vocation of the Church, and the ministry of healing ministry. Professor Emeritus Alan Guile has been engaged in the ministry of prayer for inner healing during the past 40 years.

The Church Exists in Order to Evangelise

The Church has called for The New Evangelisation and Pope Paul VI wrote that 'Evangelising is in fact the grace and vocation proper to the Church, her deepest identity. She exists in order to evangelise,'[1] and 'The Church is an evangeliser but she begins by being evangelised herself.'[2] If we are to become more completely evangelised ourselves so as to bring the Good news fruitfully to others, then we need to desire daily to encounter Jesus Christ more deeply. In this way we open ourselves more completely to His love so that we are constantly being given further grace with which to love God with all our heart and all our soul and to long only to do His will. As Pope Francis explained:

> Thanks solely to this encounter—or renewed encounter—with God's love, which blossoms into an enriching friendship, we are liberated from our narrowness and self-absorption. We become fully human when we become more than human, when we let God bring us beyond ourselves in order to attain the fullest truth of our being. Here we find the source and inspiration of all our efforts at evangelisation. For if we have received the love which restores meaning to our lives, how can we fail to share that love with others?[3]

In this passage about liberation from our narrowness and self-absorption and so attaining the fullest truth of our being, Pope Francis is writing about our need to invite the Holy Spirit to bring us progressively into deeper spiritual or inner healing, so that eventually we are restored to our true self made in the image and likeness of God. Fr Raniero Cantalamessa, Preacher to the Papal Household, wrote about this:

> Spiritual healing means, first of all, healing from sin. The term inner or spiritual healing usually signifies the healing of something that, though in itself it is not a sin, has a link with sin either as its result or as its cause or as an incentive to sin; or it signifies the healing of a state or situation which has nothing to do with sin, but which prevents, nevertheless, the full flowering of the life of grace. This kind of healing is presented by Jesus as an integral part of His messianic message when He announces in the synagogue: 'The Spirit of the Lord is upon me because He has anointed me to bring the Good News to the poor. He has sent me to announce release to the captives, and recovering of sight to the blind, to set at liberty those who have been bruised, to proclaim a year of favour from the Lord'. (Lk 4:18–19)[4]

When Jesus gave this messianic message he was not speaking about material poverty or of releasing the people of that time from the rule of the Romans but of liberating people of all times and nations from their enemies of Satan, sin, death and sickness of every kind. Similarly he was speaking of bringing spiritual sight (cf Jn 12:37–40) and freeing them from the oppression of sin and the hurts and damage resulting from it. In the last reference we have of Jesus being in a synagogue, he says of the woman possessed for eighteen years of a spirit which left her enfeebled, 'Was it not right to untie her bonds on the Sabbath day?' (Luke 13:16). It has been shown[5] that praying for inner healing includes untying many bonds just as Jesus commanded the others to unbind Lazarus, a process in which Our Lady can play a vital part in untying knots as we pray for her help. In St Mark's Gospel, the earliest to be written, and thought to be the main source for St Matthew and St Luke, around 31% of the verses concern healings and miracles.

The Mission Given by Christ to the Church Includes Healing

It was to make possible the continuation of this work after the Ascension that the Father and the Son sent the Holy Spirit. To evangelise and at the same time to be a healing instrument is the task the Lord entrusted to the Church for all ages. Even well before the Ascension He had begun to teach His disciples and to give them the authority and some experience of this mission:

> Jesus called the twelve disciples together and gave them power and authority to drive out all demons and to cure diseases. Then He sent them out to preach the Kingdom of God and to heal the sick. (Lk 9:1–2)

Later He extended the mission to others:

> After this the Lord chose another seventy-two men and sent them out two by two to go ahead of Him to every town where He himself was about to go… heal the sick in that town and say to the people there, 'The Kingdom of God has come near you.' (Lk 10:1,9)

The last words of Jesus before the Ascension repeat the dual nature of the mission:

> Go out to the whole world; proclaim the Good News to all creation… these are the signs that will be associated with believers: in My name… they will lay their hands on the sick who will recover. (Mk 16:16–18)

Again, just before the Ascension, Jesus said:

> You will be filled with power when the Holy Spirit comes upon you, and you will be witnesses for Me… to the ends of the earth. (Ac 1:8)

When this promise was fulfilled at Pentecost, the apostles at once began to proclaim Christ with power and authority. Immediately following the account of three thousand people being added to the group that day, we read that 'many miracles and wonders were done through the apostles' (Ac 2:43), as they were being empowered to continue the mission given by Christ. Beginning in the next chapter of Acts with the healing of the lame man at the temple gate, there are a number of accounts of various kinds of healings, including deliverance from evil spirits as well as miracles and wonders.

All of this was done first by the twelve and the seventy two, followed after Pentecost by the apostles and then by others beginning with Stephen and Philip, entirely in and through the name of Jesus, for this is the only source of power and authority. The name of Jesus, given by the angel before his conception, was widely used and meant Yahweh is a help. It has been claimed[6] that 'it can be translated as God saves or God heals' and thus signifies His God-given mission in life, and that because the Hebrews of

15

that time did not divide people into component parts to the extent that we do, then whenever we say the name of Jesus we are saying that His main mission was to save and to heal. 'You must call His name Jesus for it is He who will save His people from their sins' (Mt 1:21). The New Testament and other sources indicate that there was an identification or connection, although misunderstood, between sickness and sin when they tended to ask 'What has this sick person done wrong that he should be in this condition?' St Peter associated being saved with being healed, 'Christ Himself carried our sins in His body on the cross so that we might die to sin and live for righteousness. It is by His wounds that you have been healed' (1 P 2:24). Both salvation and healing are only possible through Christ taking our sins on Himself to the cross and shedding His Precious Blood.

In the translation used for the Gospel reading for the thirtieth Sunday of cycle B, Jesus does not say to Bartimaeus after restoring his sight, 'Go, your faith has healed you,' but says, 'Go, your faith has saved you.' God is always longing to do more for us, His beloved children, than we can ever ask for or ever think of. (Ep 3:20)

Reconciliation and Inner Peace

The Father sent His Son to reconcile us to Himself and then entrusted this mission to the Church, to set us free of any enemy whether internal or external, and to restore to life in all its fullness as everything harmful is stripped away so that we are restored to who we really are. As St Paul expressed it:

> For anyone who is in Christ there is a new creation; the old creation has gone, and the new one is here. It is all God's work. It was God who reconciled us to Himself through Christ and gave us the work of handing on this reconciliation. In other words, God in Christ was reconciling the world to Himself, not holding men's faults against them, and He has entrusted to us the news that they are reconciled. (2 Co 5:17–19)

It has been discussed extensively elsewhere by the present author[6] that this work of reconciliation and forgiveness, and emotional and spiritual healing requires not only the sacraments but also an effective listening and inner healing prayer ministry, because the Catechism and *Lumen Gentium* make clear that there are not only sacramental graces but also special graces given by the Holy Spirit, and both are needed for effective healing. This is a process which may take considerable time as people pray for Jesus to touch a person's wounds with His wounds and draw this pain into the suffering of Jesus on the Cross through His precious blood (Is 53:5). Then he or she may become more ready to decide to forgive and to ask God for the grace required to make this forgiveness grow more complete as time goes by, in an ongoing process which may take months or even years. The testimony given by a young man in appendix 2 describing his reconciliation with his father and mother after his experiences in a Cenacolo community, give a vivid and moving example of such a process.

There can be no inner peace and true healing of the whole person without forgiveness. Each individual needs to know in the depths of their being that with repentance and faith in the victory of Christ upon the Cross, their sins are forgiven and the record of them is blotted out by God their loving Father (Heb 10:17, Jr 31:33–34). They also need to become ready to ask for and receive more and more deeply the grace with which to forgive every person whom they have perceived as hurting them or letting them down in some way. They need the grace with which to forgive themselves and in some cases to be set free of any perception that God seemed to fail them in some way, perhaps in a painful childhood.

Thus we find connections between sin, forgiveness and healing in many encounters of Christ with various individuals, where He used the Holy Spirit's gift of discernment because of the variety of conditions in people. The prevailing view among the Jews had been to associate sickness directly with some sin of the person. In the case of the paralysed man let down through the roof Jesus does confirm some link between human sin and sickness without naming the particular sin(s) (Lk 5:20–24). On the other hand, in the story of the man born blind, Jesus clearly states: 'His blindness has nothing to do with his sins or his parents' sins' (Jn 9:3). In the case of the tenth leper who returned to Jesus to give thanks, it would appear that forgiveness only followed the outward healing, since all ten lepers are said to have been cleansed or cured when they first met Jesus, but only the tenth was made whole and saved (Lk 17:15–19). Again, when Jesus healed the man who had been lying by the pool of Bethesda, He discerned that sin played some part in the man's condition, and it would appear that forgiveness followed his physical healing (Jn 5:14–15). The letter of St James firmly establishes links between healing and forgiveness of sins (Jm 5:14–16).

It is clear, therefore, that in the mission which Christ entrusted to the Church for all ages, to evangelise <u>and</u> to be a healing instrument, the proclamation of the Kingdom of God and the ministry of healing and forgiveness are inextricably connected, and we constantly must depend upon the gifts of the Holy Spirit, including wisdom and discernment.

Sadly, after the first few centuries,[7] the Church moved, perhaps focussing mainly on physical healing, towards limiting expectations to saints, relics, 'holy places', and the sacraments now called the Anointing of the Sick and Reconciliation. Desert fathers, including St Anthony, turned away from praying for the sick in the name of humility. Thus in various ways the faith was largely lost that a baptised person could and should be ready to pray out of God's love and compassion, with someone who expresses their needs and hurts, using the power and the gifts of the Holy Spirit, so that others could become more whole as the Good News of the free gift of salvation penetrates their whole being and their way of life, instead of merely remaining a piece of information in their heads.

The healing of our immortal soul so that we can live life in its fullness (Jn 10:10) and be given the free promise of eternal life, is of a higher priority than purely physical healing alone. We can become progressively more whole in our mind, will and emotions as we are freed by grace from the damage due to sin which tends to imprison us in a false and distorted self. God wants to restore us to our real self, created in His image and likeness. He also wants to empower us through the Holy Spirit to serve Him freely and joyfully, to enable us to minister to others so that they receive the same help which we ourselves have received (2 Co 1:4). This is living out the call to constant conversion and renewal as we become more deeply evangelised, which was proclaimed by Pope Paul VI.[8]

Healing Wounds Received Before the Age of Seven

Our brokenness can start very early and can have roots before conception and during the time in the womb and then go on through early childhood. This crucially involves praying for the healing of those early roots of damage and concentrates on the wounded areas up to the age of seven. The healing of those wounds increases integration of the wounded child and the damaged adult as they both receive deeper inner healing.[9] This does not happen through any intellectual exercise but as a gift of God's love and mercy as we cry out in our helplessness and pain. It is interesting to see insights of this in the thinking of Kierkegaard:

> The primary task is not to answer the theoretical questions but to restore the unity of the self or the person; proofs for the objective

existence of God or the soul, or the historical validity of Scripture mean nothing unless the question of God grips us at the heart of our very existence; faith resolves the otherwise irresolvable tensions at the centre of human existence.

Kierkegaard borrowed the phrase from Scripture that it is a matter of *strengthening in the inner being*.[10]

Ministry of Inner Healing is a Crucial Part of Evangelisation

Vatican II stated that 'the whole laity must co-operate in spreading and in building up the kingdom of Christ'.[11] This call of the Church to lay people comes at a time when, particularly in the West (where The New Evangelisation is mainly directed) the damage in the lives of families and in society deepens and worsens generation by generation, due to many factors. The diminishing number of priests available to evangelise and of capable lay people to work alongside the priests weakens the Church further. The Church does not in general reach out with the Gospel message to others outside herself in any really significant way in most parishes, nor does it prepare its laity for the task with sufficient expectant faith in the power of the Holy Spirit. The Church has not sufficiently recognised that in order to be effective in its work its own wounds need to be healed, like the man lying by the road to Jericho. Many in the Church would say (if they thought about it all) that they recognise their present condition as being far closer to his state than to that of the Good Samaritan. They need to experience the power of the Holy Spirit transforming them through the love, compassion and healing of Christ rather than just hearing only words from the Church which operate at head level and do not lead to a new way of living out the Gospel. The Gospels and Acts show us Jesus transforming people who had previously been out of action in bringing others into the Kingdom of God, into 'good Samaritans', and He gave this mission to His Church. The healing ministry helps people to experience the power of the Scriptures as 'alive and active, sharper than any two-edged sword, piercing to the division of soul and spirit, of joints and marrow, and discerning the thoughts and intentions of the heart' (Heb 4:12).

It has recently been shown from my experience of over forty years in the inner healing ministry, involving some twelve thousand hours of listening and praying with many hundreds of people who are hurting, and from the teachings of the Church, that this ministry of healing is a crucially important part of evangelisation.[12]

This ministry is therefore, vital in two main aspects:

1. bringing deeper wholeness and conversion to Christ in practising Catholics;

2. in preparing and enabling them to co-operate with their priests in fulfilling the mission given to the Church by Christ Himself, and bringing real fruit in The New Evangelisation.

Participation in this is fulfilling the call in the Catechism:

> Lay people also fulfil their prophetic mission by evangelisation, 'that is the proclamation of Christ by word and the testimony of life'. For lay people 'this evangelisation...acquires a specific property and peculiar efficacy because it is accomplished in ordinary circumstances of the world'. This witness of love, however, is not the sole element in the apostolate; the true apostle is on the look-out for occasions of announcing Christ by word, either to unbelievers...or to the world.[13]

This chapter examines some of those areas which need attention in fulfilling the Church's objectives. The author's long experience of the inner healing ministry, and the widespread suffering of many, has given clear evidence that many practising members of the Church have needed more than the grace coming through the normal channels of the sacraments.[14] This is not surprising in the light of the teaching of the Catechism:

> Grace is first and foremost the gift of the Spirit who justifies and sanctifies us. But grace also includes the gifts that the Spirit grants us to associate us with His work, to enable us to collaborate in the salvation of others and in the growth of the Body of Christ, the Church. There are sacramental graces, gifts proper to the different sacraments. There are furthermore special graces, also called charisms, after the Greek term used by St Paul, and meaning 'favour', 'gratuitous gift', 'benefit'. Whatever their character—sometimes it is extraordinary, such as the gift of miracles or of tongues—charisms are oriented towards sanctifying grace and are intended for the common good of the Church. They are at the service of charity which builds up the Church.[15]

Among these gifts is a word of knowledge. A number of examples have been given[16] where such a gift was received a number of times by my late wife. Though that word or phrase did not convey anything at all to her, she shared it with the person needing help. It had a significance to that person, by which the Lord was able to reveal some experience from the past. This experience may have been forgotten or almost forgotten, or had been supposed to be relatively insignificant. This led to prayer which brought about a deeper healing. Others called by God into this ministry in our time experience this gift, but far more are needed.

Nominal or Authentic Christians?

Fr Pat Lynch, the founder of the Sion Community for Evangelisation, when writing to help introduce the 'Decade of Evangelisation', included a whole section entitled 'Over-sacramentalised, under-evangelised'.[17] Although this phrase has sometimes been used unhelpfully or simplistically resulting in more heat than light in discussions, honest reflection by most of us who attend the majority of the parishes in the UK and probably also in Europe, would force us to accept that there is a great deal of truth in it. Cardinal Suenens wrote:

> I do not think that we can fail to be struck by the too frequent contrast between a Christian outlined by Peter on the day of Pentecost and a Christian of today as the second millennium of the Christian era draws to a close. We have to open our eyes to this state of affairs if we hope to see the renewal of the Church become a reality.[18]

> How can we christianise today such a vast number of nominal Christians? This is at the heart of our pastoral problems: the glaring contrast between the nominal and the authentic Christian.[19]

This was written over forty years ago and the situation is even worse now. It is vital therefore to explore the possible ways in which clergy and laity can collaborate more fruitfully in receiving all the graces which God longs to pour out on the Church as it faces so much suffering, so many trials and challenges in situations which must be recognised as spiritual warfare.

The contribution presented here regarding various healings which are needed to bring about deeper evangelisation, aims towards fulfilling the vision articulated by Pope Francis in an interview which he gave in August 2013, after most of the present writing had been finished. A key passage in this interview[20] came when Pope Francis was asked 'What does the Church need most at this historic moment? Do we need reforms? What are your wishes for the Church in the coming years? What kind of Church do you dream of?' The Pope replied:

> I see clearly that the thing the Church needs most today is the ability to heal wounds and to warm the hearts of the faithful; it needs nearness, proximity. I see the Church as a field hospital after battle. It is useless to ask a seriously injured person if he has high cholesterol and about the level of his blood sugars. You have to heal his wounds. Then we can begin to talk about everything else. Heal the wounds, heal the wounds… And you have to begin from the ground up.

I believe that Pope Francis is proclaiming that the Church needs to concentrate upon showing God's love and compassion to wounded individuals, and praying with them—and through them for their families—for Christ to heal the deep underlying root causes of the disease which shows itself in innumerable aspects and forms of great human suffering today. I have described in some detail elsewhere, accompanied by many testimonies,[21] how Christ can use ordinary people to help those who cry out in their pain to become free and at peace. They in turn then desire to live in accordance with God's will and to become channels used by Him to serve and heal other wounded people.

This chapter is intended to emphasise that this is just what the Church should be concentrating on: being the field hospital in the spiritual battle to make real the victory of Christ upon the Cross, and to heal the wounds of sin, so that more people may live life in its fullness and their souls may be saved. This is real evangelisation, and it is urgently needed.

Forty Years' Experience of Inner Healing Prayer Ministry

In 1983, whilst visiting St Joseph's Parish, Stockton-on-Tees, at the invitation of the parish priest, my late wife and I, quite independently, both felt that God was inviting us to move from Leeds to that parish. I immediately asked the University if I could retire early from my post as Professor of Electrical Engineering. I was allowed to do so in 1984, and we moved into a bungalow already named Shalom on the edge of the Catholic primary school field. It was in that bungalow that we had stayed with an acquaintance the year before, and we had no need to search for a home because she had decided to move.

At first we did not know why we had been called there, although the parish priest quickly asked us to initiate and lead the first RCIA programme the parish had ever had, and I was soon elected chairman of governors of the school, to the relief of the priest. We had no family or close friends in the north-east at this time. Then, gradually at first, through the recommendation of a priest, a doctor or friend, someone in difficulties or distress would telephone to ask if they could come to our home, for us to listen to them, and then to pray with them for God to bring them help and peace and greater faith as He gave them inner healing. We had in fact been asked to pray with people since 1973, though the numbers coming had been limited by having children and a job.

The number who have come to my home for the prayer of healing has now exceeded 550. In the very early days they were almost all Catholics, although there were a number of others, including one who until then had been a Buddhist, who came into the Church after prayer ministry followed by the RCIA programme. As figure 1 illustrates, they have come from places up to hundreds of miles away because they were unable to find the help they needed nearer home. Many others asked us to pray with them whilst we were on holiday or at retreat centres, but these are not shown in figure 1.

To preserve confidentiality we have never kept any written records over the last 32 years of the people or the content of the sessions, each of which averages about two hours. However, looking over the names in diary appointments reveals that the proportion of Catholics among those coming (at the time of writing and in my ninetieth year there are appointments with over 30 people) has fallen to around 50%, as people in other churches have heard by word of mouth that help is available. Some of them had been hurt further in the healing ministry previously given to them in the church from which they came.

Figure 1: Places from which people have travelled to Norton (+) for inner healing prayer ministry.

The Need is Greater in Inner Healing rather than Physical Healing

Almost everyone who has asked to come has already had faith in God, often a genuine sense of personal relationship and a real prayer life. Hardly anyone cited some physical illness or problem as their main reason for needing God's help. They have come from places as far apart as London, Holy Island, Haywards Heath, Shrewsbury, Southport, Gloucester, Cambridge, Nottingham, Leicester and Northern Ireland, as well as two who came from Europe to stay for several days because they did not know of any similar prayer ministry available nearer to their home.

Of all these people, about half or rather less came for a very few sessions only, not yet being ready for God to begin to make really deep changes in their lives. In some cases those people would return months or years later with a new readiness and openness to surrendering more completely to Christ. God knows the right time and is patient, and never puts pressure. In some cases the period over which we would meet with them to listen and to pray would last for years, perhaps even 10 or 15 years. There would be breaks occurring during this time, where they worked through things until they again felt the need of meeting with us to deal with some aspects which hadn't fully emerged earlier, or some new painful situation.

Commissioning by Priest and then Bishop

My wife and I were commissioned in the ministry of prayer for inner healing by our parish priest within a year of arriving in the parish, and subsequently confirmed in it by our bishop. The bishop later asked us to give two courses of teaching for the diocese (as also did the bishop of a Scottish diocese two years running). He wrote to all the priests of the diocese, outlining the criteria by which they might discern which parishioners to recommend to attend the course.

Recollection of so many people going back 32 years is bound to be selective, but I would be confident that the majority of the Catholics who did continue to come for an appreciable period for ministry were regularly receiving the sacraments of Holy Communion and Reconciliation. I also believe that they would have approached Confession as an open encounter with the living Christ, not merely taking part in a formulaic manner, perhaps behind a screen. Thus the sacraments alone had not brought them the depth of inner peace and healing which they needed, and in their pain they were reaching out for more help.

The Huge Range of Pain in Lives of People

The range and depth of problems and suffering revealed by the people coming to us at home, conferences, retreats, even on holiday, are extensive. We have witnessed Jesus Christ bringing deeper healing and peace and enabling people to cope with deep wounds and great problems as they co-operate with Him through prayer ministry, their own prayer life, scripture, sacraments and fellowship with other trustworthy Christians, in all of the following situations:

- marriage problems and breakdown

- patterns of damage coming from past generations of the family

- effects of family member(s) or their own involvement in such occult practices as spiritualism, fortune telling, horoscopes, tarot cards, ouija boards, Freemasonry, reiki and so on.

- Christians living with anti-Christian or non-Christian members of their own family

- families with tragic deaths for example accident, suicide or murder

- a tremendous range of anxieties about children and grandchildren, including lack of faith, criminality, self-harming, attempted suicide, sometimes involving addictions

- families with feelings greatly repressed—unwilling or unable to face them in childhood or adulthood

- judgements and negative perceptions of parents and of others

- rejection—feeling unloved and unwanted, in some cases even stemming from the mother attempting abortion

- poor self-esteem—even self-hatred or self-rejection

- sexual abuse, incest and rape

- emotional and/or physical abuse

- depression and bipolar disorder (manic depression)

- abortion

- effects of abortion on living siblings

- unease within homosexuality and lesbianism

- guilt burdens and guilt complex

- violence and bullying, perhaps at school or at work, or on the internet, sometimes leading to suicide

- stress from work situations

- binding due to emotional bonds and soul ties with others

- anxieties and fears

- obsessive compulsive disorders and phobias

- eating disorders

- parents of children with various mental disorders

- bereavements

- distorted early perceptions about God

- unwillingness to ask for the grace of God with which to make forgiveness of others and of oneself become more complete over a period of time

- addictions, particularly to drugs and alcohol, but including gambling, computers and so on

Each one of the above bald statements or situations can cover a huge variety of pain and suffering involving a number of people, both within and outside the family. For example, in addition to the suffering and problems of an addict there will generally be a considerable number of family members (and perhaps others such as work colleagues) who are greatly affected. It soon became clear to us that God always wants to do more than one could ever ask or imagine, because each time one damaged individual came to our home, we became aware that God wanted to heal members of their past and present families, and all their convoluted bonds and relationships. Thus the role of Our Lady in untying knots, and the need to arrange for a Mass with the focus of praying for intergenerational healing, rapidly assumed great importance.

Vast Variety of Suffering and Healing Needed—Some Examples

I think, for example, of a mother whose son on drugs obtained access to credit cards, and bought goods to sell for drug money, thus running up a debt of thousands of pounds which his parents did not have. Another son who stole from his loving grandmother and has caused rifts in his family. A lady whose young teenage grandson, badly affected by family break-down and sometimes found in tears, has been committing crimes to obtain drugs, and his grandmother is desperately seeking to avoid his getting a police record. A mother who found her alcoholic child hanging and cut the rope just in time.

Then there were other families where a suicide succeeded, with all the attendant guilt among family and friends, including one mother whose only children, two sons, committed suicide within six weeks of one another. A mother whose son confessed to murder, and many others who had a child or other loved one murdered. Another mother who has at times been cut off from children and grandchildren because she is caring for, and trying to protect, the most vulnerable of her children. A mother who had to leave her husband so that her son could be released from a secure unit, because the father refused to allow him to live at home. Parents who were completely cut off from children and grandchildren for many years because of false memory accusations of childhood sexual abuse. Very many dozens have come because of sexual abuse.

The importance of uniting our suffering with that of Christ upon the cross whilst we are praying for healing, is emphasised in the appendix to this chapter.

The Need for Forgiveness of Others and of Self—God's Grace is Needed.

There is also much overlap between many of these situations. For example, the need for the grace of God with which to forgive others and oneself is clearly essential in all of the other situations listed. There may also be a distorted early perception of God which can leave many people struggling to trust God in the difficulties of later life, in a way that it seems as though they need to forgive God. In fact God never wills bad things to happen—they are the consequences of our free will, sinfulness and brokenness.

Healing Misconceptions of Who God is

There is nothing for which we need to forgive God. However, I think of the lady, wife of a Pentecostal preacher who came for ministry some 25 years ago. When we suggested to her that she was angry with God because of the dreadful things which happened to her as a child, she denied it; her husband immediately backed her up by confirming that he had used Scripture to cause her to think that she must never be angry with God. Yet, a week or two later she suddenly said, 'It was just as though God the Father came to me as a child, stood looking at the awful things which were happening and then said, "It's just too bad". Then He turned on His heel and walked away and left me.' Before she could really begin to trust God and find peace, she needed to be healed of all these desperately painful memories and emotions, including anger with God and feeling that He had betrayed and rejected her, that perhaps He didn't love her or that she was worthless, or for some reason her prayers were not answered.

People are Suffering Everywhere and We Should Meet Their Needs

In each of the above 28 situations, which are by no means a comprehensive list of all the varieties of pain which God longs to heal, there are incalculable numbers of people around us, many of them in our own parishes, who are suffering deeply, often feeling very alone and unsupported, perhaps unable or unwilling to reveal their pain to others. Others may be longing to reach out for help, but don't know anyone who would keep confidences, listen with compassion and non-judgementalism, and who has sufficient faith in the power of God to pray for him/her to bring healing and inner peace.

Family members have varying degrees of awareness of the pain and torment in others, but frequently we have to stand back, seemingly helpless, and pray for God to help those in our own family, perhaps by sending strangers for inner healing prayers who have no emotional ties to the family and its interactions. We all of us need others who can radiate the gentle loving mercy of Christ, and help us feel lovable and to be set free so as to be able to serve others. God is teaching us through the trials of life that we are weak, helpless creatures, utterly dependent upon Him. When, reluctantly, we stop trying to be in control and accept our weakness and need, and pray with humility and repentance and great praise of God,

He comes with His love, mercy and power to heal. I had to go through a succession of crises which I could not solve before I was brought to this realisation of absolute total dependence on God.

How are We to Pray for Healing?

There is no method or technique because each individual is unique. Thus there has to be considerable listening to what he or she is ready to share and also prayerful listening to God at the same time because we are completely dependent upon Him to reveal, to guide and to heal. The ministers begin with prayer for protection for everyone and for discernment and the power of the Holy Spirit.

Prayer then begins before conception when we are 'in the mind' of God (Jr 1:4–5, Ep 1:4). We are then undamaged by the brokenness of humanity and we are our real selves made in the image and likeness of God. This links up with our destiny when Christ has finally restored us to complete wholeness (holiness) to bring us to our Father.

Prayer is needed for conception because this is not always in love and peace and it then continues through the days and nights in the womb, as we pray for Christ to free this new life from any disturbances or damage or any effects through the hormones of stress in the physical or mental state of the mother, as well as any negativity from the father.

Christ can free the new life from any rejection or threat to life from possible abortion or from the attitudes of parents due to such circumstances as financial or other pressures making them reluctant or afraid to have another child. We pray that Jesus brings love, welcome and peace to this new life growing throughout the months in the womb, and then pray that He eases any undue pain or stress during delivery. It is important to pray for the baby to draw the first breaths freely because if the baby were in danger of suffocating, then years later the adult may encounter difficulties in facing new situations and challenges because they always want to retreat back to a place of safety (the womb).

We pray that the new-born baby is delivered straight into the arms of Christ to be held against His breast to experience total love, welcome and security. We pray that Jesus promises never to leave the child for one moment throughout life (Is 49:15), though they will not always be aware of His presence through their senses. Then we pray that Jesus opens His arms to embrace all the family and to bond the baby to parents and existing siblings more deeply than may have happened in actual life.

Prayer continues through each moment of babyhood and childhood up to about seven or eight years of age. We ask that if the baby needs to be touched and held, perhaps waking in fear in the dark, and no-one knew or came, then Jesus Himself will come at once and pick up the baby and restore peace, security and love.

Even if the adult is not aware of all the root causes of unease which occurred very early in life and which are now showing up in their later life, Jesus has a complete record of every hurt or disturbance because when one of His beloved children is in some form of pain He is hurting with them. Thus the prayer for healing of memories can be very relaxed and peaceful because there is no pressure on anyone. The Lord may reveal through the gift of a word of knowledge enough information to guide the prayer minister perhaps through that word evoking some almost hidden memory in the person.

We pray that Jesus touches each wound in one of these early root experiences with His wounds and draws out through His Precious Blood all of the pain and damage into His suffering on the cross.

Then the person is in a new place to ask God to give the child within the grace with which to forgive others and themselves, and even to free them from any negative perceptions of God which may have come to the young child as a result of suffering in which it appeared that God was absent or at least not helping. Even if at first they can only wish that they could want to forgive, it is sufficient for the Lord to begin to help them. Forgiveness is a process which may for some people take months or even years to reach completion. No-one can measure with certainty whether they have forgiven another person or themselves 50%, 80%, 90%, 98%. Thus part of the on-going co-operation with Christ is to pray daily for Him to bring us towards total forgiveness. The struggle with and timing of forgiveness is movingly discussed in Chapter 18.

There is need to pray for repentance on behalf of the child within for any negative perceptions which they made of parents which broke a commandment (Ep 6:2–3) and which led to the reaping in adult life of what was sown by these judgements in early childhood (Ga 6:7). This includes bitter-root judgements (Heb 12:15) and bitter-root expectations which may show up in the person realising that they have throughout their life experienced similar repeated negative patterns of treatment from a number of people. These bitter roots are explained in the appendix to Chapter 10.

Very many people have damaged or even almost zero self-esteem and need to be helped to co-operate daily with God, telling themselves the truth that they are a beloved child of God, and becoming freed by Christ of self-dislike, self-rejection and even self-hatred as they ask Him to heal the root causes. They need to repent of believing and holding onto lies about the nature of God and of lies about who they are and of the value that they are to God and to others. There is need to renounce these old wrong ideas and attitudes which became planted in childhood and to pray passages of Scripture for the renewing of the mind (Rm 12:1–2, Ep 1:17–20, Ep 4:22–24, Col 1:9–10). They may also need to renounce any involvement in occult practices followed by prayers for deliverance and receive a fresh in-filling of the Holy Spirit.

Other ways in which we are able to co-operate with Christ so that we receive the healing which He wants to give us include:

- Telling oneself daily the truth that I am a beloved child of God, and reading frequently passages of Scripture such as Zephaniah 3:14–19 and those just listed above, can be a vital part of God restoring a healthy sense of self-worth which is the opposite of self-centredness.

- People need to realise that generally inner healing is little-by-little (Dt 7:22), and requires their co-operation in many ways with Christ (see Appendix 1).

- Learning to live in the house of the creative word (Jn 8:31–32) by speaking and thinking in the positive and up-building ways inspired by the Holy Spirit instead of old habits of speaking and thinking negatively and destructively (Ps 52:4).

- Praying daily for protection by putting on the armour of God (Ep 6:10–17).

- Praying daily with the authority of Christ for strongholds in our minds and in those of our loved ones to be loosened and destroyed (2 Co 10:4–5).

- Recognising inner vows which we have made perhaps very early in life, then repenting of them, reckoning them as dead and releasing forgiveness towards anyone including ourselves. These vows frequently take the form of 'I will never…' or 'I will always…'

- Prayerfully discovering whether we have the heart and mind set of an orphan rather than the God-given heart and mind-set of sonship, out of which we can do the will of God in freedom and peace rather than in striving and stress.

- Praying with the authority of Christ and the sword of the Holy Spirit to cut ourselves and loved ones free of all unhelpful emotional bonds and soul ties between us, which can bind any of us to living or dead members of our family or to others closely connected with us.

- Praying that Christ as He sets us free will bond us more and more deeply to one another with His perfect love.

At the end of prayer ministry session the prayer ministers after the person has gone, need to pray together for God to free them from anything harmful and cleanse them and fill them afresh in mind, body and spirit with the living waters of His Holy Spirit.

These are not the only aspects which need to be addressed if people are to be helped to grow into full inner healing and conversion, but they are fundamental and essential.[22] Other areas also likely to need prayers for healing include freeing people from damaged patterns in their family line and from curses. This can best be done by prayers at a Mass for intergenerational healing (family tree Mass). These and other aspects have been discussed elsewhere[23] and in Chapter 7.

We need great wisdom and guidance from the Holy Spirit for really deep lasting healing to take place at the key roots of damage, because without this any improvement may be only superficial and temporary, leaving people in the position about which Jeremiah wrote: 'They have healed the wound of my people lightly, saying "Peace, peace" when there is no peace.' (Jr 6:14). In his final address to the Synod Fathers in October 2014, Pope Francis spoke of:

> ... the temptation to a destructive tendency to do-goodism, that in the name of a deceptive mercy binds the wounds without first curing them and treating them; that treats the symptoms and not the roots.

Genuine healing takes time, as we allow Jesus to heal our wounded memories, and to touch our wounds with His Wounds, and through His Precious Blood to draw our pain, anger, rejection and so on into His suffering on the Cross. Then we can ask him for the grace with which to forgive more completely, and to receive more and more of His love for others, which may take a long time. We need to pray daily with His authority for strongholds of damaged structures within our minds, which have up to now kept us bound like Lazarus, to be loosened and destroyed, and for Christ to cut all the emotional and other bonds which can obstruct His love flowing in us and through us to others.[24]

Reflections upon 32 years of full-time involvement in the ministry of prayer for inner healing, and 11 previous years part-time, has led to my examining what God has been revealing of His power to heal in the light of Christian teaching. Supported by 34 testimonies written by people who have experienced God's loving power in many areas of suffering, these reflections, in the light of the Church's teaching documents, show clearly that the ministry of prayer for inner healing is a necessary part of evangelisation, and is therefore an absolutely essential ministry of the Church.[25] The involvement of many more lay people in this work requires much greater awareness and openness among priests and bishops.

God is Waiting for us to Come to Him in Repentance and Humility to Seek His Help and Healing

Unless and until the Holy Spirit is allowed to bring about deep healing and genuine and lasting conversion of hearts and minds to Christ of huge numbers of people, the constantly repeated experience of the People of God is that they turn away from God, and they face apparently insurmountable disasters which are the consequence of their disobedience. God is waiting for all of us to come to Him in repentance and humility and accept our inability to sort out our own problems. 'If my people who are called by my name humble themselves, and pray and seek My face, and turn from their wicked ways, then I will hear from heaven, and will forgive their sin and heal their land' (2Ch 7:14).

The USA has had clear scripture-based warnings[26] connecting 9/11 and the stock market collapse of 2008, but so far has reacted with arrogance and pride. This country and others need to learn from this. We read of many examples of how God reveals His mighty power when the people and their leaders acknowledge their sinfulness and helplessness and stop trying to win spiritual battles with purely human resources: Moses, Gideon being told by God to cut his army from 32,000 to 300, and David who faced Goliath are examples. God is constantly reminding us 'Not by might or by power, but by My Spirit says the Lord' (Zc 4:16), and 'Fear not and be not dismayed at this great multitude; for the battle is not yours but God's... You will not need to fight in this battle; take your position, stand still, and see the victory of the Lord on your behalf' (2Ch 20:15,17).

We all of us in the Church, clergy and laity, need to keep proclaiming that what we are going through is spiritual warfare, and that our weapons are in focused, specific prayers, for example those collected together by Bishop Porteous,[27] which are set in repentance and humility with great praise and thanksgiving to God that His Son Jesus Christ has won the victory. We can and should pray with His authority, as His Holy Spirit teaches and guides us, to bring deeper conversion to Christ with consequent healing to more and more of His beloved broken children, so that they in turn are empowered by the Holy Spirit to bring the Good News to others.

Pope Francis has called for spirit-filled evangelisers[28] flowing from a personal encounter with the saving grace of Jesus, who wants us to touch human misery, to touch the suffering flesh of others,[29] and to do so with gentleness and reverence.[30]

In this work of praying for inner healing one sometimes meets a person who has been looked down upon, used and rejected by the rest of the family, perhaps treated as a scapegoat. He or she may never have experienced love and support and understanding from anyone close to them all their life. They may have found very few, if any, people to listen to them when they become ready to speak of the pain, much of which they may have had to suppress. It is a humbling experience and a great privilege to be asked to listen when such a victim begins to speak and perhaps to weep. We begin to see God revealing more and more of the wonder of their being and we can join with them in praising and thanking Him for this (Ps 139). It can become evident that this amazing person who once was crushed is now revealed as the key to a vast amount of healing and restoration which the Lord wants to do in their past, present and perhaps future family. This appears to be so because often he or she seems to be the sole member of the family who is turning to God and praying for healing and reconciliation, from a place of deep need but also of great faith. As we accompany such a person on their journey, for months or longer, we experience what it is, in the words of Pope Francis, 'to enter into the reality of other people's lives and know the power of tenderness'.[31] Sometimes we can be privileged in joining in praising and thanking God as signs of His healing in one or more members of the family begin to emerge.

The Pope 'invites everyone to be bold and creative in the task of rethinking the goals, structures, style and methods of evangelisation in their respective communities'.[32] He writes at some length about personal spiritual accompaniment in processes of patience and compassion which need us to practise the art of listening whilst helping others along the paths of true growth.[33]

When discussing difficulties in finding people to undertake the apostolic work of evangelisation, Pope Francis describes[34] the biggest threat of all which gradually takes shape, using some words of his predecessor before he was elected Pope Benedict—'the grey pragmatism of the daily life of the Church in which all appears to proceed normally, while in reality faith is wearing down and degenerating into small-mindedness'. Pope Francis continues: 'a tomb mentality develops and slowly transforms Christians into mummies in a museum'. The present author has described in some detail[35] how Christ wants us to pray to free ourselves and one another from the many layers of binding which have held us prisoners like mummies, so that like Lazarus we become unbound by the love and prayers of others and we can live life in its fullness.

Four decades of experience and many personal testimonies examined elsewhere[36] clearly show that prayer for inner healing of deep early roots is an essential and effective part of evangelisation. It has brought forth considerable fruit entirely in accordance with the paths which Pope Francis has now set before the Church. It is urgent that the Church should take active and widespread steps to make this healing evangelisation available to many more people both within and outside the Church.

Appendix

The Catechism teaches that suffering can become a participation in the saving work of Jesus[37] as we unite our suffering with His on the cross and learn that in our endurance we follow St Paul 'in my flesh I complete what is lacking in Christ's afflictions for the sake of His Body, that is the Church' (2 Co 12:19, Col 1:24).[38]

Pope Paul VI in his closing address to Vatican II included this Message to the Poor, the Sick and the Suffering:

To all of you, brothers [and sisters] in trial, who are visited by suffering under a thousand forms, the Council has a very special message. It feels that your pleading eyes are fixed on the Church, burning with fever or hollow with fatigue; questioning eyes which search in vain for the why of human suffering and which ask anxiously when and whence will come relief. Very dear brothers [and sisters], we feel echoing deeply within our hearts as fathers and pastors your laments and your complaints. Our suffering is increased at the thought that it is not within our power to bring you bodily help nor the lessening of your physical sufferings, which physicians, nurses, and all those dedicated to the service of the sick are endeavouring to relieve as best they can.

But we have something deeper and more valuable to give you, the only truth capable of answering the mystery of suffering and of bringing you relief without illusion, and that is faith and union with the Man of Sorrows (Is 53,3), with Christ the Son of God, nailed to the cross for our sins and for our salvation. Christ did not do away with suffering. He did not even wish to unveil to us entirely the mystery of suffering. He took suffering upon Himself and this is enough to make you understand all its value.

All of you who feel heavily the weight of the cross, you who are poor and abandoned, you who weep, you who are persecuted for justice, you who are ignored, you the unknown victims of suffering, take courage. You are the preferred children of the kingdom of God, the kingdom of hope, happiness, and life. You are the brothers [and sisters] of the suffering Christ, and with Him, if you wish, you are saving the world! This is the Christian view of suffering, the only one which gives peace. Know that you are not alone, separated, abandoned, or useless. You have been called by Christ and are His living and transparent image.[39]

Notes

1   Pope Paul VI, *Evangelii Nuntiandi*, 14.

2   *Ibid.*, 15.

3   Pope Francis, *Evangelii Gaudium*, 8.

4   R. Cantalamessa, 'Spiritual Healing' in *Prayer for Healing* (International Colloquium, Rome: International Catholic Charismatic Renewal Services, 2003), pp. 219–20.

5   A. Guile, *Journey into Wholeness: Prayer for Inner Healing—An Essential Ministry of the Church* (Leominster: Gracewing, 2013).

6   *Ibid.*

7   F. MacNutt, *The Nearly Perfect Crime—How the Church Almost Killed the Ministry of Healing* (Grand Rapids, MI: Chosen Books, 2005).

8   Pope Paul VI, *Evangelii Nuntiandi*, 15.

9   Guile, *Journey Into Wholeness*.

10 G. Pattison, 'Passionate Thinker', in *The Tablet* vol. 267 no. 8995 (2013), pp. 6–7.

11 Vatican II, *Lumen Gentium*, 35.

12 Guile, *Journey Into Wholeness*.

13 *Catechism of the Catholic Church*, 905.

14 Guile, *Journey Into Wholeness*.

15 *Catechism of the Catholic Church*, 2003.

16 Guile, *Journey Into Wholeness*.

17 P. Lynch, *Awakening the Giant in Evangelism and the Catholic Church* (London: Darton, Longman and Todd, 1990), pp. 96–100.

18 L. J. Suenens, *A New Pentecost* (London: Darton, Longman and Todd, 1975), p. 122.

19 *Ibid.*, p. 125.

20 Pope Francis, 'A Big Heart Open to God', interview with Antonio Spadaro, in *America Magazine*, 30 September 2013.

21 Guile, *Journey Into Wholeness*.

22 *Ibid.*

23 *Ibid.*

24 *Ibid.*

25 *Ibid.*

26 J. Cahn, *The Harbinger*, (Lake Mary, Florida: Front Line, 2011).

27 J. Porteous, *Prayers for Those Experiencing Spiritual Affliction*, (London: CTS, 2012).

28 Pope Francis, *Evangelii Gaudium*, 259.

29 *Ibid.*, 270.

30 *Ibid.*, 271.

31 *Ibid.*, 270.

32 *Ibid.*, 33.

33 *Ibid.*, 169–173.

34 *Ibid.*, 83.

35 Guile, *Journey into Wholeness*, pp. 131–160.

36 Guile, *Journey into Wholeness*.

37 *Catechism of the Catholic Church*, 1521.

38 *Ibid.*, 1508.

39 Pope Paul VI, *Closing Address to the Second Vatican Council* (8 Dec 1965).

3

The Role of Priests in the Healing Ministry

Alan Guile

Since the Second Vatican Council the ministries of laymen and women in the Church have been receiving a growing recognition and acceptance. In this chapter, Alan Guile asks searching questions about how seminarians, on the road to the priesthood, are being trained to exercise their healing ministry and to collaborate with laymen and women who are gifted by the Holy Spirit with charismatic gifts for the whole parish. The priest is not the only minister of healing grace in the parish.

The Priests Alone Cannot Meet All the Needs of Inner Healing Ministry

It is natural for Roman Catholics seeking help in their pain to look initially toward their priest(s). Most parishioners have great compassion for their priests who are carrying many burdens, some unknown to their parishioners, and doing their best through very difficult situations. Thus people understand that it is generally impossible for a priest to be able to offer personally all the prayer ministry and ongoing support which is needed outside his work in the healing sacraments. Many factors play a part in this. Among them are:

- Priests are increasingly overworked, with two or even three parishes to run.

- Whilst the suffering of people is continually increasing with further breakdown of family relationships, poor parenting, greater temptations of materialism and increasing spiritual warfare, the availability of priests is constantly decreasing. The average age of priests keeps rising, and they are being moved so frequently to plug gaps left by death or retirement, that they are often not long enough in one parish to get to know at any real depth family members and their situations and needs.

- Whilst the number of priests is decreasing, calls upon their time have often increased for duties which some years ago hardly existed.

- The morale of the priests and the trust of people in them have been adversely affected by the sexual abuse by priests and its cover up.

- There seems to be a crisis of identity and authority in many priests. How often have people heard homilies about the desperate spiritual battle in which we are all caught? How often has a homily lifted their spirits with hope and trust in the victory of Christ upon the Cross, and of how we can trust Him, praise Him, pray for protection and use His weapons of prayer with His authority? How often have people been warned of the dangers of involvement in specific occult activities?

- Some priests have not had very much first-hand personal experience of the multitude of painful situations and difficulties facing lay people and their families, especially if they entered a seminary very young. Awareness of this can tend to be an obstacle to some people opening up beyond a certain point to some priests.

- People frequently feel unable to reveal to their priest the depths of their problems and pain. They may perceive him as far too busy so they are reluctant to seek to take up his time. Sometimes when they catch him for a moment in church, his eyes and attention are elsewhere. They may feel that he wouldn't fully understand the problems of their own and family lives, and would not be likely to know how to give effective ongoing help and support.

I recall a day when I had two hours of ministry in the morning with a young man, another two hours in the afternoon with a lady who had been sexually abused by several men when very young, and at 5.40 I was relaxing when my doorbell rang. It was a lady I hardly knew, and who talked almost non-stop until 9.25 pm about non-significant events. Then suddenly she told me something which she said she had thought she would never be able to tell anyone in her whole life, and which she would have to take to her grave. It was too late and I was too tired to begin prayer ministry at that time of night, particularly after almost eight hours of ministry that day, and I had so many appointments that I could not see her for two weeks. She accepted the delay gratefully. Before that appointment arrived for us to begin prayer ministry, she met me in the street and telephoned once. On both occasions she said, 'I can't believe how much better I feel now that I have told someone'. Psalm 32 contains the line, 'When I kept silent, my bones wasted away through my groaning all day long'. In her case she had done nothing wrong: she was an innocent victim.

When I spoke to a senior priest about my surprise that in many years of coming regularly to Mass and to the sacrament of Reconciliation she had not become unburdened, he said that he was not surprised because many people feel embarrassed to speak of some aspects of their lives to a priest. A very experienced Catholic GP came to the conclusion that some people feel more comfortable speaking of their pain and needs to someone other than a priest in confession—if they don't know of anyone with a prayer ministry then it may be a doctor or a counsellor. Thus it would not be altogether surprising if many priests, and perhaps especially bishops, do not have full awareness of the depth and variety of pain which their people are carrying, in some cases in desperation.

This lack of awareness is often accompanied by the feeling within many people that they are the only one with this particular problem and that no-one would spare the time to listen in-depth and understand with compassion, if they were to reveal all their hurts and struggles. Furthermore, many think that if others really knew about them, then they would feel rejected and perhaps worthless. In fact, if the people doing the listening and the prayer ministry are called by God (as with priests in the confessional), they do not judge but instead feel more love and respect for the sufferer as he/she takes the risk of opening up, as the listener gets deeper insights into the wonderful creation of God gradually emerging within this person who is damaged.

I had a vivid experience of this over 35 years ago when I had been invited to go to Hawkstone Hall for a week, to lead a group consisting of sisters, a priest and a brother who were attending the three-month renewal course. After several meetings, no-one had opened up about their need for help through prayer, until suddenly one sister had the courage to do so. The love and compassion in the group was then palpable and others began to reveal their needs. It is not surprising that many people find it hard to open up to their priests about their sufferings and burdens.

It is vital that any discussion or prayer about the situation of priests or their training is not in a spirit of judgementalism or criticism. Instead we need to ask God to give us more and more of His love for His priests and this will lead us to help them and pray for them. An example of a senior priest being blessed and changed by God when we and others prayed for him has been described.[1]

Seminary Training and Priestly Formation

It follows from the teaching of the Scriptures outlined in the previous chapter which shows that Jesus gave the Church the mission to bring the Good News and to heal, including bringing inner or spiritual healing, that it is vitally important that teaching clearly establishes this dual call in the minds of the seminarians. It would also be helpful if whilst training they learn to pray with one another, as is now happening at Oscott College. The teaching of the Scriptures can be reinforced by relevant passages in the Catechism, Vatican II documents and other sources on such matters as grace and gifts of the Holy Spirit.

It is very encouraging that since this was written, Pope Francis has issued *Amoris Laetitia* where he calls for seminary formation to enable the exploration of psychological and affective background and experiences, and the Rector of Oscott College has already written in The Tablet about this taking place. This important development is referred to in chapters 6 and 10, and at the end of the present chapter.

Some Aspects for Consideration for Inclusion in Seminaries

There are sources from which to draw sound teaching about prayer for inner healing, so that seminarians learn how to seek the guidance of the Holy Spirit so as to be able to pray for the whole person. They can grow in faith that God always wants to accomplish inner spiritual healing, peace, faith and ongoing growth in Him, although physical healing may or may not happen. They can learn that the sufferer may need ongoing encouragement and prayer ministry to become free of obstacles to God bringing about deeper healing. These may include:

- being unwilling or unable initially to listen to God and to want to surrender more completely to Him

- lack of forgiveness (towards others, self, God)

- poor sense of self-worth (true identity as a child of God)

- being unable to 'live in the creative house' (Jn 8:31–2) by being disciplined in speaking and thinking positively as God does

- fear or other negative perception of God from childhood learning and experiences together with the behaviour of one's own father

- unrepented sins

- unwillingness to face up to repressed or partially repressed feelings and hurt and to let God reveal roots which need healing

- not letting go of strongholds of wrong patterns of thinking, attitudes, ideas desires, beliefs, habits and behaviours and damaged reactions

- and recognising, repenting of, reckoning as dead and releasing forgiveness where there was any inner vow made earlier in life, often taking the form of 'I will never...' or ''I will always...'

- subconsciously not wanting to be healed because of the challenges and responsibilities which would follow, and wanting to hold on to attention which present disabilities bring

- some hold of Satan

We have all the encouragement needed to pray for the healing and unbinding that the Lord wants in the teaching of the Church, which is entirely compatible with taking up our cross and uniting our suffering with that of Christ upon the Cross when and how God chooses that it remains. The Catechism includes:

> Christ invites His disciples to follow Him by taking up their cross in their turn. By following Him they acquire a new outlook on illness and the sick... He makes them share in his ministry of compassion and sharing... The risen Lord renews this mission ('In my name they will lay their hands on the sick, and they will recover')... The Lord gives to some a special charism of healing so as to make manifest the power of the grace of the risen Lord.[2]

Again we have:

> It is part of the plan laid down by God's providence that we should
> fight strenuously against all sickness and carefully seek the blessings
> of good health, so that we can fulfil our role in human society and
> in the Church.[3]

This teaching appears at the beginning of the General Introduction to
Pastoral Care of the Sick, of which each priest has a copy, and it was
quoted by Cardinal Ratzinger in the Instructions on Prayers for Healing,
issued by the Congregation for the Doctrine of the Faith, and approved
by Pope St John Paul II.[4] Perhaps we have too often narrowed our
understanding and appreciation of these teachings towards physical
suffering and sickness, and assumed they are part of redemptive suffering
and to be 'offered up' instead of allowing God to make the decisions as
we pray for healing. We have not sufficiently appreciated that God always
wants to answer our prayers for emotional, psychological and spiritual
healing, so that we experience deeper conversion to Christ through the
power of the Holy Spirit.

Inner Healing and Early Root Causes of Damage

It needs to be taught in seminaries that whatever the nature of pain and
suffering that we may encounter during adult life, we can never approach
full healing which Christ longs to give us unless the vital early root causes
are healed. Clearly, people also need prayer for healing of hurts and
experiences which occur later in life after these early roots, but it is always
the latter which play a major role in our damaged reactions and behaviours
to the stresses and traumas of adult life.

These early roots, which frequently need to be the first priority in
prayer ministry, lie in:

a) damaged patterns of behaviour coming from past generations of
our family

b) effects arising in the womb and at delivery

c) experiences from birth through babyhood and early childhood up
to the age of about seven.

Prayer for Jesus to bring healing can start before conception because
Jeremiah 1:5 and Ephesians 1:4 tell us that we were known to Him before
the creation of the world. Thus, beginning our prayer there, when we
were undamaged by human sin, connects us with our own eventual

restoration by Christ to our real selves when all of God's work of healing and cleansing us has been accomplished and we can be admitted to our home in Heaven.

The significance of these three areas (a), (b) and (c) and how they establish early roots in our subconscious mind, and thus control how we react to the sufferings and problems of everyday life, and how we can pray for Jesus to heal them, have all been extensively described and illustrated by the present author elsewhere.[5]

Some further aspects which are dealt with there,[6] and which it would help priests to learn about, are now listed and commented upon briefly:

a) Generational healing. It has been established for decades, following the age-old traditions of the Church, that it is vital to pray at a Mass celebrated especially for the intention that the families of those present may be healed of damaged patterns of behaviour. Books have been written about this by priests.[7] I know people in many parts of the country struggle to find a priest who is aware of the vital importance of celebrating a Mass at which all the participants can pray with expectant faith for all their own family, past, present and yet to be born, so that damaging patterns of behaviour cease to be experienced by succeeding generations. Yet the importance of this has been highlighted by priests, doctors and others for over thirty years.[8] When the evening Mass in our parish is known to be an opportunity for this, the attendance can rise from 25–30 to over 100, with people travelling from many places up to 150 miles away.

b) It is essential to know the vital significance in affecting human life of breaking the commandment, 'Respect (honour) Your father and mother', which is the first commandment that has a promise added: 'so that all may go well with You and You may live a long time in the land' (Ep 6:2–3). No one, apart from Christ Himself, has had perfect parents, so that every one of us has wittingly or unwittingly made some negative perceptions of our parents. However mild or innocuous they might appear, they bring consequences in our adult life. I had learnt the theory of this commandment and the consequences of breaking it, and of 'whatever a man sows that he will also reap' (Ga 6:7) many years before, when, approaching seventy, I was suddenly shocked to learn that an apparently mild perception of my father as weak had lead to many years of pain and difficulty when dealing with male authority figures in my 34 years on the staff of universities. It even affected my health through stress.

c) Bitter root expectancy and bitter root judgement (Heb 12:15), play a major role in how our lives can be affected and only Jesus can heal us. This needs to be taught and understood, particularly in marriage but also in our other relationships.

d) We need to teach how to pray about becoming free of strong-holds (2 Co 10:4), and how essential it is to take the authority of Christ to cut our emotional bonds, soul ties and any unhelpful binding to others. These prayers are needed every day, as none of us can say that we are unaffected by some binding.

e) Priests do not always know how to handle their own feelings or those revealed to them by suffering parishioners and over fifteen have come to me for prayer ministry. In the 1970's an elderly priest told me how an HMI had gone to his seminary president whilst he himself was a seminarian. After the inspection, the HMI said, 'Academically very good, but what do You do about the emotions of Your students?' 'We crush them', was the president's reply. Effects on this particular elderly priest and his painful experiences were clear to be seen. When I mentioned this to a priest trained in the same seminary in the last two decades, he told me that this conversation between the HMI and the president was still being talked about in that seminary in his day.

f) Over forty years ago my wife and I became close to our bishop in Leeds, and we suggested to him that there needed to be some place within the diocese with a small community including perhaps a priest, a nun and a married couple, to which any priest could go at any time when he was greatly stressed. If he wished simply to remain a while in silence he could do so. If he chose to share some concerns with community members they would listen, and would pray with him if he wished. This was during a period when a number of priests were leaving the priesthood. The bishop very much welcomed the idea, and felt that it did not necessarily have to be confined to a single diocese. It never materialised.

g) Priests may not always have had sufficient training in listening techniques, basic ideas connected with counselling, or in spiritual direction or guidance of people encountering so many temptations and suffering in their lives, following many deep hurts very early in their lives. Priests often do not know how Christ can heal these deep root causes which underlie their struggles to cope with their present problems and suffering. They are left to do their best as they try to help their people, learning by experience and prayer.

h) In many seminaries there seems to have been little awareness of the realities of spiritual warfare for example that the first main aim of satanists is the destruction of priesthood and seminaries. Many priests have had no teaching about, or experience of, deliverance ministry and exorcism. When I asked one priest to pray with someone for deliverance from evil spirits I was told 'I'm afraid to do it—you do it'. Other priests have told me that they don't want to have anything to do with it. Priests sometimes seem unaware that they have a greater spiritual authority than is given to anyone else, and that they are meant to use it to protect their people and to set them free.

Few priests seem to know about or take seriously the remarks of Pope Paul VI, who posed the following question at a General Audience in 1972: 'What are the greatest needs of the Church today? His answer was:

> Do not let our answer surprise You as being over-simple, or even superstitious and unreal: one of the greatest needs is defence from that evil which is called the devil. It is contrary to the teaching of the Bible and of the Church to refuse to recognise the existence of such a reality—or to explain it as a pseudo-reality, a conceptual and fanciful personification of the unknown causes of our misfortunes.[9]

Several priests trained in the last twenty years told me how whilst students they managed to 'smuggle' the diocesan exorcist into the seminary to give a talk. They did not dare to invite him to a meal so he just slipped quietly away afterwards. One short, unofficial talk is very far short of what is desperately needed. The course now being given in Rome involves not only teaching, but also spending many hours in the company of an appointed exorcist while he is dealing with a variety of suffering people.[10]

The Faithful are not Warned Often Enough or Even At All About the Dangers and Consequences of Contact and Dealings with Practices such as Spiritism, Fortune Telling, Horoscopes, Reiki Healing and so on. These Require Deliverance from Evil Spirits.

Despite this warning of Pope Paul VI and other teaching of the Church, one frequently finds Catholics, many still attending Mass, who are involved in such dangerous and wrong activities as spiritualism, fortune-telling, horoscopes, ouija boards, tarot cards, Reiki healing and so on. They have neither been warned of the dangers nor set free from the influences of evil by their priests. Other totally innocent people need deliverance because of demonisation from childhood trauma or because of a curse. Many dioceses throughout the world have not had or still do not have any exorcist appointed by the bishop. Fr Rufus Pereira, a founder of the International Association of Exorcists, wrote:

> Nevertheless there is not a single exorcist appointed in most countries, and even in most dioceses in many of the other countries, and so our people in their need have no alternative but to go to either spiritists or to neo-Pentecostal healers.[11]

Only a very few years ago there were only six exorcists in the whole of the USA, but recognition of the need in Italy has led to the training of priest exorcists, 500 in Italy and others from elsewhere.[12] A priest told me recently that Ireland had been without officially appointed exorcists.

Our Own Unhealed Wounds Can Intrude and Interfere With the Free Flow of God's Love to Others

Furthermore, although God only has wounded people whom He can use in various ways in the ministry of bringing healing to others (or in any other capacity, come to that!), it is fundamental that one who is being used most powerfully by God should get most of their own damage healed first. If they do not do so, their own unhealed wounds and needs can intrude and interfere with the free flow of God's love to heal others. We must die more and more to ourselves. Priests, like every other human being, need healing, and it may be harder for them than for many others to admit their own hurts and weaknesses, and to find a safe place to go for help. Too often, when the Church has appreciated some of the needs of priests for help, they have been sent for professional counselling or psychotherapy, instead of calling on the power of Christ through prayer. In 1991, when I wrote a letter to the Tablet (at the request of the deputy editor) about the power of Christ to heal, a priest's letter was also published, part of this was:

> Being a professional psychotherapist as well as a priest, I never mix the two. I will go further. I never pray with people because I wouldn't know where to start. That may shock some readers but it illustrates that each priest has to make do with the attitudes and talents he happens to possess.

Only Christ Can Heal the Whole Person—Has the Church Sometimes Seemed to Have Forgotten This?

One can find accounts by priests needing healing of hurts who attended psychoanalysis sessions with a therapist over a long period, even once a week for eighteen months, almost certainly at very considerable cost, when prayer ministry within the Church should have been a completely free alternative, or could have accompanied fewer sessions with a therapist. A similar approach has been followed in the cases of numbers of priests and religious in various situations of need. Counselling by professionals who are not permitted to pray with their clients and who rely upon human wisdom, techniques or programmes, is never likely to be wholly sufficient because we are body, soul and spirit, and only Christ can heal the whole person through His suffering and death on the cross. The question of whether or not we are getting the right balance between human and divine resources is discussed by the author in chapter six.

Priests and Lay People Working Together

Of course priests were never expected to meet all the huge variety of the needs of a vast number of damaged people. However, those in the Catholic Church tend to look first to their priests for guidance as to where the help can be provided by others in the Church. Furthermore, it is very difficult in the Catholic Church for lay ministries to flourish unless they have the support and preferably active help and encouragement from the priesthood. In the Decree on the Ministry and Life of Priests, Vatican II stated:

> While trying the spirits if they be of God, they must discover with faith, recognize with joy, and foster with diligence the many and varied charismatic gifts of the laity, whether these be of humble or more exalted kind...Priests should also be confident in giving lay people charge of duties in the service of the Church, giving them freedom and opportunity for activity and even inviting them, when opportunity occurs, to take the initiative in undertaking projects of their own.[13]

The Priests Need to be Taught to Recognise Charismatic Gifts in the Church

Unawareness of this Vatican II statement can hardly be claimed because Pope Benedict XVI included this passage in a letter which he wrote to all priests on 18 June 2008. Unfortunately, despite much theorising and talking about collaborative ministry, many priests do not seek to discover with faith, recognize with joy and foster with diligence any gifts of a charismatic kind, but instead often may react negatively. Some have been badly let down by lay people. Perhaps many are unaware of the further teaching:

> It is not only through the sacraments and ministrations of the Church that the Holy Spirit makes holy the People, leads them and enriches them with His virtues. Allotting His gifts according as He wills (cf 1 Co 12:11), He also distributes special graces among the faithful of every rank. By these gifts He makes them fit and ready to undertake various tasks for the renewal and building up of the Church, as it is written 'the manifestation of the Spirit is given to everyone for profit' (1 Co 12:7). Whether these charisms be very remarkable or more simple and widely diffused, they are to be received with thanksgiving and consolation since they are fitting and useful for the needs of the Church. Extraordinary gifts are not to be rashly desired, nor is it from these that the fruits of apostolic labours are to be presumptuously expected. Those who have charge over the Church should judge the genuineness and proper use of these gifts, through their office not indeed to extinguish the Spirit, but to test all things and hold fast to what is good. (cf 1 Th 5:12,19–21).[14]

Of course, for reasons given above, it is extremely difficult for priests to get to know people in sufficient depth to know who can be trusted in such delicate ministry and who is gifted and called by God. However, priests who are aware of the needs and great blessings which can follow, do find that the Lord guides them to the right people through prayer.

In 1999 our bishop wrote a letter to all the priests of the diocese inviting them to discern which of their parishioners might be called by God to pray for inner healing, and to send their names recommending them for a 12-week course which he had asked my wife and me to give. He wrote,

> I think it is important that attendance at the course should be by invitation only because those taking part will need to be well-balanced and with a real prayer life and people who could be trusted never to break confidences and who would be willing to listen and pray non-judgementally out of love and compassion and not out of any wrong motives such as curiosity, or the desire to give advice or their own need of satisfaction.

The Decree on the Apostolate of Lay People Stresses the Importance of Lay People Using the Gifts which God Gives

The Holy Spirit sanctifies the People of God through the ministry and through the sacraments. However, for the exercise of the apostolate He gives the faithful special gifts besides (cf 1 Co 12:7), 'allotting them to each one as He wills' (1 Co 12:11), so that each and all, putting at the service of others the grace received may be 'as good stewards of God's varied gifts'(1 P 4:10), for the building up of the whole body in charity (cf Ep 4:16). From the reception of these charisms, even the most ordinary ones, there arises for each of the faithful the right and duty of exercising them in the Church and in the world for the good of men and the development of the Church, of exercising them in the freedom of the Holy Spirit who 'breathes where He wills' (Jn 3:8), and at the same time in communion with his brothers in Christ, and with his pastors especially. It is for the pastors to pass judgement on the authenticity and good use of these gifts, not certainly with a view to quenching the Spirit but to testing everything and keeping what is good. (cf 1Th 5:12,19–21).[15]

There is the Right and Duty to Exercise the Gifts of the Spirit

This passage stresses that gifts of the Holy Spirit are given to every member of the Church to be used in service to others. And it is a duty of all to exercise them when they are being given those gifts. God doesn't make any spare parts in the Body of Christ. As the same Vatican II document puts it:

> In the organism of a living body no member plays a purely passive part, sharing in the life of the body it shares at the same time in its activity. The same is true for the Body of Christ, the Church; 'the whole body achieves full growth in dependence on the full functioning of each part' (Ep 4:16). Between the members of this body there exists, further, such a unity and solidarity (cf Ep 4:16) that a member who does not work at the growth of the body to the extent of his possibilities must be considered useless both to the Church and to himself.[16]

If I had been aware some years ago of this particular teaching of the Church, I would almost certainly have felt it to be harsh, judgmental and unrealistic because I was convinced that I had nothing to offer. There are probably many in the Church, like I was then, who are still feeling that even if God and the Church expect more of them then they haven't anything to offer, and that in any case their life is too busy to consider the possibility of serving the Church in some new way. However, God frequently uses in His plans those who previously were crippled by such things as poor self-esteem, and hurts, and who through this have learnt that without Christ they can do nothing. He puts His treasure in earthen vessels to make it clear that the new life and power come entirely from Him not from human beings.

In most of our parishes in the UK we have a sizeable and even sometimes a high proportion of people who would describe themselves as practising Catholics, who have been led to believe that all God and the Church expect of them is to attend Mass once a week, and that they do not need to give any further time and effort. It is my considered conclusion that many priests hesitate to disturb and challenge their people with the true demands of Christ upon His followers. I have seen a priest flinch when I mentioned this last quotation from Vatican II, when he was asking me to consider speaking to his parishioners. That statement[17] is not in fact judgemental or unrealistic but arises from God's infinite love for each person to whom He has given unique gifts, and God needs that person to use his gifts for the healthy growth of the Church.

Perhaps many priests, having been subjected to grumbling, criticisms and even complaints (some to bishops) from their people, and from parishioners leaving the Church, have become restricted by fear. Jesus certainly did not hesitate to challenge and disturb and gave people the freedom to walk away if His teaching was too disturbing for them. However, it is vital that we remember the words of St Paul: 'By speaking the truth in a spirit of love, we must grow up in every way to Christ, who is the head. Under His control all the different parts of the body fit together, and the whole body is held together by every joint with which it is provided. So when each separate part works as it should, the whole body grows and builds itself up through love'. (Ep 4:15–16). Thus our emphasis should be on God's love, compassion and mercy for each one of His precious but wounded children rather than appearing to place harsh and unloving demands and challenges on them.

Fr Ronald Rolheiser wrote in the Catholic Herald in 2008 about his reflections on the most important thing which the Church should be saying to the world today. He concluded that it should be speaking words of understanding, consolation and comfort, and that one of the major tasks should be to console the world and to comfort its people rather than stressing challenge. 'Comfort, O comfort my people, says our God. Comfort them. Encourage the people of Jerusalem. Tell them they have suffered long enough and their sins are now forgiven.' (Is 40:1–2). Fr Rolheiser wrote of how many years earlier he heard an echo of these words in the reflections of a very saintly priest, ordained over fifty years before. When he asked, 'Father, if You had Your life as a priest to live over again, would You do anything in a different way?', Fr Rolheiser expected his answer to be 'No', because he had been such a wonderful priest. To his surprise, the answer was, 'If I had my priesthood to live over again, I would be gentler next time. I would console more, and challenge more carefully. I regret that sometimes I was too hard on people and ended up laying further burdens on them when they were already carrying enough pain. I would be gentler. I would spend my energies more trying to lift pain from people. They need us first of all to help them with that.'

What Type of Lay People Could be Used in Healing Ministry?

Letters written in 1999 and again in 2000 by our bishop to all priests in the diocese asking them to invite suitable parishioners to a 12-week teaching and training course given by myself and my wife on praying with people for inner healing, include the following paragraph:

> I think it is important that attendance at the sessions should be by invitation only because those taking part will need to be well-balanced and with a real prayer life, and people who could be trusted never to break confidences and who would be willing to listen and pray non-judgementally out of love and compassion, and not out of any wrong motives such as curiosity, or the desire to give advice or their own need of satisfaction.

We need our priests to bring us the gentleness and compassion of Christ working in partnership with lay people who have themselves experienced the loving power of Christ in their own lives lifting pain and burdens from them. People who have suffered deeply and perhaps feel they have sinned greatly can be the very people whom God can use most powerfully to bring the Good News to others. This was expressed by St Paul: 'Let us give thanks to the God and Father of Our Lord Jesus Christ, the merciful Father, the God from whom all our help comes. He helps us in all our troubles so that we are able to help others who have all kinds of troubles, using the same help that we ourselves have received from God. Just as we have a share in Christ's many sufferings, so also through Christ we share in God's great help.' (2 Co 1:3–5).

It must be recognised that God inspires and uses lay people in many ways which can be channels of evangelisation and healing. They include the SVP, the Legion of Mary, marriage counselling and Marriage Encounter, drug and alcohol counselling, Youth 2000 and other Youth ministries, HCPT, Faith and Light movement, among many others. In all of these a greater awareness of experiences of Jesus bringing inner healing[18] could help those involved. The more parts of the Body of Christ that are praying with expectant faith in the power of the Holy Spirit for Jesus' inner healing and peace, the more deeply greater numbers of people will be evangelised.

However, there is no Catholic residential centre in the UK which exists solely to provide wide-ranging healing ministry to people who could stay for at least some days. By contrast there are around ten 'homes for healing' run by other Christians, some large and also offering training courses in healing ministry as well as residential ministry, staffed by a community augmented by other trained people. There is no Catholic diocese in the UK with a healing team of the kind recommended by the Anglican Church and including psychiatrists and other doctors as well as priests and lay people.[19] A case for a Catholic residential healing centre is made in chapter 18. It would help priests if there were such a centre to which they could recommend parishioners to go when they have deep hurts and needs, which do not seem to be responding to the prayer ministry which is available locally.

God not only hears the cries of those who are lost and in pain, but He is suffering with them. How can we who claim to be His body on earth believe that we are becoming more united with Him, and seeking to do His will, when we fail to listen to pain and respond with compassion, so that God can use us as channels of His healing love to His beloved children? It is genuinely very difficult for many Catholics at present, even those who do not have particularly deep wounds, to awaken and respond to new possibilities. This situation is not a new one, as Pope Benedict XVI, reflecting upon Gethsemane, wrote:

> The Lord says to His disciples: 'My soul is sorrowful, even to death; remain here and keep watch' (Mk 14:33–4). The summons to vigilance has already been a major theme of Jesus' Jerusalem teaching, and now it emerges directly with great urgency. And yet, while it refers specifically to Gethsemane, it also points ahead to the later history of Christianity. Across the centuries, it is the drowsiness of the disciples that opens up possibilities for the power of the Evil One. Such drowsiness deadens the soul, so that it remains undisturbed by the power of the Evil One at work in the world and by all the injustice and suffering ravaging the earth. In its state of numbness, the soul prefers not to see all this; it is easily persuaded that things cannot be so bad, so as to continue in the self-satisfaction of its own comfortable existence. Yet this deadening of souls, this lack of vigilance is what gives the Evil One his power in the world. On beholding the drowsy disciples, so disinclined to rouse themselves, the Lord says: 'My soul is sorrowful even to death'.[20]

The Church itself must bear some responsibility for this drowsiness, this unwillingness to be disturbed and to serve—the *acedia* strongly deplored by Pope Francis in *Evangelii Gaudium*. A number of factors in this taking hold in individuals have been suggested elsewhere.[21]

The Challenge to Deeper and Specific Prayer

Twenty two years ago a priest suggested that my wife and I should give an all-day seminar on the power of Christ to heal, and that secular organisations as well as churches from Newcastle-upon-Tyne to York should be invited to send members. I wrote to our bishop asking whether the invitation letter could say that we had his blessing and support. He wrote back to say that not only could we say that, but also that he would attend the early part of the day. The day before the seminar, he telephoned me to say, 'I find I am free all day tomorrow. If I'll be any use, I'll stay with you all day'. He listened to our talks, took part in small groups and the plenary sessions of 60–70 people. At the end, the priest who was chairing the day asked the bishop if there was anything that he wanted to say. 'Yes', said the bishop, 'as a result of today I now understand why it is necessary to pray specifically and in detail for inner healing'.

Catholics Need to Awake to the Reality and Power of the Holy Spirit

The great majority of practising Catholics receive very little teaching and opportunities to grow into any real (not just theoretical, head knowledge) awareness of how much God has gifted them and needs them. The weekly homily is of very variable quality and quantity, and only rarely lifts their spirits with such new hope and faith that it opens their hearts and lives to the reality of the power of the Holy Spirit, and changes their lives in ways which are commonly happening in the evangelical and Pentecostal churches.

How often are the people at Holy Mass stirred to their depths to hear that each one is God's work of art, created in Christ Jesus (Ep 2:10); that each one is a wonderful masterpiece uniquely gifted and needed by God to bring the Good News of the free gift of salvation and new life to others; that there really is life in all its fullness which Jesus promised to bring us (Jn 10:10); that they will begin to experience that real life and peace and joy which only Jesus can bring if they allow Him to take control of their lives and allow Him to amaze them by using them to bring the Good News to others; that as God does deeper inner healing and conversion to Christ within them He will use them to evangelise and heal others; that Pope Paul VI wrote[22] that the Church exists in order to evangelise; that *all Christians* are called to this witness and in this way can be real evangelisers; that Vatican II taught that the 'whole laity must co-operate in spreading and in building up the kingdom of Christ'.[23]

All too often Catholics have learnt to speak and think in impersonal terms, for example the Mass, the faith, the sacraments, instead of explicitly speaking and thinking about Jesus actively working in and around us in a variety of ways. Too few opportunities are provided and encouraged to hear powerful witnessing by other Catholics of amazing experiences of Christ working in their lives through the power of the Holy Spirit.

The Need to be a Community and a Family of Believers, Not Just People Who Meet at Mass

This will require inspired teaching and leadership by priests as can sometimes be found[24] but it also needs opportunities for Catholics to become able to meet regularly with other Catholics (or other Christians) for prayer, scripture reflection and sharing and mutual up-building, instead of merely exchanging 'how are You' with a few others on the way into or out of the only Mass they attend in the week. Models of helpful experience are available, for example in the parish of St Joseph's, Guildford, where parish renewal through small groups has been developing for over 15 years, with over 100 people involved in ministries within and outside the parish.[25] This model of a parish with vibrant internal life and outreach has been greatly developed both theologically and in practice by Fr James Mallon in Canada.[26]

There is a group on the inner healing prayer ministry which I have been leading weekly in the Blessed Sacrament Chapel for over ten years. This was initiated by our former parish priest. Our late, newly appointed bishop, having been told of our ministry, invited my wife and me to visit him. Our parish priest accompanied us. The bishop said that he had studied all the correspondence and records of his predecessor, knew all about the ministry, had no reservations or questions and wanted to build it up. When we asked him what he wanted of us, he asked us to invite priests in the diocese with any interest in healing to a meeting and to send him a report with recommendations. This we did subsequently, but as we drove home our parish priest suddenly suggested that our teaching tapes (now CDs) should be used to start a group in the parish. I then said, 'Only this morning a lady from the parish was in our home for ministry and she made the same suggestion'. A friend reminded me later that he had made the same suggestion six months earlier, but I had completely forgotten. This group provides teaching which helps to equip those members called by God into this ministry, and also provides opportunities for all who come to ask for prayer ministry themselves.

It is vital that a parish offers more than a casual contact or brief chat over coffee after Sunday Mass. I am privileged to belong to another group in our parish which was begun by the same priest who started the healing group, and which meets fortnightly in a home. The depth of sharing and praying for the deep needs and suffering of members and their families is a wonderful support as God's love grows between us. God frequently uses our contact with other Christians in order to pour graces into our lives—it is the experience of many people that it is through the flow of God's love and compassion for one another that we may be led to deepen our awareness of God's love and power and brought into growing intimacy with our Saviour Jesus Christ. There is much we could learn from other churches where small supportive groups are a regular and vital feature.

Mothers Prayers are an amazing work of God which is of vital importance because more and more I and so many others encounter the deep suffering of mothers over their families. This prayer group movement began in the Catholic Church with two grandmothers in England in 1995 and has already spread to over 200 countries. Up to eight meet, usually weekly, and in confidentiality share their burdens and pray for one another's families. Amazing answers to prayers have been experienced. In a recent meeting the following message was given in prayer: ' My children, I see the pain. I see the wounds. I see the healing that is needed in Your own lives and in those You bring to Me. It gladdens My heart that You bring wounded souls to me. When You pray for them, pray with faith and trust in My power to save. Believe that My light can penetrate all darkness; nothing can withstand my power. Mine is the victory. You have My authority on earth so use My power and command the light to penetrate the darkness and bring healing and wholeness'. There are now some Fathers prayer groups.

There is Need for Priests to Encourage Lay People to Meet in Groups, to Foster Their Faith and to be Prepared for Spiritual Battle

We need priests to recognise that more people should be encouraged to meet in small confidential groups, and that they should foster their faith in Jesus and in using His authority with which to fight in the spiritual battles of our world. Priests and lay people need to be ready with answers to possible questions which may be put to them by other Catholics who would see themselves as very orthodox or perhaps 'middle of the road'. Such possible questions as 'Why are You discussing and suggesting these new things when we have all we need in the Church already?' These questions have indeed been answered fully in the clear evidence of deeply suffering people choosing to travel hundreds of miles for inner healing prayer ministry, as well as the testimonies that they have been greatly blessed by God.[27] This ministry has been clearly demonstrated,[28] from the documents of Vatican II and the teaching of Popes, to be a vital part of evangelisation, which is the reason for the existence of the Church. It is therefore part of the great commission given by the Church by Jesus Christ to give the Good News and to heal. Of course it can then be asked how one can expect to meet or approach the goals of Church and scriptural teaching, in the face of increasing mismatch of clerical resources and the constantly increasing damage and chaos of mankind, both at home and throughout the world, but God is asking us to trust Him and to desire to do His will in total openness to the Holy Spirit.

The Need for More Heartfelt Loving Prayer for Our Priests

Our priests need and deserve our prayers which should begin whilst they are still in formation. The need for prayer has always been there but it is far more vital today than it used to be. Canon David Oakley has drawn attention in Chapter 5 as to how very different and complex the family and other experiences of seminarians frequently are today, compared with former times. Pope Francis himself wrote about this in his encyclical *Amoris Laetitia*:

> Seminarians should receive a more intensive inter-disciplinary, and not merely doctrinal formation... Some come from troubled families with absent parents and a lack of emotional stability. There is a need to ensure that the formation process can enable them to attain the maturity and psychological balance needed for their future ministry.[29]

It is very encouraging that this situation is being addressed in its various aspects at Oscott College, as described by the Rector in his Chapter 5 as well as elsewhere.[30]

All of us in the Church should be praying for seminarians and priests involved in their formation. A well-known prayer already said daily by many lay people is reproduced here:

> Lord Jesus, You have chosen Your priests from among us and sent them out to proclaim Your word and to act in Your name. For so great a gift to Your Church, we give You praise and thanksgiving.

We ask You to fill them with the fire of Your love, that their ministry may reveal Your presence in the Church. Since they are earthen vessels, we pray that Your power shine out through their weakness. In their afflictions let them never be crushed; in their doubts never despair; in temptation never be destroyed; in persecution never abandoned. Inspire them through prayer to live each day the mystery of Your dying and rising. In times of weakness send them Your Spirit, and help them to praise Your heavenly Father and pray for poor sinners. By the same Holy Spirit put Your words on their lips and Your love in their hearts, to bring good news to the poor and healing to the broken-hearted. And may the gift of Mary Your mother, to the disciple whom she loved, be Your gift to every priest. Grant that she who formed You in her human image, may form them in Your divine image, by the power of Your Spirit, to the glory of God the Father. Amen.

Notes

1   A. Guile, *Journey into Wholeness: Prayer for Inner Healing—An Essential Ministry of the Church* (Leominster: Gracewing, 2013), pp. 175–76.

2   *Catechism of the Catholic Church*, 1506–8.

3   *Pastoral Care of the Sick—Rites of Anointing and Viaticum* (1983), p. 10.

4   Congregation for the Doctrine of the Faith, *Instruction on Prayers for Healing* (2000).

5   Guile, *Journey into Wholeness*.

6   *Ibid.*

7   R. DeGrandis, *Intergenerational Healing* (Self-published: 1989). See also J. H. Hampsh, *Healing Your Family Tree* (Everett: Performance Press, 1986).

8   Guile, *Journey into Wholeness*.

9   Pope Paul VI, *General Audience* (15 November 1972).

10   M. Baglio, *The Making of a Modern Exorcist* (New York: Simon and Schuster, 2009).

11   R. Pereira, 'Exorcism and Deliverance, Reconciliation and New Life' in *Prayer for Healing* (International Colloquium, Rome, International Catholic Charismatic Renewal Services, 2003), pp. 237–251.

12   Baglio, *The Making of a Modern Exorcist*.

13   Vatican II, *Presbyterum Ordinis*, 9.

14   Vatican II, *Lumen Gentium*, 12.

15   Vatican II, *Apostolicam Actuositatem*, 3.

16   *Ibid.*, 2.

17   *Ibid.*

18   Guile, *Journey into Wholeness*.

19   House of Bishops of the General Synod of the Church of England, *A Time to Heal—A*

Contribution towards the Ministry of Healing (London: Church House Publishing, 2000).

20 Pope Benedict XVI, *Jesus of Nazareth—part 2* (London: Catholic Truth Society, 2011),pp. 152–153.

21 Guile, *Journey into Wholeness*, pp. 158–9.

22 Pope Paul VI, *Evangelii Nuntiandi*, 14, 21.

23 Vatican II, *Lumen Gentium*, 35.

24 T. Philpot, 'Priorities', in *The Pastoral Review* vol.1 no. 3 (2005). See also J. McManus, 'The New Evangelization and the Healing of the Whole Person', in Goodnews 220, July/August 2012.

25 M. Harrison, 'Parish Renewal Through Cell Groups' in *Goodnews* 206, March/April 2010.

26 J. Mallon, *Divine Renovation* (Toronto: Novalis, 2014).

27 Guile, *Journey into Wholeness*.

28 *Ibid.*

29 Pope Francis, *Amoris Laetitia*, 203.

30 D. Oakley, 'Grounded in Reality' in *The Tablet* vol. 270 no. 9149 (2016), p. 13.

4

Exorcism and Deliverance

Fr John Abberton

We believe that Jesus Christ gave his disciples the power to 'drive out evil spirits'. (Mk 3:15). Christ's disciples today are sent out with the same divine power. As Jesus said, 'These are the signs that will be associated with believers: 'In my name they will cast out devils...' (Mk 16: 17) In this chapter Fr John Abberton, an experienced diocesan exorcist, shares with us both his knowledge of and his experience of the ministry of exorcism and deliverance.

Introduction: Ministry or Ministries?

I have been a diocesan exorcist for over sixteen years. Most of my work is concerned with some form of deliverance. People who come to me asking for help sometimes need to be delivered from evil spirits connected with places, occult activities, or other people. Sometimes they need to be freed from curses and sometimes delivered from spirits that have been passed down through the family line in some way. The ministry of deliverance is exercised by many priests who are not exorcists and also by religious as well as lay people. In this sense it can be distinguished from exorcism although, in practice, there is much overlapping and quite often, it seems to me, what begins as prayer for deliverance results in an exorcism.

In the context of praying for healing, 'deliverance' includes many things. The activities of demons or evil spirits are varied. Destructive habits of thinking can be encouraged by demons. In this case healing or deliverance will not always involve praying over a person but may be brought about through the power of the Holy Spirit in the course of a conversation, or a series of conversations, akin to counselling. In the case of Christian healing this would usually involve the use of Holy Scripture, so it could be said that healing may come through prayerful listening to the Word of God and the subsequent discussion. I believe that this kind of ministry can open the sufferer to deliverance and healing. There must always be prayer, but not necessarily as we would imagine it in the sense of praying over someone. Healing may well take place as the sufferer encounters the Truth as it is presented in the Word of God.

The ministry of exorcism is more clearly defined. Exorcist priests are appointed by bishops to act in their name and through the bishops in the name of the whole Church. Exorcism is concerned with those people who can be classed as possessed. Each time the appointed exorcist intends to use the Formal Rite of Exorcism, he must have his bishop's permission. Ideally he should have consulted others, especially, in the case of suspected mental illness, a psychiatrist or some other qualified and experienced mental health professional. Unfortunately this is not always possible and rarely happens. The exorcist must try to discern each case in accordance with the symptoms given in the introduction to the Rite. These symptoms are taken both from Scripture and from the experience of the Church going back centuries. In many cases it is not possible to be certain about an apparent possession. Father Gabriel Amorth, the former chief exorcist of Rome, admitted to using the Rite as a kind of diagnostic tool.[1]

Although we can see reasons for speaking of 'ministries', in practice, where exorcists are concerned, we can speak of one 'ministry'. In this chapter I will speak of one ministry whilst not losing sight of the distinctions I have made above.

My main purpose in this presentation is not to give a description of the ministry of Exorcism and deliverance, but to make the case for its necessity in the life of the Church. This case needs to be made if only because some bishops and priests do not see the need for it. In trying to make this case I will refer to some particular cases (always being careful to respect the requirement of confidentiality).

My first point in making this case is taken from the parable of the sheep and goats and the Last Judgement (Mt 25:31–46). Christ identifies with people in great need. At the end of the passage His words are, 'Truly, I say to you, as you did it not to one of the least of these, you did it not to Me.' The demon-possessed are not mentioned in the list of suffering people in this parable, but, surely, no right-minded Christian would exclude any seriously needy people from the list of those we are required to help if we are able. In any case, in commissioning the Apostles in the missionary discourse the Lord Jesus commands, 'Heal the sick, raise the dead, cleanse lepers, cast out demons' (Mt 10:1). I will return to this later.

Evil Spirits or Mental Illness?

It is true that some bishops and priests, and perhaps some theologians and Scripture scholars, will want to argue that what was then described as possession was probably something like mental illness. I suppose one of the reasons for this is the case of the young boy cured of epilepsy. Epilepsy is not a formal mental illness, although it is often associated with psychiatric disorders. It is a physical condition producing what in ancient times were regarded as signs of demonic activity and beyond the enlightenment were usually seen as symptoms of madness. Since it is a named condition in Scripture, it provides us with a way of discussing the relationship between mental and/or physical disorders and the activity of evil spirits. This story is found in Matthew 17, Mark 9 and Luke 9. Some argue that Jesus would not have disturbed the common belief at that time that such conditions were produced by demons, probably because they would not have understood anything else. Jesus, so the argument goes, would have simply accepted what the boy's father said about the presence of a demon since the Lord's main concern was to heal the boy. There are problems with this interpretation especially with regard to Mark's Gospel.

In the Gospel according to St Mark we have the story of the healing of a boy possessed by what the boy's father calls, 'a mute spirit'. The symptoms produced by the spirit's agitation look like epilepsy. In healing the boy, Jesus dismisses a 'mute and deaf spirit' and the spirit is described as 'unclean'. When the disciples ask Jesus why they could not cast it out, Jesus tells them that such a spirit can only be cast out by prayer (In Matthew's Gospel it is because the disciples had such little faith, and we have the necessary combination of prayer and fasting). Taking into account all the details of this story I cannot accept the sceptical argument. To stretch the argument against the presence of a demon by suggesting that anyone who reads the story as presented must therefore believe that epilepsy is always caused by an evil spirit is unreasonable. There are a number of possible, and reasonable, explanations in favour of accepting the story at face value. One of these is the suggestion that an evil spirit may produce symptoms that look like epilepsy. Another, not too distant from this, is the possibility that in some cases the condition of epilepsy might be caused by the presence of a demon. Another suggestion is that a spirit not necessarily connected with this condition (such as a 'mute and deaf' spirit) might cause the kind of disturbance that looks like epilepsy. I am not dismissing the argument that the people of Our Lord's day would normally, and often erroneously, have associated some illnesses with evil spirits, but neither am I dismissing the idea that evil spirits may sometimes be present alongside such illnesses or may even contribute to the onset or severity of such illnesses.

Francis MacNutt is clear that mental disturbances can be caused or made worse by evil spirits.[2] This is not to say that every mentally ill person needs deliverance, and exorcists and those who exercise the ministry of deliverance must take great care in discerning the cases that come before them. Mistakes in this area can be serious. Where there is real doubt about the advisability of exorcism or deliverance prayer, advice should be sought from a mental health professional, preferably from one who knows the person concerned. Some psychiatrists are willing to consider the question of exorcism in some cases, if only because they are open to the possibility of some therapeutic value for their patients. Exorcists are expected to have some knowledge of psychology and mental illness but they cannot always rely on this and it is sometimes dangerous to do so.

When I was a priest in one parish in Bradford I was able to meet, on a fairly regular basis, with some psychiatrists and psychiatric health workers. This was made possible through a Catholic social worker and mental health counsellor who worked for Catholic Care. Members of the group included, at different times, a Methodist lady psychiatrist, an Anglican Evangelical male psychiatrist from Leeds, a Muslim male psychiatrist from Bradford, and several male health workers, one of whom was also a Lutheran Bishop. Both the Evangelical and the Muslim told me that they believed in the reality of evil spirits. The Evangelical said that he was sure that some of his patients were in need of some kind of exorcism. The Methodist was less convinced but was open to the exercise of the ministry if it would help her patients. From the outset I wanted to broaden the purpose of the group. I tried to encourage them to consider meeting to discuss the topic of 'spirituality, mental illness and healing'. I did not want the meetings to be simply a consultative group for problem cases.

From a purely secular viewpoint a Christian exorcist will have to struggle to make a case for his ministry, but within the wider Christian family and especially within the Catholic Church there should be no pressure on the exorcist to prove his case. We have the authority of the Scriptures as well as the testimony of the saints, so the pressure to provide a convincing argument rests on those who do not believe in evil spirits and do not accept the ministry of exorcism and deliverance. As far as the

Catholic Church is concerned exorcism is recognised as a real ministry. It has its own authorized rite, and the exorcist must be officially appointed by his bishop. To my mind there is simply no room for equivocation here, and, with respect, those bishops, priests and deacons who do not accept the validity of the ministry must take care that they are not allowing the continuation of what is sometimes horrendous suffering as they simply advise those who ask for deliverance to visit their doctor. I regard this as a serious matter for the reasons I will now outline.

A Ministry Required in Justice as well as Charity

Earlier I drew attention to the parable of the Sheep and the Goats (Mt 25:31–46); I said that no Christian in his or her right mind would ignore anyone in serious need on the basis that he or she is not included in the list of suffering and needy people presented in this passage. I also pointed out that in sending out the Apostles Christ gave them not only the authority but the command to expel demons. As the New Testament tells us, key aspects of Our Lord's public ministry were exorcism and deliverance or unbinding from evil spirits. As we read in the Acts of the Apostles, from its beginning, the work of evangelisation included healings and deliverance.

The Christian message is one of liberation. Although this has famously been politicised I would like to suggest that we do allow for a broad understanding of the word 'liberation', not excluding political and social considerations and of necessity including an awareness of the activity of Satan and his cohorts. The liberation won for us in Christ has been described as freedom from 'sin, death and the devil', Luther's 'unholy Trinity'. I am not able to investigate this understanding of liberation here, but I would like to suggest that recognising the presence of evil in the world and acknowledging that we are sinners and therefore partly responsible for that is not enough. St Paul warns us that we have spiritual enemies to deal with, and we ignore them, sometimes literally, at our peril.

Limiting the action of Satan to the area of personal sin, almost to the exclusion of his activity in society, is to be dangerously blind to the power of evil in the world and the contagion of sin. Treating possession by evil spirits and demonic interference in people's lives as a medieval myth is to be blind in another sense. It means that we do not discern correctly the source of some people's very real suffering and run the risk of bearing some guilt for neglecting their cries for help. It is ultimately the responsibility of bishops to ensure that the ministry of exorcism and deliverance is made available in their dioceses. It is the bishop, as successor to the Apostles, who is the exorcist. The priests he appoints act in his name. As Fr Amorth has remarked, very few bishops have ever conducted an exorcism. It has to be said that they are responsible for providing the ministry and considering the urgent need for it, recognised by the last three Popes and the failure to make this a priority is a serious mistake.

In Catholic social teaching we do not speak of feeding the hungry as an 'optional extra'; it is expected of us and is a matter of justice. In Catholic understanding at least, helping those in need is not a case of 'doing good' but a matter of following Christ as He directs us to work, preach and heal in His name. Caring for those in need is a sacred duty. Helping those who are severely troubled by evil spirits is likewise not only something we do 'out of the goodness of our hearts'; they are in great need, and we are bound to help them. Recently the brother of a lady who came to me for help said that bishops who fail to offer this kind of ministry in their dioceses are surely guilty of neglect. The background to this remark was the more than twenty years of severe suffering endured by this lady, a devout Catholic, who had received inadequate help from the Church and was now affected by what she described as useless medication.

I would also like to add here something else which is of great importance today. In my experience as an exorcist many of those in need of deliverance and sometimes formal exorcism, are victims of sexual abuse. I have known three cases of women who have been abused by priests and I was once asked to help a young man with the same problem. Many others have been abused by family members or friends of the family. In the context of the family most abuse takes place in early childhood and the pre-teen years. As we know, clergy abusers sometimes target children, but many crimes of this kind are visited on teenagers and adults. Where adults are concerned the victims are usually women, including women religious. Many of these are in need of deliverance. I know of one case where formal exorcism was needed. The woman concerned exhibited classical signs of possession by an evil spirit and I was given personal proof that there was a demon present as she said two things about me which she could not possibly have known. The priest whom I was assisting, and whom I knew quite well, was surprised, saying 'I did not know that. How did you know it?' The answer was obvious.

I would like to use this presentation to appeal to bishops to be more open to the need for exorcism and deliverance in the Church. In particular

I would urge them to take seriously the wishes of Pope St John Paul II and Benedict, the Pope Emeritus that there be an adequate number of exorcists in their dioceses. The work involved in this ministry is often arduous. It is certainly demanding. Parish priests who are exorcists cannot be expected to work alone. Running a parish is work enough for many of them, and much is demanded if we are to care for the suffering people who need our help. There must be time allowed for preparation. In the case of formal exorcism, some fasting is recommended. I have already mentioned the occasional need to consult others. The Rite of Exorcism assumes there will be after-care. Parish priests, acting alone, cannot always provide this. Even in the case of less serious needs, other kinds of care are sometimes required; for example counselling or ongoing prayer for inner healing. Many times inner healing is necessary before exorcism and deliverance, which suggests the need to recognise and promote the healing ministry in our dioceses. Ideally, the exorcist will work as a member of a team, but, again, this is often difficult for a parish priest who is the sole exorcist in his diocese. I hope I have made the case here for at least two exorcists in each diocese. I know this was the wish of Pope Benedict. There is another reason why there should be more than one; priests need to support each other, and in some places a priest-exorcist may feel somewhat isolated since some of his acquaintances may regard his ministry as 'quaint' or unnecessary. Some exorcists have found it wise or necessary from time to time to ask another exorcist to pray with them for deliverance after they themselves have ministered to someone else.[3] I was fortunate in recent years to have a spiritual director who was more than willing to listen to stories which other priests might have regarded as either too frightening or far-fetched.

Praying for the Dead

From the beginning of my time as an exorcist I found that many cries for help involved praying for the dead. One of the clearest examples of this is a case involving a 'haunting' in a family home in North Yorkshire. The lady of the house told me that an old woman had been seen by one of the children. At first the husband and father of the house had refused to take this seriously. He changed his mind when on going in and out of the kitchen in the process of making a hot drink he found that all the fridge magnets had been disturbed by an unseen hand. This was when I was asked to help. I sat in the small lounge where there was a huge roaring fire so that my left leg was beginning to burn. On the right side, however, the small room was suspiciously cold. I asked the usual questions about who had lived there before, and it was then that the wife and mother told me that an old lady had lived there before and had been murdered in that very room by three youths, whom she knew and who then robbed the house. I invited everyone to pray for the deceased woman that she might be able to forgive her murderers. After this the apparition vanished and the atmosphere in the house changed.

St Pio of Pietrelcina was often visited by Holy Souls who asked his help. We do not know how Purgatory works in practice, and we do not know if some souls 'in Purgatory' are actually, in some way or other, showing themselves to us 'on earth'. One theory, based on the writings of St Thomas Aquinas, is that such apparitions and manifestations are angels taking the form or identity of deceased people. There is much to commend this theory especially since I had to deal with one case where a man was actually physically pulled from his bed by the apparition of a household maid. We do not know if God would empower a soul to do this (Aquinas suggests not), but we do know that angels have the power to move objects (as do evil spirits).

In some cases, praying for the dead brings real relief to someone who is being troubled in mind or body. This brings up the question of generational healing and Masses celebrated with the intention of such healing (see Chapter 7). My own experience is that such Masses have a real impact on people's lives. Of course there needs to be specific mention of certain problems, but the priest concerned will usually offer the Mass for the intention of family healing. I believe that it is possible for individuals and families to be suffering in certain ways because of what has been 'passed down'.

I would like to give another example of this. I was once asked to assist with the deliverance of a man some distance away from me. Another priest and a religious were also present. During the course of the discussion and prayer I suggested that there was a generational spirit involved. This man had shown very strong aggression without any good reason and without warning. He had finally frightened his wife so much that she was simply unable to cope with the situation. Though he had not attacked her he had damaged things around her. The final straw came when, without warning, he pushed his fist through a wardrobe door. He told us that his grandfather had been very angry over the sale of a piece of land. I thought this may have been the source of the problem but the others disagreed. I had to leave to travel home, but I found out that the priest and the religious had finally decided to pray against a generational spirit of anger. They told me that the man had responded so violently that he had coughed up some blood. It's possible that whatever happened could have involved some kind of occult oath or a curse. Whatever it involved, it was praying against a generational spirit which began the healing.

Other Important Considerations

I would like to conclude by drawing attention to some serious problems in the Church with regard to what is called 'New Age'. In recent years I have become convinced that one of our main problems in the Catholic Church is the toleration of non-Christian forms of spirituality and healing. Some important books have been written on this subject, and the Vatican produced a study document entitled, 'Jesus Christ, The Bearer of the Water of Life'. Sadly this document is not widely known and its recommendations are not being followed. I would urge bishops to consult with their exorcists about this. There are some Catholic retreat centres, hospices and religious houses using spiritually dangerous techniques. These dubious practices are taken up by members of the laity and this is often when the real trouble begins.

As a basic principle we might ask if it is compatible with Christianity to seek healing from something that is patently false. It seems to me that truth is an essential component of Christian spirituality. For example, there is no real evidence for the existence of the energy centres in the body called chakras, and some other beliefs are also highly dubious if not obviously wrong. There are some important scientific studies of homeopathy which show it to be 'quack medicine'. There are good books written about the possible dangerous effects of Yoga, Tai Chi and similar practices, and although certain beliefs, like superstitions, can bring some emotional relief, when people open themselves up to the possibility of other 'forces' or 'energies' there is the danger of welcoming something destructive. Some studies of Reiki healing suggest that it is one of the most spiritually dangerous techniques of all. I have personally witnessed the effect of Reiki on a whole family; it provides an open door for evil spirits. It is essential that bishops, priests and deacons are aware of the dangers. I especially recommend the book by Dr Rhonda McClenton.[4] A good introduction to the dangers of Yoga and Martial Arts has been written Dr Vito Rallo.[5] One of the best books on Reiki and Tai Chi has been written by Bro Max Scully.[6]

Most discerning people will accept the principle that prevention is better than cure. Allowing for the magnificence of God's Mercy and the way that healing and deliverance often bring other benefits, I would argue that in the realm of spirituality much unnecessary suffering can be avoided by being well-informed and by remaining in the Christian way rather than wandering off the path into what, for most, is unchartered and dangerous territory.

Notes

[1]   See G. Amorth, *An exorcist tells his story* (San Francisco, CA: Ignatius Press, 1999).

[2]   F. McNutt, *Deliverance from Evil Spirits—A Practical Manual* (Grand Rapids: Chosen Books, 1995).

[3]   C. Neil-Smith, (Private Communication, 1977).

[4]   R. J. McClenton, *Reiki and Christ-based Healing* (Bala Cynwyd, PA: Icthus Press 2011).

[5]   V. Rallo, *Exposing The Dangers Behind Martial Arts & Yoga* (Lancaster: Sovereign World, 2011).

[6]   M. Scully *Yoga, Tai Chi and Reiki: A Guide for Christians* (Ballan Vic: Connor Court Publishing, 2012).

5

Healing Ministry in Seminary Formation

Canon David Oakley

As the ministry of priests is so vital for the life of our Church people who have experienced the healing ministry always ask, 'how are our future priests being trained for this ministry?' In this chapter the Rector of Oscott College gives us a reassuring insight into how the seminarians in his college are being introduced to the different dimensions of the healing ministry.

The Seminary

Since the Council of Trent, the usual way that a man is formed for the life and ministry of an ordained priest is within a seminary college. The etymological root of the word seminary suggests a nursery for fragile seedlings, a place where these seedlings can grow strong and able to withstand the challenges of life when they are transplanted outside of the protective environment of the seminary. Originally, seminaries were established for the formation of priests in many different challenging political and ecclesial contexts in the sixteenth century. Men who wished to become a priest for ministry in the British Isles, during the sixteenth through to seventeenth centuries, had to travel abroad and focus on a deepening of the spiritual life to prepare themselves for martyrdom. Even during the eighteenth century, when death was no longer a threat, there were still no established seminaries in this land. Those preparing for ordination lived abroad in a more or less monastic environment, being educated in accordance with a Tridentine programme delivered in the Latin tongue. Increasingly since the Second Vatican Council, some of this formation takes place within other settings too, outside of the seminary building, notably that of the parish.

Pope St John Paul II on Seminary Training

In 1992, Pope St Pope John Paul II published the document that defines our work in seminary formation in this age, *Pastores Dabo Vobis*, or *I will Give you Shepherds*. In this document we read these words:

> The seminary can be seen as a place and a period in life. But it is above all an educational community in progress. It is a community established by the bishop to offer to those called by the Lord to serve as apostles the possibility of reliving the experience of formation, which our Lord provided for the Twelve. In fact, the Gospels present a prolonged and intimate sharing of life with Jesus as a necessary premise for the apostolic ministry. Such an experience demands of the Twelve the practice of detachment in a particularly clear and specific fashion, a detachment that in some way is demanded of all the disciples, a detachment from their roots, from their usual work, from their nearest and dearest (cf. Mk 1:16–20; 10:28; Lk 9:23, 57–62; 14:25–27).[1]

These very contemporary words about seminary formation still reflect an important Tridentine tradition. The seminary is a privileged and unique community of faith within the Body of Christ. First of all, it is a place of intense personal discernment alongside formation. A man arrives at the seminary after an initial period of discernment and assessment of his suitability to become a candidate for a diocese or religious community. After an initial inquiry, the potential candidate enters a time of accompaniment and spiritual direction. This time varies from diocese to diocese and there are a number of models and different practices involved in this initial period of vocation exploration. At some point, the candidate is asked to make a formal application to the diocese or religious community. Along with a full curriculum vitae, references are sought and a psychological evaluation is made of the candidate. The journey to this moment varies from candidate to candidate. After a selection interview process, a successful candidate is informed that he will be admitted to the seminary.

A Faith Community for Self-discovery

If the seminary is a place and a period in a person's life, then there have been many other places and periods beforehand. In former times, it was almost taken for granted that a candidate for priesthood was raised within a committed Catholic family. This is certainly not the case today. Many candidates have experienced the wounds of a broken family, with parents who have separated and often formed new relationships. A significant number of men are converts to the Catholic Church, and sometimes only for a little period of time before they begin the journey towards becoming a priest. Look at their contemporaries and ask yourself, what do you see in them? Young people today are often materialistic, consumed by social media and technology, and they reflect all the signs of a post-modern society. They have often experienced sexual encounters, sometimes hardly deserving the title of relationship. They may have advanced in careers, professions and jobs, with their own income and means of self-support. They are used to their own personal accommodation and living a lifestyle with freedom of choices that is distant to that of the seminary and the presbytery. What does this suggest about our candidates for priestly ministry? They rarely have roots deeply planted within an authentic understanding of the ecclesial tradition. They are 'bruised fruit' to use a term of St Francis de Sales. They are in need of inner healing themselves.

If all this is true, then there is another narrative to consider too. Today's seminarian has often experienced a very real conversion experience. He may have belonged to a prayer group, an apostolic group, a movement such as Youth 2000, he may have experienced the faith community of a university chaplaincy. There are many different ways in which his faith has been ignited and fanned into a flame. He often has experience of ministry and pastoral care, of evangelisation and catechesis, of prayer ministry with others. He may have already exercised leadership in the life of a community of disciples. He may be well down the road of becoming an experienced and mature pastoral minister.

A Time of Discernment

Discernment continues for the candidate from the moment he arrives at the seminary. Life here is very different to life within a parish community, a university, a monastery or indeed a public school. There are however, some similarities with all these different institutions. As the Rector of St Mary's College, Oscott, I often suggest to a seminarian that parish life is very different to life in the seminary. However, if you are unable to cope with life in the seminary then it may be a challenge to live the life of a priest in a parish setting. Of course, there is a definite sense of institutional organisation—there has to be, if we are going to make living along with seventy or so others possible. Some find this community organisation claustrophobic and restrictive, a little limiting and shockingly different to life as they have experienced it before they enter seminary.

The man who arrives at the seminary door is entering a very different world to the one he has been used to. He finds there is a different culture to that of his family and life in an educational institution or workplace. He must discover the history of the particular seminary he has entered. There is a whole new pattern of life and even a new language with its own specialised terminology. Another factor that needs to be taken into consideration is that the seminary is a predominantly male community. In this respect, it is a narrow and limited experience of the human community. Fortunately, many candidates are able to visit the seminary beforehand for discernment weekends. Even then, it takes some considerable time for a man to adjust to this very different way of life when he arrives to live and study here. Above all, he may experience a loss of independence and the heightened awareness of his own 'baggage'. It is difficult to articulate fully this idea of baggage—but typically it consists of a network of cultural and social experiences, a pattern of feelings and emotions that belong to a post-modern secularised society. Some of this is introduced above. Needless to say, a man does not leave his cultural, social and emotional baggage at the seminary door when he is taken to his room on arrival. Candidates may arrive from many different places in the Church, with a variety of spiritual and liturgical traditions and preferences. Almost immediately, simply by living in a seminary community, a man may feel challenged by others' traditions and viewpoints dissimilar to his own. This is an important part of the formation journey towards ordination.

The seminary formation staff live alongside those who are in discernment and formation within the seminary. They have the mandate to accompany the individual seminarian in his discernment. From time to time, and in a very formal canonical setting, they are charged with the duty of scrutiny and assessment. My own personal preference is to see this work very much along the lines of discernment. This discernment, which springs from a real knowledge of the individual being assessed, is a prophetic ministry—we are asking the Holy Spirit to enlighten our minds, in order to recognise a genuine vocation of the Lord or otherwise. This is not a duty the seminary formation staff take lightly. It demands of us a real intimacy with the Lord and a seeking of His will and purpose.

A Time of Formation

The seminary is a community of formation. Since the publication of Pope St Pope John Paul II's inspirational post-synodal apostolic exhortation, *Pastores Dabo Vobis* in 1992, the Church recognises four different areas or strands of formation:

1. Intellectual Formation

The intellectual area consists of the academic programmes which enable a disciple to become a credible apostolic witness to the mysteries of faith. It is not his own word that he will preach and teach, but that which he has received from the Lord in the Scriptures and the unfolding ecclesial tradition. There are many philosophical and theological courses over a six year period of formation. There are altogether, eighty-seven individual courses over the six year period of formation. Here at Oscott, our courses are validated by a secular institution, Birmingham University and an ecclesiastical institution, the Pontifical University of Leuven. Perhaps the aim of the intellectual strand of formation can best be presented in the words of Pope Benedict XVI:

> 'Be transformed by the renewal of your mind' (Rm 12: 2). Two very important words: 'to transform', from the Greek *metamorphon*, and 'to renew', in Greek *anakainosis*. Transforming ourselves, letting ourselves be transformed by the Lord into the form of the image of God, transforming ourselves every day anew, through his reality into the truth of our being. And 'renewal'; this is the true novelty which does not subject us to opinions, to appearances, but to the Grace of God, to His revelation. Let us permit ourselves to be formed, to be moulded, so that the image of God really appears in the human being. 'By the renewal', St Paul says, in a way I find surprising, 'of your mind'. Therefore this renewal, this transformation, begins with the renewal of thought. St Paul says 'o nous': our entire way of reasoning, reason itself must be renewed. Renewed, not according to the usual categories but to renew means truly allowing ourselves to be illuminated by the Truth that speaks to us in the Word of God. And so, finally, to learn the new way of thinking, which is that way which does not obey power and possessing, appearances and so on, but obeys the truth of our being that dwells in our depths and that is given to us anew in Baptism. 'The renewal of your mind'; every day is a task proper to the process of studying theology, of preparing for the priesthood. Studying

theology well, spiritually, thinking about it deeply, meditating on Scripture every day; this way of studying theology, listening to God himself who speaks to us is the way to the renewal of thought, to the transformation of our being and of the world.[2]

The purpose of intellectual formation, therefore, is nothing less than complete personal transformation; in the words of St Paul, nothing less than the 'renewal of your mind'. It calls upon all of us involved in this work to take on a new way of thinking, 'to permit ourselves to be formed' in order to renew ourselves, leading to 'the transformation of our being and of the world'. This is never then, an academic work similar to the work of a secular university. Intellectual formation within a seminary setting involves a real conversion of the mind. It takes time and prayerful reflection.

2. Spiritual Formation

The spiritual area consists of the development of a disciple's personal relationship of prayer within the interior life. It is 'a prolonged and intimate sharing of life with Jesus' that alone can prepare a man for all aspects of pastoral ministry, especially those in which he will act and speak in the name of the Lord. Spiritual formation is at the core of formation for the priesthood and is central to the future priest's identity and mission. Because it is chiefly the work of the Holy Spirit in cooperation with human freedom, the responsibility for spiritual growth and formation lies principally with the seminarian. The aim of the Spiritual Formation Programme is thus to help the individual learn the life-long habit of living in intimate union with Jesus Christ, constantly seeking his friendship. This involves:

a) Learning the genuine meaning of Christian prayer and prayerful reflection upon the Word of God, as put forward in the Church's Scriptures and Tradition, so as to become a man of God and one who can help others turn to God.

b) Learning how to participate lovingly and actively in the sacred mysteries, above all in daily Mass, the 'summit and source' of the sacraments and the Church's life; how to cultivate the virtue and discipline of the Sacrament of Penance; how to recite the Liturgy of the Hours so as to become inserted in a living way into the Paschal Mystery.

c) Developing a spirit of humble and disinterested service of others, especially the poor, with a love that is both strong and tender, in imitation of the Sacred Heart of Jesus, so as to become a man of charity living in obedience, celibacy and self-denial. Spiritual formation will also pay particular attention to preparing the future priest to know, appreciate, love and live celibacy out of genuine evangelical, spiritual and pastoral motives and in accordance with its true nature and purpose.

3. Pastoral Formation

The pastoral area consists of the formation of the seminarian through pastoral theological reflection and opportunities to exercise pastoral care in various settings, to develop the gifts and skills he will need to become a pastoral priest. The pastoral placement is the real pastoral care of a disciple—it is not about pretending to be a priest! Here at Oscott, every student belongs to a house group with a member of the formation staff. This is not a group of close friends. Rather, the house group is a gathering of seminarians from across the six-year programme, who have the opportunity to share experience and offer pastoral care to each other. Each house group is attached to a local parish and celebrates Sunday Mass with the parish community every month of the college year. From time to time, students join with one of the formation staff priests, during praise and worship gatherings in the college chapel, in order to offer prayer ministry to those who seek this. Fellow students and others from outside the college community often approach a 'prayer team' and real ministry takes place. The student is not seen in this situation as an apprentice (although he will perhaps learn from his prayer ministry companion, one of the formation staff priests). This is an opportunity for the student to discover how to pray in the Spirit for real needs, with real people, and with a real expectation that the Lord will act with sovereign power. I have seen myself how this experience encourages an individual student to grow in confidence and enthusiasm to pray with others for others. There is another significant development here in our seminary. Final year students receive a seminar course from the spiritual directors here at Oscott, concerning deliverance ministry and exorcism. This is an introduction to the Church's liturgical prayer and some practical reflections on this important aspect of spiritual healing ministry.

4. Human Formation

The human area of formation is the one I have left until last—even though it is of primary importance. In essence, the purpose of this area of formation is a personal lifelong growth in a process of change towards becoming the person we are created by God to be. The start of this journey is self-knowledge—interestingly, the beginning of the spiritual journey of prayer according to St Teresa of Avila in *The Interior Castle*. There is a need for honesty, an appreciation of self-truth that leads to deeper conversion of life. Of special importance is the capacity to relate to others. This is truly fundamental for a person who is called to be responsible for a community and to be a 'man of communion.' This demands that the priest not be arrogant, or quarrelsome, but affable, hospitable, sincere in his words and heart, prudent and discreet, generous and ready to serve, capable of opening himself to clear and brotherly relationships and of encouraging the same in others, and quick to understand, forgive and console (cf. 1 Tm 3:1–5; Ti 1:7–9).[3] The growth towards affective maturity includes an education in sexuality and an appreciation of the virtue of chastity by which a man becomes 'capable of respecting and fostering the 'nuptial meaning' of the body'. Consequently, human formation implies developing true, serene friendships in which the student learns to bring to human relationships a strong, lively and personal love for Jesus Christ. The community life of the seminary itself encourages this by fostering that essential training in freedom and self-responsibility by which we learn to master ourselves, to become more maturely open to others and to resist, fight and defeat selfishness and individualism.

This brief introduction to the four areas of formation enables us to appreciate the journey of inner healing that must take place if a man is to respond to the demands of seminary formation. We hear in the Gospel how the disciples had to make a painful journey, coming to a deeper understanding of their own weaknesses and emotional struggles. Perhaps the greatest area of healing was in the area of their collective shame and guilt after the resurrection—they had run away during the trial and crucifixion of the Lord. As we hear clearly in the Gospels and in the Acts of the Apostles, the first disciples were unable to grow in their human formation by their own efforts. They needed the power of the crucified and risen Lord to enable them to come to new life in their areas of brokenness. They needed the Pentecost power of the Holy Spirit to complete this work and to enable them to minister effectively to others.

A Way of Discipleship

When a man responds to the Lord's invitation to enter deeper into the way of discipleship and to become a priest, there are many opportunities in the seminary to find the inner healing necessary if he is to become a missionary-disciple, an apostle of the Lord. Like all disciples, a seminarian can experience the healing power of the sacraments, especially the Sacrament of Reconciliation. Furthermore, he is assigned a spiritual director and a human formation director. The spiritual director accompanies a man as he responds to the Lord and develops a prayer life and the interiority needed to enter into the life of an ordained priest. His human formation director is a trained counsellor who can help the candidate for holy orders to unpack the baggage mentioned above, and to reflect on the ways he needs healing. We hope that the newly ordained priest will continually seek spiritual direction after ordination. We hope too, that human formation will continue as the priest learns how to deal with the challenges he faces within ministry. From this perspective, human formation is often called accompaniment or supervision.

Pastoral Reflection on Healing Ministry

The spiritual and human elements of formation are important parts of a seminarian's preparation for priestly ministry. We do not offer pastoral ministry to others from outside the perspective of our own need for healing. Opportunities are taken within pastoral theological reflection and courses on the sacraments for a more formal reflection on the ways in which a priest can exercise the ministry of healing. This may be within the formal context of sacramental celebration—especially the Sacraments of Reconciliation and Anointing. There are regular praise and worship sessions in the seminary and sometimes, seminarians are invited to exercise a ministry of healing within this context. There are examples of individuals exercising ministry with each other within the community.

What is offered here, by way of reflection on the formation programme, is but a beginning. The seminary is an important place of formation. It is not the only place. Within pastoral placements, a seminarian can experience examples of prayer for healing. There is an ongoing dialogue between his own experience and journey on the one hand, and the formation programmes and experiences he enters into on the other hand. When the seminarian becomes a priest through ordination, he leaves the seminary and begins a very different way of life. The experience could be compared with passing a driving test—it doesn't mean he knows *everything* about the priesthood, but has now reached a point where he can drive without someone sitting next to him all the time! A newly ordained priest will not know everything about the ministry of healing. Hopefully, he will know enough to seek support and encouragement to exercise this ministry through prayer and the laying on of hands.

A Seamless Garment

In the latest thinking about priestly formation, a reflection that will guide formation throughout the whole Church, formation is now seen as a 'seamless garment' from initial discernment of a vocation, through seminary community life, and onwards throughout a priest's life and ministry. This suggests to me, that we should not become despondent about our work of formation in a seminary setting, and the many aspects of this which still need development in an individual's life. We cannot be expected to do everything in the several years a candidate for ordination journeys with us towards priesthood.

There is a growing concern in formation circles about the early years of priestly life and ministry. So much is won or lost within the first five years. There is growing evidence to suggest that diocesan priests often feel alone and isolated in a presbytery setting, even though they may be sharing this space with a parish priest. Life is very different in the parish to the life previously known in the seminary. Whilst most newly-ordained priests welcome release from the organisation and structures of seminary life, they discover the many ways in which seminary life was actually quite supportive and protective of them. In a presbytery, food does not appear on the table three times each day. One must accept responsibility for many of the practical aspects of life, once taken for granted in the seminary college. There is a culture of support and encouragement within the seminary, from the bishop and the formation staff. Many of the newly-ordained soon feel the icy blast of indifference from many of those they are sent to serve. Maybe they also feel an overwhelming sense of inadequacy—can they really be prepared for the demands of pastoral and prayer ministry in the confessional and at the sick bed? They feel challenged by the variety and magnitude of the demands on their time and energy. Personal prayer time becomes squeezed and unsupported. The inner spiritual life, preaching and pastoral ministry, draws much from a depleted well that soon runs dry without prayer, study and theological reflection.

The Young Priest's Need of Spiritual Support

This is a depressing picture and totally unnecessary. It seems to the mind and heart of this seminary rector, that much of our work in the seminary is fragile and may soon turn to waste if it is not looked after. If a priest is to become a life-giving agent of spiritual and pastoral care for others, then he must find that same care and spiritual support himself. This essay is about the seminary rather than priestly life. Nevertheless, it is good that we should consider the fundamental experience of community that underpins the seminary institution and will support a man as he takes his first steps into priesthood. It is only within a meaningful experience of community that a priest will be encouraged to put aside time and space to develop his own relationship with Jesus. It is only within a community setting that a priest will hear God's word in a new and life-giving manner, and find new meaning and depths within the biblical word. It is only within a community of intercessory prayer, that the priest will be supported in his own prayer ministry with others. Very quickly, the treadmill of pastoral life becomes a management of the many demands made upon the individual priest. The mindset becomes one of survival, dealing with the very real feelings of failure when everything is not done, and that which is done is not done well. It is precisely from this situation, the priest learns to pray with his Lord and Master:

> At that time Jesus said, 'I thank you, Father, Lord of heaven and earth, because you have hidden these things from the wise and the intelligent and have revealed them to infants; yes, Father, for such was your gracious will. All things have been handed over to me by my Father; and no one knows the Son except the Father, and no one knows the Father except the Son and anyone to whom the Son chooses to reveal him.'Come to me, all you that are weary and are carrying heavy burdens, and I will give you rest. Take my yoke upon you, and learn from me; for I am gentle and humble in heart, and you will find rest for your souls. For my yoke is easy, and my burden is light'. (Mt 11:25–30)

The eleventh chapter of Matthew's Gospel paints a very bleak picture of life for the Lord and His disciples, at that time on Jesus' ministry. We cannot fail to notice, the Lord's ministry of healing continues after this prayer, indeed perhaps because of this prayer. The same is true of the priest. It is my hope that the seminary will enable a man to echo this prayer of Christ, a prayer that arises from a heart that knows the Blessed Trinity, a prayer that may issue the same invitation, that those who seek inner healing will find in the priest, a gentleness and humility that is a vehicle of God's healing power.

Notes

1 Pope St John Paul II, *Pastores Dabo Vobis*, 60.
2 Pope Benedict XVI, *Lectio Divina*, 15 February 2012.
3 Pope St John Paul II, *Pastores Dabo Vobis*, 43.

6

Seeking Balance in Human and Divine Resources in the Healing of our Wounds

Alan Guile

When we are dealing with a person's relationship with God we cannot ignore God's presence in him or her. Neither should we ignore God's presence in our relationship with the person who is seeking our help with some trouble or inner pain. Christian ministers, both clerical and lay, have to be aware not only of psychological and medical dimensions but also of the spiritual dimensions of the person. As Pope St John Paul II said, 'The body can never be reduced to mere matter: it is a spiritualized body, just as man's spirit is so closely united to the body that he can be described as an embodied spirit.[1] *In this chapter Alan invites us to take a fresh look at how we seek to integrate our faith and trust in God's healing love and mercy with our own natural skills for helping people. Do we have the balance right?*

The Balance Between Human and Divine Resources

The Scriptures, for example 1Ch 20:15–17, Zc 4:6, call upon us to put trust in God rather than relying on human strength and resources alone. The Church has largely moved from the dependence on the Holy Spirit in the Acts of the Apostles and the very early years, towards increasing stress and reliance upon intellectual, academic and business orientated approaches. However, God generally expects us prayerfully to co-operate with His grace-filled power, by using all the knowledge and experience which He has Himself given us the means to acquire. We have a particular example of His power blending with human knowledge and resources in the field of healing in Sirach 38: 1–15.

It is not always easy to find the best balance in this blending. In fact in healing two opposite extremes are sometimes met. One is where Christians with a fundamentalist approach have told a sufferer to stop medication after they have been prayed with, and have accused this person of not having enough faith in God if they later say that they have not been healed. Thus, they now have an additional burden of guilt to carry together with their original problems. There are far larger numbers of people who refuse or are unwilling to acknowledge the presence and power of God. Thus they and others are led to rely solely upon human resources and if these do not produce satisfactory results, there is no turning to God in prayer. I have had to help people who were damaged in the first of these extremes. The hundreds who have come to my home in the last thirty years have included many who were searching for the right blend of all the resources of medicine, psychiatry, psychology and counselling, alongside praying for God both to guide the professional and to heal deep underlying roots of unease.[2]

Are We Getting the Balance Right?

Over twenty years ago I led an all-day seminar on this very topic to which people from medical, counselling and prayer ministry backgrounds in organisations from Newcastle down to York had been invited. The invitation letter contained a supportive message from our bishop, who was himself present all day. At the end he spoke of how much he had learned that day about the need to pray specifically and in detail concerning early roots of hurt and damage. We must be constantly seeking to learn from God and from one another.

The question can legitimately be asked, 'Are we in general as well as in individual cases, getting the balance about right in our attitudes and practices, between using all the resources of medicine, psychiatry, psychotherapy, psychology and counselling, and prayer for Christ to bring that healing to the whole person which leads to true peace and wholeness?' We should be prepared to use all of these resources as appropriate for those suffering individuals who are open and ready to receive God's powerful help and are willing to continue becoming disciplined to go on co-operating with that grace. The areas and origins of individual suffering are frequently very complex and multi-faceted, so we need to understand that what the individual initially perceives to be the main problem is likely to be the tip of an iceberg or not the main problem at all. Healing prayer ministry enables Christ to reveal the factors and root causes lying behind the person's present suffering.

Experiences of Healing in Depression

I have personally known many people over the last forty years who were receiving psychiatric and psychological treatment for depression, sometimes very severe, who on all the evidence available, would say, and it is supported by their experience and progress over following years, that they have been greatly helped by prayer for inner healing, including in some cases, deliverance prayer.[3] There is further support for this in the literature. I was present in 1975 when a priest who was out of action due to depression and under a psychiatrist's care, was prayed with, very briefly, by another priest and lay on the floor of a church in Manchester for over two hours, 'resting in the Holy Spirit'.[4] He spoke to me about his experience during that time the next day and he went on to have a powerful ministry for about 40 years as a priest, as a part of which he wrote about healing and prayed with very large numbers of people. A significant part of this healing was that he reported that whilst 'resting in the Spirit', the Lord showed him that some painful experiences which he had thought to be important were relatively unimportant, but certain nearly forgotten incidents had left a deeper imprint.[5] Clearly if this can be the case for some sufferers then their psychiatrist, psychotherapist, psychologist or counsellor is not going to be in possession of all the relevant information. I have given some examples[6] of how the Holy Spirit's gift of a word of knowledge can sometimes reveal some deep cause of present unease, which the sufferer would not have been able to disclose to a professional who had care of them. A testimony supporting this was given.[7]

One man had gone on suffering severe repetitive attacks of depression for very many years. Before he came to us about twenty years ago he had already been treated by four psychiatrists and two psychologists, and he has been looked after by others since then as some depression has continued at lower levels. Although he had felt some fulfilment through belonging to the SVP and the Teams of Our Lady, and had been helped by one particular priest, he found that when he was again pitched down into darkness he found there was no-one in the Church attempting to bring him out of it. They would wait until he came out of it, which left him questioning whether anyone really cares. 'Where is the love?' and 'I do really wonder where God is in all this'. He wrote recently that when a friend had recommended him to come to see us, 'I knew things would happen, and they did. Somebody did care, and not just one person, but two'. He explained that on his first visit he glanced at my late wife and knew that she was looking into his soul and that she was different to people he had talked to before. He wrote, 'Both of you were so kind and if ever I felt down and in despair prior to seeing you, I came away refreshed, ready to face the world once again.' Despite the recurring attacks of deep depression during which 'my faith takes an enormous step backwards' he finds that time spent in his own company brings faith back again relatively undamaged. There is a great lesson in his experiences which all of us in the Church need to learn. We send people off to the doctor, the psychiatrist, the counsellor, but as this man wrote, 'Where is the love?' 'This is my commandment: love one another, just as I love you' (Jn 15:12). This points to a very significant difference between human professional care and powerful help motivated by God's love for each one of us.

We Sometimes Ignore the Power of Prayer

Even in an examination by very experienced Christians with professional qualifications and experience of suffering in many areas of human damage and distress, the discussion may use psychological approaches and sociological issues and solely human ways of treatment. This can tend to swamp and even perhaps almost obliterate any consideration of praying for help and healing from Christ for those who are open and ready for this, and where the professional is in a position to be free to offer this. Obviously, many are under legal and professional restrictions which prevent or hinder any Christian prayer ministry. In one Christian handbook[8] eight experts each discuss in the light of their own expertise the following areas:

- child sexual abuse
- domestic abuse
- alcohol and other substance abuse
- gambling addiction
- sexual addiction and internet pornography
- dealing with difficult people
- adult bullying
- violence in the workplace

Each of the eight chapters has a section entitled "A Christian Response". However, in only one of these, the one on gambling, is there any reference to or discussion of the possible role of prayer to help those offenders who are willing.[9] It is worth quoting part of this particular section.

> Recovery from pathological gambling is a lifetime process frequently complicated by the presence of another psychiatric illness, and nearly always complicated by fractured relationships and catastrophic financial damage. Prayer is not and never should be a first line of defence: attention must be paid to the overall suffering of the individual. But there is research that demonstrates that prayer helps to restore personal well-being to compulsive gamblers, and the restoration of personal well-being is the foundation for establishing gambling abstinence. If the compulsive gambler is to stop the gambling behaviour, it will only be accomplished by the the restoration of a sense of satisfaction with life, a restoration that has been shown to be helped by an active and fulfilling prayer life.[10]

We Must Understand that Root Areas Need Healing

The preceding comments are helpful, because in all the areas of damaged and troublesome human behaviour, the causes and factors involved are likely to be many and very complicated and interwoven, and will vary from one individual to another. However, it is well-established that growing into inner peace and true self-esteem which leads to personal well-being, can be greatly helped by praying for Christ to heal underlying root causes,[11] which supports the findings quoted above.[12] The key underlying root causes are known to be in the three areas of (i) past generations of our family (ii) our time in the womb and our birth, and (iii) babyhood and about the first seven years of our childhood.[13]

Childhood Factors

Three of the other seven chapters[14] refer to childhood factors and experiences.

> A number of psychologists have also observed that if a child is exposed to inappropriate sexual activity or material, this can affect normal sexual development, especially around eight years of age. Sex offenders often come from a disturbed family background, and

difficulties in early attachment have been shown to be a feature of child molesters.[15]

The author adds that child abusers writing about their experiences suggest that personal stress also contributes to their offending behaviour. Among factors when trying to understand the origins of the offending behaviour of child molesters are self-esteem and intimacy defects. Similarly, in the chapter on sexual addiction and Internet pornography,[16] we read:

> Sex addicts have become dependent on sexual behaviour as a way of dealing with the stress, grief and pain they faced in the past. Most sex addicts found sexual behaviours in early life to be a solution to eradicate pain that was overwhelming to them. Very often these addicts find themselves being triggered into these same feelings of shame, loss and stress as adults and find themselves reaching for the same solutions. Until they learn to deal with these past feelings and hurts in ways that are healthy, they will continue to struggle with addiction. Wounds from abuse suffered as children will affect adults for the rest of their lives unless they understand and come to terms with them. Full recovery from sexual addiction won't take place until a person comes to a consciousness of what happened to them in childhood.

The same authors go on[17] to discuss two kinds of childhood abuse, invasion and abandonment. In invasion children feel afraid, alone and ashamed, and the stress and trauma lead them to look for relief and consolation in unhealthy ways. In abandonment, while people may remember traumatic experiences, it is harder for them to identify normal healthy things which should have happened but never did. Abandonment occurs when children do not feel the love, attention and nurturing they need to thrive. When children are not listened to, when they receive few (if any) displays of affection, when they are left alone for extended periods of time and are deprived in other ways, they grow up confused and damaged. When they are too small and helpless to defend themselves against such injuries they may come to a very logical conclusion: 'If this is happening to me I must be bad because bad people are punished', or 'If no-one loves me it must be because I am bad and unlovable.' It can lead in some cases to a very damaged view of God and my relationship to Him, if as a child it doesn't seem as if He answers my prayers for help.

All of these areas of early damage can be healed by Christ through prayer ministry.[18] There are many aspects to this ministry including praying for

Jesus to heal and transform the damaged memories and experiences, touching our wounds with His wounds and so through His precious blood drawing out the child's pain into His suffering on the Cross; receiving healing of damaged perceptions of God developed in early childhood; becoming free of reaping what we sowed in childhood judgements of our parents; being freed of bitter root judgements and bitter root expectations; praying for the child to desire the grace to forgive themselves and those who hurt him or her; receiving the grace to love and accept themselves in the way that God does so; using stronghold prayers to become free of damaged strongholds and patterns of thinking attitudes, desires, beliefs, habits and behaviours; the sacraments of Reconciliation and Holy Communion; and becoming disciplined in daily prayer in a desire to enter into deeper relationship with God and surrender to His will.

It is not about a quick fix but many testimonies bear out the help and healing which God can give as people go on co-operating. Compared with human means of seeking help such as counselling, Christian prayer has so much more to offer directly, including the healing which only comes from the suffering of Christ, asking God for the grace with which to forgive and receiving the sacraments.

Further information about childhood damage playing a vital part in adult offending is given in the chapter on adult bullying.[19] This refers to research which suggests that childhood bullies develop into adult bullies with greater risk of negative outcomes including anti-social behaviours and involvement in crime. A study of 500 children suggested that children who were aggressive at eight years of age were more likely to be involved in criminality when they were thirty.[20] There is considerable discussion of the importance of early attachments in childhood, particularly in the first years of life.[21]

Patterns of Damage in Our Family Generations

A further area of root cause of damage involves patterns of damaged behaviour occurring in a number of generations of a family, which can be addressed by prayer at a Mass held particularly to pray for intergenerational healing.[22] It may be difficult to determine whether these are genetically determined biological factors, or due to experiences and learned behaviours such as the way one treats one's spouse and children may have a great deal to do with one's own childhood experiences and relationships at home, and in particular how the adult, whilst still a child, perceived his or her parents.

There are indications of family or genetic factors in three of the chapters.[23] Although it is difficult to be exact in explaining the reasons for someone's deviant sexual interests, when discussing child sexual abuse[24] it mentions the fact that a brother also abused a child as suggesting the possibility of genetic influence. In the chapter on domestic abuse,[25] it is said that a widespread assumption, much contested in the literature, is that there is a 'cycle of violence' transmitted from one generation to the next. In the chapter on alcohol and other addictions[26] it is said that among the causes of dependence are genetically determined biological differences between people which render some of us more vulnerable than the rest to dependence on one drug or another, but that it is clear that the environment in which we live is hugely important. Individual victims of addiction may be aware also of possible childhood traumas. One recovering addict, himself an eminent biochemist, mentions[27] a traumatic happening when, aged 2, he was separated from his parents for three weeks due to meningitis. He screamed his head off for all this time in insecurity. Then, aged about 12, his otherwise happy childhood was interrupted by a year of compulsive behaviour rooted in either shame or guilt.

Anger and Aggression

In both of the other two chapters,[28] namely those dealing with difficult people,[29] and violence in the workplace,[30] there is naturally a great deal of discussion about anger and aggression and learning to control them. It is likely that again there will be early roots of anger and frustration which the child could not deal with fully and much of which became buried. All of these kinds of experiences contribute to an adult becoming powerless to change damaged attitudes and behaviours, as layers like those on a mummy have formed. This can be healed by Christ through prayer[31] and reminds us of Christ instructing others to unbind Lazarus.

Relevance to Clerical Sexual Abuse

Evidence has been quoted above,[32] that early childhood experiences have been reported as playing a direct role in three of the eight areas of damage, in particular with those dealing with sexual abuse, sexual addiction and Internet pornography, and it is known that Christ can heal the early roots of damage through prayer.[33] Thus it seems particularly appropriate to ask about the level of awareness in various parts of the Church, in regard to the significance of this in the case of sexual abuse by clergy. The offenders as seminarians or as priests might well be more open to receiving prayer ministry than many other sex offenders who may have little or no faith in God. Prevention is always better than cure and here the benefits are beyond measure if potential victims never in fact suffered abuse, and potential offenders could actually live fulfilled healthy priestly lives because of healing before ordination. If the significance of prayer for inner healing were sufficiently appreciated, then would it not seem necessary to be ready to discover the roots of hurts in all seminarians, and to make sure that they could receive on-going prayer ministry and support to whatever extent each one required and was ready and open to receive?

There is a recent study of the current crisis in the Church over the sexual abuse of children by priests and other Church personnel.[34] Seventeen skilled and experienced Christian practitioners have contributed twenty-five chapters. However, prayer is only mentioned in three of these chapters. In the conclusion of the chapter dealing with research on the clerical sex abuses,[35] it is stated that there have been two main groups in the Church examining the data to serve their own political agendas: conservative writers who want to use it to exclude homosexuals, and liberals who want the Church to relax its rules on celibacy and pave the way for women priests. It is said that neither group appears to know specifically what sort of quantitative and qualitative data exist in this field. An example is that there is no well-designed study comparing the level of sexual, physical and/or emotional abuse experienced by priest sex offenders during their childhood versus priests who had similar experiences but did not offend in their role as priests. It is stated:

> We are only beginning to consider the various and complex situational factors, seminary training, family dynamics, social influences and personal histories that are relevant to a fuller understanding of the clerical offender. The past histories of the clerical offender might combine or interact to create and predict various types of perpetrator but we are unsure how and in what way. This point cannot be overstated.[36]

It should be clear to all concerned that we not only need all that is available from the best medical, psychiatric, psychological, social study sources to deal as best we can with such complex matters, but that the very last thing we should do is to omit God, or leave prayer as almost a last and not always used resort.

It is in this same chapter,[37] that it is reported that a clerical abuser of children sometimes has a history of being sexually abused. In a 2006 report, single-incident clerics were found to be less likely to have a recorded history of abuse (physical/sexual abuse and substance abuse) than clerics involved in more than one incident. The group of single-incident clerics include 4.2% who had suffered physical or sexual abuse as children, compared to 8.2% for clerics with multiple incidents. It is stated that it should be noted that these rates are well below rates for male lay victims of sexual abuse who later went on to abuse others, (16.6% for males before the age of 21). Thus it is said that the data do not support use of a childhood history of sexual abuse as an exclusionary criterion for candidacy to religious life and priesthood.

However, we should not be too ready to use this data to dismiss the importance of inner healing prayer ministry with seminarians. For one thing, even for the majority who would never go on to become an abuser, such ministry could only be beneficial.

Furthermore, returning to the reduction even in the small likelihood of any of them ever becoming abusers, we may need to look beyond childhood sexual abuse being the only cause of that person later becoming an offender. In the study of child sexual abuse,[38] it is not only stated that a number of psychologists have observed that if a child is exposed to inappropriate sexual activity or material, this can affect normal sexual development, especially around eight years of age, but also that sex offenders often come from a disturbed family background, and difficulties in early attachment have been shown to be a feature of child molesters, and it quotes a father's service in the army which could have been a contributing factor. It is, sadly, possible for a child to come from a stable, church-going family where, although no-one is to blame, it can happen that financial circumstances, work commitments, parents' personality and their own childhood, separation due to illness, and perhaps other factors, bring about a situation where the young child does not perceive and experience all of his or her needs being met. In some families, for example, the parents did not receive hugs or other nurturing contact from the grandparents, and perhaps their children in their turn feel such a lack. The present author has published[39] a number of testimonies of the benefits of prayer ministry which clearly show that childhood incidents thought to be insignificant at the time have affected a person's behaviour for decades. Although these did not lead to any of these victims becoming an abuser, it would hardly seem possible to rule out that an abuser might come from a home with good caring parents.

Prayer for Healing in Seminaries

It would seem to require fewer resources of the Church to have regular inner healing prayer ministry in the seminaries, perhaps even to offer it before candidates enter them, rather than to design and formulate research investigations into all the complicated and inter-related factors which may combine in a given individual so as to make him become a potential abuser. It would certainly seem to be more immediate, and also to help to build up the foundation of a seminarian's spiritual growth into a deepening relationship with, and dependence upon, Christ. Rather than trying to disentangle through psychological investigations the many inter-related and tangled components in family relationships and experiences, the candidates could be encouraged to recognise the role of Our Lady in untying the knots and entanglements in unhelpful bonds in families and their individual members. This recognition, going back to the time of St Irenaeus, has become an important feature of the life of Pope Francis. The majority of the candidates who would never become abusers could be helped towards the development of their faith in a happy, fulfilled life as a priest if such prayer ministry were available to them while studying. It is very much to be welcomed that prayer ministry for inner healing is already beginning to become available in some seminaries.

Since this was written Pope Francis has issued the apostolic exhortation *Amoris Laetitia*, in which he calls for the formation in seminaries to 'explore the psychological and affective background and experiences'. The Rector of Oscott College has already written of how this is now being done not only for the seminarians but also for the staff.[40]

Growing Recognition of the Need for Prayer for Inner Healing

If all priests had become aware of prayer for inner healing whilst in seminary, as is now well-established in one of our seminaries, and if perhaps they had experienced blessings and benefits themselves, or observed them in others, then it would be likely to contribute to their awareness of the importance of this ministry in the Church. There certainly hasn't been the awareness in many, perhaps most, countries and dioceses. In 2000, the Congregation for the Doctrine of the Faith issued Instructions on Prayers for Healing, signed by Cardinal Ratzinger and approved by Pope St John Paul II.[41] It speaks of sickness and disease throughout, but there is no mention of inner healing. Then in 2001 the Pontifical Council for the Laity collaborated with the International Catholic Charismatic Renewal Services to convene a meeting in Rome of Prayer for Healing, which was presided over by Cardinal Stafford, the President of the Council. Eighty-seven participants were invited and nineteen papers were presented. Apart from a paper on exorcism and deliverance, there is one single seven-page paper on inner healing in the published proceedings of close to 300 pages. There is also a five-page paper on psychological healing by a doctor who prays with people.[42] He writes:

> The best research carried out in psychiatry has helped me to examine the issue of psychological healing and the power of the Holy Spirit. These studies have made me more aware of the effectiveness of prayer of healing in psychology, and of the therapeutic importance of genuine Christian prayer to people suffering from psychological problems. This is a truth of the faith, but also of experience which all baptised Christians can endorse.

Having reminded us that we should always pray for the whole person, he adds:

> If the graces of bodily healing are obtained during the time of prayer for the sick…, the graces of psychological healing are more frequent still. But the distinction to be drawn is that the former are less noticeable as a sign of the power of Christ's love working through the Holy Spirit.

He also says that the grace of psychological healing should not merely be 'recovered' by professional psychologists, because although its internal dynamism coming from the Holy Spirit working in the injured psyche is fully compliant with the psychological dimension of human nature, it is not the same as that promoted by human sciences left to themselves. This is because psychological healing should offer a providential and peace-giving sign, inviting the individual to embark upon a Christian spiritual path. He urgently and strongly advocates the need to elaborate a theology and a pastoral ministry of healing, so that we can better discern the specific work of the Risen Christ in obtaining the grace of psychological healing.

More Recognition by Doctors than Priests?

It is intriguing that although the clerical contributors of the papers at the Rome Colloquium in 2001 outnumbered lay contributors by 2.8:1, it was one of the latter, a doctor, who brought out the points outlined in the last section. This is, however, in line with comments made elsewhere[43] on relatively recent developments in medical research almost entirely in the US:

> The healing ministry, which had, up until very recently, very little support in the medical world or sadly in the Church, now has strong supporters in many medical schools and teaching hospitals.

There was extensive reporting[44] on publications by doctors which included such information as 'courses on the role of religious devotion and prayer in healing are currently (1999) being taught in approximately fifty US medical schools.' It was reported in 1996 by a professor of medicine at Harvard that he calculated that the American health system would save $50 billion a year if good pastoral care was available to all those in hospitals. The comment was made:

> Wouldn't it be a supreme irony if doctors in the future felt more comfortable than priests and lay ministers in praying for healing?[45]

There is a balancing move forward in the role of prayer by the Church in the US as evidenced by the foreword to a book published[46] in 2005 by a priest who speaks of the relatively new inner healing ministry in the Catholic Church in America as having exploded in the last few years (ten years ago at the time of the present writing) beyond charismatic circles. One could not say that about the UK and Western Europe.

Fellow Sufferers not Foes

How should we approach our problems? How are we to regard the available data? We must not fall into the trap of using what we have learned to serve our own agendas as some conservative and liberal writers have been trying to do.[47] Instead of coming up with entrenched certainties about who is right and who is wrong so that we appear to be opponents, arguing about statistics or the relative merits of various studies or approaches we need to acknowledge that we are all sinners, all weak and fallible and in need of God's grace to free us from the adversaries of our own self-centredness and the devil. Then we can come in repentance, praising God for the victory of Christ on the cross and humbly asking for the guidance of the Holy Spirit. It is the infinite love of God flowing between the members of the Body of Christ which can bring about healing of wounds in individuals and which can heal divisions between different parts of the Body. It is only God who can bring us to a healthy and harmonious balance of the resources which He enables us to learn about through study, together with the powerful gifts of the Holy Spirit which He may give us if we pray humbly with expectant faith.

Notes

1 Pope St John Paul II, *Letter to Families*, 19.

2 A. Guile, *Journey into Wholeness: Prayer for Inner Healing—An Essential Ministry of the Church* (Leominster: Gracewing, 2013).

3 *Ibid.*, pp. 42–3.

4 F. MacNutt, *The Power to Heal* (Notre Dame: Ave Maria Press, 1977), pp. 207–8; Guile, *Journey Into Wholeness*, pp. 46–7.

5 F. MacNutt, *The Power to Heal*, pp. 207–8.

6 Guile, *Journey into Wholeness*, pp. 101–4.

7 *Ibid.*, pp. 123–4.

8 B. Geary & J. Bryan (eds), *The Christian Handbook of Abuse, Addiction and Difficult Behaviour* (Stowmarket: Kevin Mayhew, 2008).

9 J. M. Walsh, 'Gambling Addiction' in Geary & Bryan, pp. 113–146.

10 J. M. Walsh, J. W. Ciarrocchi, R. L. Piedmont and D. Haskins, Spiritual Transcendence and Religious Practices in Reducing Pain or Enhancing the Quality of Life? *Research in the Social Scientific Study of Religion*, 18, pp. 155–175.

11 Guile, *Journey into Wholeness*; J. McManus, *The Inside Job—A Spirituality of Self-Esteem* (Chawton: Redemptorist Press, 2004).

12 J. M. Walsh et al, *Spiritual Transcendence.*

13 Guile, *Journey into Wholeness.*

14 Geary & Bryan, *The Christian Handbook of Abuse.*

15 B. Geary, 'Child Sexual Abuse' in Geary and Bryan, pp. 13–47.

16 M. Brouwer and M. Laaser, 'Sexual Addiction and Internet Pornography' in Geary & Bryan pp. 147–175.

17 *Ibid.*

18 Guile, *Journey into Wholeness.*

19 B. Geary & E. Montgomery, 'Adult Bullying' in Geary & Bryan, pp. 209–246.

20 L. D. Eron, L. R. Husemann, E. Dubow, R. Romanoff & P. W. Yarmel, 'Aggression and its correlates over 20 years' in Crowell, Evans & O'Donnell (Eds), *Childhood Aggression and Violence; Sources of Influence, Prevention and Control* (New York: Plenum, 1987), pp. 249–262.

21 Geary & Montgomery, 'Adult Bullying'.

22 Guile, *Journey into Wholeness*.

23 Geary & Bryan, *The Christian Handbook of Abuse*.

24 Geary, 'Child Sexual Abuse'.

25 L. Orr, 'Domestic Abuse' in Geary & Bryan, pp. 49–82.

26 C. C. H. Cook, 'Alcohol and Other Addictions' in Geary & Bryan, pp. 83–111.

27 C. Graymore, *Alcoholism—Insight into the Addictive Mind* (Newton Abbot: David & Charles, 1987).

28 Geary & Bryan, *The Christian Handbook of Abuse*.

29 J. Bryan, 'Dealing with Difficult People' in Geary & Bryan, pp. 177–208.

30 M. Fitzsimons, 'Violence in the Workplace' in Geary & Bryan, pp. 247–274.

31 Guile, *Journey into Wholeness*.

32 Geary & Bryan, *The Christian Handbook of Abuse*.

33 Guile, *Journey into Wholeness*.

34 B. Geary & J. M. Greer, *The Dark Night of the Catholic Church—Examining the Child Sexual Abuse Scandal* (Stowmarket: Kevin Mayhew, 2011).

35 G. J. McGlone, 'The Clerical Sex Abuser: A Review of Research' in Geary & Greer, pp. 109–140.

36 *Ibid.*

37 *Ibid.*

38 Geary, 'Child Sexual Abuse'.

39 Guile, *Journey into Wholeness*.

40 D. Oakley, 'Grounded in Reality' in *The Tablet* 270/9149 (2016), p. 13.

41 Congregation for the Doctrine of the Faith, *Instruction on Prayers for Healing*, (2000).

42 P. Madre, 'Psychological Healing' in *Prayer for Healing* (International Colloquium, Rome: International Charismatic Renewal Services, 2003), pp. 231–6.

43 J. McManus, *Healing in the Spirit* (Chawton: Redemptorist Press, 2002), pp. 5–19.

44 *Ibid.*

45 *Ibid.*

46 B. McCarthy, *A Catholic Compendium of Inner Healing* (Goletta CA: Queenship Publishing, 2005).

47 McGlone, 'The Clerical Sex Abuser, pp. 109–140.

7

Intergenerational Healing Mass—
Healing the Family Tree

Alan Guile

In his Apostolic Exhortation, The Joy of Love, (Amoris Laetitia) Pope Francis discusses at great length the love that unites husband, wife and children. The family is a community of love. But the Pope is also well aware that families can be struggling with deep wounds and negative attitudes passed on from generation to generation. In this chapter Alan Guile discusses his experience of promoting and participating as a layman in Mass celebrated for the healing of the family tree. Members of families who have participated in and experienced these Masses testify to the healing and peace it brought them. Alan laments the fact that very few priests invite families to share in Masses celebrated specifically for the healing of their family trees. He believes it is time to look again at how the Mass can bind up the wounds in families and deeply renew their faith in the love and mercy of God the Father.

Introduction

The publication in 1982 of the first of two books[1] by the psychiatrist Dr Kenneth McAll led to a priest celebrating Mass that year in our home, particularly for two children we had lost in miscarriage. A friend who was present subsequently reported that relationships with several members of her family began to improve markedly from then on.

Two Catholic priests, having read the first of these books, wrote books of their own during the 1980s.[2] During the last thirty years I have arranged with priests for more than one hundred Masses to have their main intention focused on intergenerational healing. Many were additional to the regular weekly Mass schedule, and were celebrated in church for people coming to our home for prayer for inner healing. In our parish three of the regular evening Masses have been celebrated for this intention each year for many years. The congregation at this Mass is normally 25–30, but when advance information is sent out beyond the parish that the Mass is to be for intergenerational healing, between 70 and 110 people come, some travelling forty miles or more.

There still appear to be only a small number of places in the UK where such Masses are available either regularly or occasionally, even after all these years of heightened awareness. Despite extensive enquiries, no priest could be found to write this paper. The very small number of priests known to me who do have the awareness and the experience were unable to write it because of health and the pressure of their duties.

Why Do We Pray for the Dead?

Some years ago Fr Ronald Rolheiser, writing in the *Catholic Herald*, addressed the question put to him by a woman whose son had been killed in an accident: 'Does it make sense to pray for the dead?' He wrote that the Christian answer is an unequivocal yes. His first reason is that such prayer helps us, the living. Closely tied to this is a second reason, that we pray for our dead loved ones to help heal our relationship to them. He said that this takes us to the heart of the matter, that we pray for the dead because we believe in the communion of saints, an essential Christian doctrine that asks us to believe that a vital flow of life continues to exist between ourselves and our loved ones even beyond death. Love, presence and communication reach through death. It is out of love that we pray for them to be purified as the Catechism teaches.

We know that it has been the custom of the Church from the very earliest times to pray for the dead. There is evidence of this in the catacomb and other inscriptions and epitaphs from at least as early as the second century. The importance of praying for the dead was taught by many of the early fathers of the Church and is emphasised by our praying for them at every Mass today.

The vital importance of loving prayer for the dead has been well documented throughout the centuries. One book,[3] for example, cites tradition beginning with the second book of Maccabees (2M 12:42–46); Jesus himself praying for the widow of Naim (Jn 7:11–17) and for Lazarus (Jn 11), and mentions St Cyprian, Tertullian, St Monica, St Teresa of Avila, the Curé of Ars, and St Perpetua. St Malachy held a series of requiem Eucharists for his dead sister. St Bernard writes of this sister being so worldly-minded that her brother, St Malachy, determined not to see her any more as long as she lived. However, after her death he heard a voice in a dream telling him that his sister was complaining that she had

had nothing to eat for thirty days, and when he awoke he realised that it was exactly thirty days since he had last offered the sacrifice of the Living Bread for her. He now began again to do this until finally he saw her in a dream, clad entirely in white and surrounded by blessed spirits.[4] Thus St Malachy discovered how the Eucharist heals the deceased.

This awareness is not confined to the Catholic Church. Kenneth McAll himself was Anglican and other Anglicans have written on this subject.[5] They discussed two difficulties raised through the work of Dr McAll in the minds of evangelicals:

a) On the idea that prayer can lead to the freeing and releasing on the journey towards Heaven even of the 'unsaved or uncommitted dead', they conclude that the picture which evangelicals have of a God whose love has no further claim upon the 'lost' when they die, does need to be challenged.

b) To those who claimed that Dr McAll's work had connection with spiritualism, they refute this firmly.

On the first of these two points, I have a letter written to me twenty or more years ago by a dear longstanding friend who is a Baptist minister who has also served as a minister in the Methodist Church. He concludes that there are scriptural indications that there is more to be said than some evangelicals and other Christians assert. He cites the statement of St Peter that Jesus went to preach to 'the spirits in prison' in between the Crucifixion and the Resurrection (1P: 3:18–20), and that Jesus descended to the lower regions (Ep 4:9).

Fr Michael Gwinnell, in responding to people's needs and their requests for prayer for deceased family, found that the Christianity-long tradition of praying for the dead was saying to him 'have compassion on the unquiet dead'. He began to ask himself what happens to those who die unsurrendered to God, who are still in their sins, yet who are not fully committed to evil. This self-questioning led him also to 1 Peter 3:18–20, and he concludes that those among the dead who are not in touch with Christ but are in touch with one of his disciples may thereby be able to have the 'gospel preached to them' and so be granted repentance unto life (Ac 11:18). Thus he writes that he has come to accept that through the ministry of his disciples, Jesus rescues people after physical death as well as before it.[6] He discusses the unbaptised in the light of the writing of St Paul (1 Co 15:19).

Who Should be Included in Our Prayers?

We may ask, 'who should we include in our prayers?' The answer is that we include not only those relatives we knew in life but also those of earlier generations. There can be influences upon us from earlier generations which cause patterns of unloving or unhelpful behaviour or attitudes which seem to occur in a number of generations. Many of us may have said something like 'oh yes that runs in my family'. Some families come from communities where throughout generations even to the present day, there has been great bitterness, unforgiveness, injustice and even cruelty. We need to look no further than Northern Ireland to see this in reality. This reminds us that we need to pray for healing grace and forgiveness for all those who have gone before us that they may find rest in the love of God. Some of our earlier ancestors, unknown to us, may have died in tragic circumstances or died alone without the prayer of others.

In the Scriptures, we find in many passages in both the Old and New Testament, reference to 'He punishes the children and their children for the sin of the fathers to the third and fourth generation' (Ex 34:7). For this reason Fr Hampsch and Fr DeGrandis offer a genogram listing our ancestors back to the fourth generation. However, Fr Hampsch cautions about excessive literalism in the understanding of such phrases, which could lead to contradictions and confusion in the application of God's word. He also writes that 'it is helpful but not necessary to outline one's family tree by using a structured genogram, listing in particular any who may have strongly influenced the family members in a hurtful way causing emotional, physical or spiritual problems.'[7] Where we have knowledge of particular members of our deceased family where there was discord and damage, we clearly will focus our prayers on them. Most of us do not have sufficient information to draw up a complete genogram to the fourth generation. We can put our faith in God who can embrace in our prayers all past members of our family, whether known to us by name and behaviour or not.

Freedom from Unhealthy Bonds with Past Family

It is vital that any Mass for this intention includes prayers to cut the living members of the family free from any unhelpful bondages connected with deceased members. To help us think about this, we can reflect upon experiences which we may have had of knowing someone who never seems to become free of the influence or control of one person, for example, the mother. We can probably all think of at least one adult son or daughter who has shown signs of not being able to break away from the mother's influence, and so is not free to develop fully and thus become what God gave them the potential to be. There can be restrictive influences of varying levels between two living individuals. Such restrictive influences can continue to exist if one person, say the mother, dies. There is no doubt that we can cut these restricting influences by the authority and power of Christ through prayer, leaving those concerned free to ask God's help to forgive and to be joined together by Christ's life-giving love.

In some circumstances, some things may not have been said or done before death took place. This may have included forgiveness or reconciliation or telling the person that they were loved. Those still alive may be hurting from this and can pray to forgive and to be forgiven, so that the healing grace of the Lord can come into their life in a new and dynamic way, through their loving prayer for the dead.

It has long been realised by doctors that certain unhealthy patterns of living and behaving towards others can recur in succeeding generations of a family. We will all be particularly aware of some of these such as alcoholism, depressions, broken marriages etc. Discussions of damaged patterns and controlling bonds can be found in a wide literature.

There are many ways in which bonds within past family members may be affecting those now alive. Some have already been mentioned. Others can include compulsive habits, mental health, disease, criminality, unhealthy sexual behaviour, lack of wholeness in marriage.

When we speak of these bonds or a bondage to someone in our family line whom we never met in life but whose guilts can affect us, we do not mean that the present person is bound to an ancestor in some way. However, the present person may have their own weakness (physical or moral defect) and these can be activated by a demonic spirit which has obtained access through the weaknesses inherited because of the sins of our ancestors. Also learned experiences, habits and attitudes can pass down the generations as we base our behaviour with our children on what we experienced from our own parents.

Freedom from Bonds Due to Occult or Other Evil Practices

If any of our ancestors have had direct contact with powers of evil through involvement of some occult activity such as satanism, witchcraft, spiritualism, freemasonry, astrology, fortune-telling, tarot cards, ouija boards, Reiki healing etc, then there can be serious consequences within the family. The most tenacious disorders transmitted demonically are those resulting from the sins of occultism practised by ancestors. Dr Kurt Koch gives a great deal of evidence about this based on his forty years experience in over a hundred countries.[8] Fr Hampsch distinguishes four levels of occultic contamination.[9] It is essential to pray at each intergenerational Mass for the cutting free of families from all such influences. This does not rule out the possible need for more prayers for deliverance being needed for individuals in our present family.

Prayer for Lost Babies

Another area we need to look at is that there has often been a lack of prayer for children who have died through still-birth, miscarriage or abortion. These children are also part of our family tree, and it is very right and loving to pray for them. In this way we invite the Lord Jesus into this area of family life where a particular healing may need to take place.

Fr Hampsch reports remarkable changes which have happened in some families when deceased children were prayed for at a family Mass. These have included the clearing up of learning disabilities, fertility problems, behavioural problems, hyperactivity and even character disorders.[10] Most families will have lost babies over the generations and some of these may never have been given names or had prayers for them. Now at such a Mass they can be welcomed into the family by whatever name God may give in prayer. A lady who attended some of these Masses wrote the following letter:

> I am writing to say how greatly I have benefited from the Masses for the family tree.

> I am an Anglican. It was comforting for me to find out that I can pray for the deceased members of my family, but the greatest benefit was the thought that I already have babies in Heaven, instead of grieving. I now feel blessed.

> These Masses must give great comfort to the many women who have had miscarriages, still-born or aborted children.

> I am eternally grateful to God.

Among the bidding prayers at a Mass for intergenerational healing in our parish, the following prayer is said by the whole congregation together.

Prayer for Intergenerational Healing

In the name of Jesus Christ I renounce all the works of the devil together with any occult, freemasonry or witchcraft practices there may have been in my past family.

I consecrate myself to Jesus Christ, my Lord and Saviour, both now and forever.

In the name of Jesus Christ and with the authority of Jesus, I now break any curses and all psychic heredity and any demonic hold upon my family line as a result of the disobedience to God of any of my ancestors.

Father in heaven, I stand before you a sinner through my own faults. I bring before you my ancestors, and I ask forgiveness for their sins and mine. I forgive them for any disobedience to you which has brought harmful patterns into my family.

I ask you, Father, to give them a fresh opportunity to receive your pardon, and to be reconciled with you and with one another.

I pray that all present members of my family and any to be born in the future will be set free of disobedience to you, and of all harmful patterns of living, and through repentance of their sins and the gift of faith, they may come to know Jesus Christ as Saviour and Lord, and experience the power of the Holy Spirit working in their lives.

I praise and thank you, Lord, for everyone in my past family, including any babies who were lost, together with those alive now and those to come.

In this prayer we include asking God for forgiveness of not only our sins but also those of our ancestors. This concept of repentance for sins which we did not commit has been examined by Mgr Peter Hocken in the light of the letter *Tertio Millennio Adveniente* issued by Pope St John Paul II in 1994. Mgr Hocken quotes[11] Elie Wiesel 'While no man is responsible for what his ancestors have done, he is responsible for what he does with that memory'. He also writes that the purpose of unofficial acts of repentance is to begin breaking the grip of spiritual forces at work in conflict, as we follow the Old Testament prophets who confessed 'we and our fathers have sinned', and we affirm the spiritual link between the generations of the past and our generation today.

Testimonies

Dr Kenneth McAll had more than a thousand case histories of many patients which bore evidence that, following the loving prayer of the living at a Eucharist for those who had died in previous generations, there were sometimes improvements, even very marked ones, in the physical and emotional health of one or more members of the present family.

Among those who came to the monthly family tree Masses celebrated by Fr Benedict Heron OSB since about 1984 was a lady whose son did not communicate with her, and just lay in bed staring at the ceiling. During the Mass she shouted out, 'I know my son has been healed'. Nothing more was heard from her until one of the team bumped into her one day and asked whether in fact her son had been healed, 'Yes', she replied. When she had arrived home after the Mass her son actually opened the door to her and said 'hello mum', as if nothing had ever happened.

Many people have provided testimonies over the years of blessings coming to members of their family following attendance at these Masses. One source of these testimonies is the Family Tree Ministry newsletter. As far back as issue 4 in Summer 1991, there is an account of a conference held at a Catholic church in Bradford. One lady had travelled many miles to witness to her experiences of healings in her own family tree and healings amongst the Aborigines of New Zealand. Even in the first three years of these newsletters one can read testimonies written by Anglican priests, a Harley Street counsellor and clinician, a Catholic psychiatrist, and a journalist among others.

There is no doubt that many people have experienced blessings through prayer for intergenerational healing, but there are many factors involved which vary from person to person. In the case of histories reported in the Family Tree Ministry one finds that many people had the great benefit of spending a considerable time with the late Dr McAll himself, his wife and members of their team. One lady writes, 'Dr McAll spent hours with me going through my family tree', and she writes of colossal help from four of the team. Others who also had direct ministry from Dr McAll write about how this began a sometimes painful pilgrimage which was still going on years later.

Very few people will ever have access to a team as gifted by God with wisdom, discernment, gifts of the Holy Spirit such as word of knowledge, and deep awareness of the intricacies of family damage and bonds, as the group then around the late Dr McAll. Sometimes the need for prayer at an intergenerational Mass will emerge from ongoing prayer for inner healing over months or years, as has happened to a high proportion of the hundreds coming to the home of the present author.[12] Several teams are always available in our parish church after the end of each of these Masses so as to continue the work of prayer for healing, and great appreciation of benefits from attending these Masses is frequently expressed. Fr Hampsch gives two testimonies of a person who received physical healing after a family tree Mass at which they have prayed for their whole family.[13]

Conclusions

Numbers of people do respond when a priest is known to be celebrating a Mass particularly for this intention, and many believe that they and their family have been blessed. Many more would come if priests spoke about the importance and gave some explanation about why they were planning to celebrate a Mass with this intention.

Even if the priest does not speak in his homily at the Mass about intergenerational healing, or gives no homily at all, the bidding prayers offer a powerful opportunity to pray with expectant faith.

The Catechism, writing about the charge 'Heal the Sick' which the Church received from Christ, says: 'This life-giving presence of Christ, the physician of souls and bodies, is particularly active through the sacraments, and in an altogether special way through the Eucharist.'[14] In the Mass of Monday in the first week of Lent, the prayer after Communion is 'Lord, through this sacrament may we rejoice in your healing power and experience your saving love in mind and body'. This is the faith of the Church. It is vital that we build up expectant faith in priests as well as in lay people so that it becomes the lived experience of more people that the truth (Christ) really does set us free and make us whole.

It may be that the relatively rare opportunities provided in the UK for families to be blessed by opportunities to pray for their families at such a Mass are not unconnected with the generally lower level of expectant faith in the power of the sacraments here compared with the faith in many other parts of the world. In 2001, an International Colloquium on Prayer For Healing was convened in Rome by the Pontifical Council for the Laity together with the International Catholic Charismatic Renewal Services. Part of the colloquium was devoted to testimonies from around the world, which were reported in the proceedings.[15] There was considerable discussion of the importance of such genealogical or family tree Masses in the report from Africa[16] and in Asia where it was said that it is now a very common practice, widely accepted by the Church as normal for Christians to do.[17] The bishops who gave reports on North America[18] and on Oceania[19] both stressed the role of the Eucharist in healing. The latter reported on powerful healings taking place after a Eucharist was celebrated asking the Lord's forgiveness for hurts experienced at the time when Tasmania was a penal colony.

Another factor which is likely to have held back the provision of intergenerational healing in some countries has been the lack of serious study of the subject by bishops and theologians. Such study would successfully counter and dispel doubts, confusions and misunderstandings, and establish this most important ministry as a normal part of the loving actions of God through his Church.

Notes

1 K. McAll, *Healing the Family Tree* (London: Sheldon Press, 1982); Idem, *A Guide to Healing the Family Tree* (Goleta Ca: Queenship Publishing, 1996).

2 J. H. Hampsch, *Healing Your Family Tree* (Everett Wa: Performance Press, 1986); R. DeGrandis, *Intergenerational Healing* (Self-published, 1989).

3 M. J. Linn, D. Linn and M. Linn, *Healing the Dying* (New York: Paulist Press, 1979), pp. 72–73.

4 M. Linn, D. Linn and S. Fabricant, *Healing the Greatest Hurt* (New York: Paulist Press, 1985), pp. 54–55.

5 M. Mitton and R. Parker, *Healing Death's Wounds—How to Commit the Dead to God and Deliver the Oppressed* (Grand Rapids: Chosen Books, 2004).

6 M. Gwinnell, *Ministering to Deceased Relatives and Forbears*, unpublished paper for a seminar, April 1992.

7 Hampsch, *Healing your Family Tree*, p. 17.

8 K. Koch, *Occult Bondage and Deliverance* (Grand Rapids: Kregel Publications 1972).

9 Hampsch, *Healing your Family Tree*, pp. 154–157.

10 Hampsch, *Healing your Family Tree*, pp. 183–189.

11 P. Hocken, *Healing the Wounds of History* (London: Goodnews Special Publication, 2005).

12 A. Guile, *Journey into Wholeness: Prayer for Inner Healing—An Essential Ministry of the Church* (Leominster: Gracewing, 2013).

13 Hampsch, *Healing your Family Tree*, pp. 116–117.

14 *Catechism of the Catholic Church*, 1509.

[15]   *Prayer For Healing* (International Colloquium, Rome: International Catholic Charismatic Services, 2003), pp. 255–297.

[16]   *Ibid.,* p. 262.

[17]   *Ibid.,* p. 277.

[18]   *Ibid.,* p. 270.

[19]   *Ibid.,* p. 291.

8

Healing the Loss of Babies

Eileen Brydon

This chapter addresses the deep grief and hurt following the loss of babies through induced abortion. Although this is arguably the most common medical procedure in the world, most mothers and the public know little or nothing of the reality of abortion and how it impacts mothers, fathers, grandparents and society in general. The chapter is written by someone who for decades has worked with the mothers struggling to decide whether or not to go ahead with the abortion, or who are coming to terms with deep distress many years later. Eileen has long been at the forefront of listening to and teaching young people and others, so that this is a detailed examination of the issues written by an acknowledged expert practitioner who has been engaged in crisis pregnancy and post-abortion counselling during the past 23 years. She is an accredited counsellor with the Association of Christian Counsellors (ACC).

Introduction

Children are a gift from the Lord, they are a real blessing (Ps 127:3)

The loss of a child is the greatest pain and it echoes down through the years of family life, casting a shadow over every sunny occasion. We can all empathise with this and try and reach out to those who experience it. The hurt experienced following the loss of an unborn baby is also very real, whether the loss is due to accident, miscarriage, stillbirth or an induced abortion. Understanding, support and help are available to parents grieving the loss of babies due to accident, miscarriage and stillbirth; however the remit of this paper is to focus on the grief and hurt following the loss of babies as a result of induced abortion, and what we as a church can offer in the way of support and healing.

No one would doubt that following the loss of a baby due to accident, miscarriage or stillbirth, both parents and especially the mother, suffer greatly in the aftermath. Generally, they receive a great deal of sympathy from family and friends in the form of cards, flowers and love, which will help them to grieve openly. In stark contrast however, there is little or no sympathy if the loss of the baby occurs from an induced abortion. The parents and especially the mother will usually suffer in silence, knowing that she chose the option and signed her baby's life away. In the aftermath of such a loss as this there will be no cards, no flowers, no love and no opportunity to grieve openly. Those who knew of the decision to abort will assume that, since she herself made the decision, there shouldn't be any negative impact in the form of pain, suffering or regret. Indeed the whole attitude of most individuals and society at large is that she has solved the problem and can happily get on with her life. This is a very grave deception and it seems the whole world is fooled by it.

The Abortion Act 1967 was given Royal Assent in Britain on 27 October 1967 and was implemented on 27 April 1968. Within a matter of months London became known as the abortion capital of the world. The Department of Health has recorded to date a total of 8.5 million abortions in Britain alone.[1]

Induced abortion is arguably the most common medical procedure in the world and yet women worldwide as well as the public at large know little or nothing of the reality of abortion and how it impacts on the lives of mothers, fathers, grandparents, siblings and society in general. How can something so common, occurring an estimated 50 million times every year throughout the world,[2] be so hidden, that very few people are aware of the deep wounds and hurt experienced in the aftermath of each personal abortion experience?

The Cloak of Secrecy

The whole topic of abortion is and has always been cloaked in secrecy. The truth has always been withheld and this is the deliberate strategy of the pro-abortion industry. The Abortion Act was passed because its political advocates used lies, deception and the prevailing widespread public ignorance.[3] This cloak of secrecy has always, and still is, maintained with the cooperation of the mass media that are very silent and unwilling to shed any light on the subject despite the volume of information available to them. Pro-abortion advocates always deny that there are any physical or psychological problems for women following an abortion. They declare that any woman who claims to be struggling, must have had prior psychological and emotional problems unconnected with what they refer to as 'a termination of pregnancy' and most women, they claim, put it behind them and get on with their lives. This kind of attitude leads the grieving mother to think that she is an oddity because all other post-abortive women are seemingly coping well. Political correctness which insists on promoting a double deception adds further to the silence, secrecy and denial by forcefully claiming that abortion is good for women.[4] This total deception is severely condemned by the Holy Spirit in the book of the prophet Isaiah: 'Woe to those who call evil good and good evil' (Is 5: 20). In order to see how deceptive the widely held perception regarding abortion is, we can do so using the following equation:

crisis pregnancy + abortion = problem solved, end of story

In the past 23 years, listening to post-abortive women, it is clear to see that nothing could be further from the truth. Lifting the veil of this silence, secrecy, ignorance and deception is not easy due to the prevailing attitudes, media silence and denial of pro-abortion advocates.

The Modern World View Versus the Christian World View

Here in Britain, attitudes towards abortion may vary but the majority of people believe that in certain circumstances abortion is regrettable but the right choice. In order to understand why this is so, it is necessary to understand the mind-set of our times. Historically the laws of our land were based on Christian principles inherited from generations of God-fearing men and women and on the perceived and received wisdom from the past:

> When Gentiles, who do not possess the law, do instinctively what the law requires, these, though not having the law, are a law to themselves. They show that what the law requires is written on their hearts, to which their own conscience also bears witness; and their conflicting thoughts will accuse or perhaps excuse them. (Rm 2:14-15).

The understanding of right and wrong was founded upon absolute biblical principles. However, since the so-called Age of Enlightenment of the eighteenth century, these principles have gradually been eroded by humanistic thinking. Faith and intuitive understanding have been exchanged for a modern world view no longer seeing the need for God. Mankind sought to become increasingly independent and autonomous. The biblical view, where right and wrong are clearly defined, has been overtaken by this relativistic approach. It is very important to understand these two value systems, as illustrated in the diagram below.

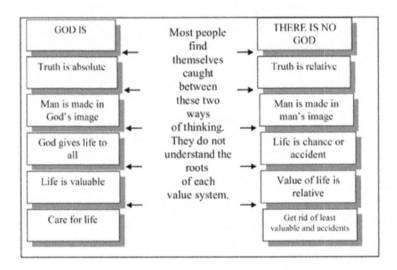

Relativism and Humanism, a man-centred world view, asserts that there is no God, and that life is accidental and chance. The choice of abortion involves an assumption that the lives of unborn children are of less value than other human lives and are therefore expendable. Unborn children no longer have an intrinsic worth by virtue of being created by God but their worth depends on the needs, desires and opinions of the pregnant mother and those close to her.

The biblical and humanistic world views are total opposites. In reality most people find themselves caught somewhere between these two ways of thinking. For example many people would agree with abortion if a pregnancy resulted from rape, but may oppose it as a choice for a happily married, financially solvent couple who already have one child. It is therefore crucial that we understand the roots of each value system in order to appreciate the dilemma in which so many people are caught.

In recent years the assertion of a woman's right to control her own body has had many repercussions. The advent of the contraceptive pill was a major breakthrough in helping women control whether they became pregnant and such contraception brought freedom to pursue other goals. Abortion similarly became acceptable as a means of expressing the power to choose and to exercise control. It is perceived as a means of increasing individual freedom and yet abortion has not delivered this freedom.

The Reality and Impact of Abortion

The reality of abortion and its impact on post-abortive mothers in particular must be grasped before we can begin to talk about the healing process and the journey to wholeness. Everyone needs to face the truth of this tragedy that every abortion kills a baby and endangers the mother. Every baby dies, every mother is wounded and some mothers die from the choice our culture urges her to make. The whole abortion procedure is a real attack on her delicate maternal nature beautifully crafted by God who has called her into His procreative plan: 'Be fruitful and multiply.' (Gn 1: 28–30).

According to current government statistics around 4,000 unborn babies are killed by abortion every week in Britain.[5] The statistics which are published annually show that as many as 98% of abortions are authorised under Clause C which states that:

> the pregnancy has not exceeded its twenty-fourth week and that the continuance of the pregnancy would involve risk, greater than if the pregnancy were terminated, of injury to the physical or mental health of the pregnant woman.[6]

Yet The Royal College of Obstetricians and Gynaecologists wrote in their first report on Unplanned Pregnancy in 1972 that 'there is no such danger of injury in the majority of these cases as the "indication" is purely a social one'.[7] Also the UK's leading mental health experts who reviewed all the international evidence found that abortion of an unwanted pregnancy was not good for women's mental health.[8] They went on to say that if pregnant mothers had mental health problems they should be properly assessed, not just sent for abortions. The Department of Health and the medical profession are ignoring the huge amount of evidence that abortion can make mental health problems worse.

The following is an example of the death experience that every mother endures when she succumbs to abortion. One mother's true personal story describes the events of her reluctant journey through the beginning of the death experience:

> I went to the GP when I was pregnant. I told him I was stressed. Five minutes later he referred me for an abortion. I didn't feel

strong enough to cope, so I went along with it. Since then I have been falling apart. I allowed my baby to be killed and that's hard to live with. What makes me angry is that everyone said 'it's your decision', but I was never offered any other choice. Now I have the memory, and I still don't feel strong enough to cope.[9]

Pregnant mothers who succumb to abortion have to submit either to surgical or medical abortion procedures decided upon by the medical practitioner. Vacuum aspiration or suction abortion is the most commonly used surgical abortion technique in Britain and is used in pregnancies up to 14 weeks. The cervix (neck of the womb) is dilated with instruments and a tube connected to a strong suction pump is inserted into the womb. The fluid around the baby is sucked out along with the dismembered baby. In later pregnancies which exceed 14 weeks, a method known as Dilation & Evacuation (D&E) is performed using crushing forceps to remove limbs and other body parts, as the skeleton has now calcified.[10]

The abortion drug RU486 marketed under the name of Mifepristone or Mifegyne is given to the mother in tablet form at the hospital or clinic. It is recorded as anti-progesterone and works by blocking the effects of the natural hormone progesterone, which is required to maintain the lining of the womb during pregnancy. Typically it is used with another substance, prostaglandin, which assists in dilating the cervix, causing contractions and expelling the dead baby.

The mother is involved in the whole process and is fully aware of the effects that the drugs are having on her body. The baby may be aborted at home and this will be very traumatic for the mother particularly as she will have to deal with the body of her dead child and all that it implies. In the words of Edouard Sakiz the Chairman of the company making RU486 in 1990:

> As Abortifacient procedures go, RU486 is not at all easy to use. In fact it is more complex to use than the technique of vacuum extraction... a mother who wants to end her pregnancy has to live with her abortion for at least a week using this technique. It's an appalling psychological ordeal.[11]

At a news conference on 17 May 2002, Dr Richard Hausknecht, medical director of Danco, the company which manufactures RU486 for the American market, admitted, 'it [RU486] is not safer than a surgical abortion'.[12]

Unresolved Grief

Although on the surface it appears that abortion solves the problem of an unplanned pregnancy, below the surface countless mothers are hurting, grieving and suffering in silence. In the late 1980s around 20 years after the Abortion Act was implemented, statistics revealed that 3.3 million mothers were living in the aftermath of a personal abortion experience. Their pain and grief was such that the walls of denial subconsciously built by them began to crumble on a national and international scale which made it possible for everyone to catch a glimpse of the truth hidden beneath cloak of secrecy. Agony Aunt columns in newspapers and magazines began to print letters from mothers revealing the very real grief and pain associated with their own abortion experiences. A few examples of the headlines were:

- My abortion still haunts me

- I can't cope with this abortion guilt

- Hardly a day goes by when I don't think of my baby who would have been five years old now.

- Why didn't anyone tell me my baby had a beating heart?

- Why didn't anyone tell me that I would feel worse after the abortion?

- How can I live for the rest of my life knowing that I have killed my baby?

- How can I be a good mother to my children when I have killed their brother or sister?

- Will my baby ever forgive me?

During her relationship with world renowned singer Robbie Williams, Nicole Appleton from the girl pop group *All Saints* became pregnant and caved in under pressure, aborting the baby she and fiancé Robbie desperately wanted to keep. Nicole, who was four months pregnant, described the abortion as 'the worst day of my life' and revealed that it left her feeling suicidal:

> I was horrified, violated by what I felt was the power of an industry
> that leads a mother to sacrifice her child to keep the band's

commitments. After having my abortion I was in shock...I wanted to kill myself.[13]

Paradoxically, at the same time, increasing numbers of post-abortive mothers turned for help to the Society for the Protection of Unborn Children (SPUC) the first pro-life organisation in the world formed in 1966. In 1987 SPUC held its Annual National Conference and one of the guest speakers was Olivia Gans who founded the group American Victims of Abortion (AVA). Her presentation involved a testimony of her own personal abortion experience and the subsequent emotional and physiological damage that ensued. Following her presentation, women delegates at the conference approached SPUC senior staff and said that Olivia could have been talking about their own lives as they too had been hurt by abortion. As a result of this encounter British Victims of Abortion (BVA) was launched as a sister organisation of SPUC under the umbrella of SPUC Educational Research Trust. The post-abortive mothers recognised their babies as the first victims of abortion but they also felt they were victims as well. BVA publically advertised free helpline and counselling support to individuals, and frequently initiated and responded to media coverage on the subject. Some years later BVA was renamed ARCH (Abortion Recovery Care and Helpline) as it was felt that this name better reflected the free services they were offering.[14] Many post-abortive mothers who called the helpline said 'I was offered no choice except abortion' and 'they might as well have put a gun to my head rather than a pen in my hand.'

Informed Consent

In general medical law, an Informed Consent Form must be signed following an assessment of the patient before any medical procedure including an abortion can take place. This is all to comply with the following guidelines:

NHS The Patient's Charter & you, page 4, providing information states:

You have the *right* to have any proposed treatment, including any risks involved in that treatment and any alternatives, clearly explained to you before you decide whether to agree to it.

NHS Patients' rights—Citizens Advice states:

> The doctor must inform you of the nature, consequences and any substantial risks involved in the treatment or operation, before you give your consent. It is for the doctor to decide exactly how much to tell you, the patient.

The Care of Women Requesting Induced Abortion—Evidence-based Clinical Guideline Number 7 November 2011 states in Recommendation 4.13:

> Staff providing abortion services should provide up-to-date evidence-guided information, supported by local data where robust, about complications and sequelae of abortion.

and in Recommendation 4.14:

> Women should have access to objective information and, if required, counselling and decision-making support about their pregnancy options.

Evidence supporting recommendations 4.11–4.14 state:

> All women attending an abortion service will require a discussion to determine the degree of certainty of their decision and their understanding of its implications as part of the process of gaining consent. Careful and sensitive enquiry as to the reasons for requesting an abortion should be made, with the opportunity for further discussion, especially where women express any doubts or suggestion of pressure or coercion. All information provided at the initial consultation must be backed up by good-quality, accurate, impartial written information that is well presented and easy to understand.[15]

The post-abortive mothers all state that they were rushed into the decision with great urgency, receiving no information on the development of their unborn baby, or on the possible risks to their own health and well-being.

It is important to note that an unplanned pregnancy doesn't become a crisis pregnancy until all the back-up support which the mother thought she would have from her partner, parents, doctor, family and friends, is withdrawn or non existent, and then it becomes a crisis. This crisis makes the mother very vulnerable when the crucial support structure that should surround her is absent or withdrawn and she is left alone feeling that the door of the abortion chamber is the only one left open to her.

Once again the great deception of the old equation: 'Crisis Pregnancy + Abortion = Problems Solved' proved to be very far from the truth. What then is the truth contained in the volume of information which is available to all in the public domain? As mentioned earlier, abortion is typically carried out by the dismemberment, or deliberate premature delivery of the unborn baby. It is an invasive procedure for the expectant mother which, even in the best hospital conditions, presents risks to her physical and psychological health. It is clear to see from the list below how deep the physical and emotional hurts which can be experienced by mothers; they are all deeply damaged in varying ways and degrees.

Physical Harm of Abortion Includes:

- Haemorrhage—often leading to the need for a blood transfusion
- Infection
- Infertility
- Increased risk of miscarriage and premature birth in subsequent pregnancies
- Increased risk of ectopic pregnancy
- Breast cancer
- Death

Dr Warren Hern, an American abortionist noted:

> In medical practice, there are few surgical procedures given so little attention and so underrated in its potential hazards as abortion. It is a commonly held view that complications are inevitable.[16]

Psychological and Emotional Harm of Abortion include:

- Depression
- Guilt
- Grief
- Anger

- Drug and Alcohol abuse

- Sleep disturbances

- Suicidal ideation

The majority of calls by far on the ARCH helpline are from mothers struggling with emotional and psychological problems the symptoms of which are collectively known as Post Abortion Trauma (PAT). Post Abortion Trauma has been clearly defined as a category of Post Traumatic Stress Disorder (PTSD).[17]

Many post-abortive mothers tried filling the void left by the loss of their babies with many activities including holidays, changing jobs, regularly moving house, and constantly redecorating the home. Eventually after years or even decades, they may have a death experience, for example a grandparent or even a family pet, which suddenly triggers the beginning of the breaking down of the wall of denial that has served as a coping mechanism and has kept them from moving on. In order for everyone to remain healthy and whole, we need to grieve all our losses. For mothers who have experienced abortion this can be very difficult. This breaking down of the wall of denial often unlocks the unresolved grief which manifests itself in uncontrollable crying bouts which neither they nor the people around them can understand why and where it is all coming from. 'A voice was heard in Ramah, wailing and loud lamentation, Rachel weeping for her children; she refused to be consoled, because they are no more' (Jr 31:15). A good example of this hidden and often forbidden grief of our nation manifested itself in the televised funeral following the death of Diana Princess of Wales in 1997. It was as if the nation was given permission to grieve and many mothers admitted to counsellors at the time that it was not simply the death of Diana for whom they were grieving; they were grieving all their personal losses, particularly the loss of their babies through abortion.

In her book[18] Dr Theresa Burke describes how family, friends and society forbid any expression of grief following abortion. Reflecting on her own silent struggle, one woman, Patty, shared her experience:

> I thought that if I had an abortion everything would be over with and my life would go back to normal. That's what everyone at the clinic promised. But now I know that after an abortion your life is way different. My abortion didn't end my pain; it began it. For the longest time I thought I must be completely nuts. When I tried

to confide in friends about my anguish, they shook their heads with disapproving looks. It made me feel so alone, so weird. Sometimes I felt like I was going crazy.

Patty had believed the myth that abortion is nothing more than the removal of a 'blob of tissue'. Indeed some abortion clinic counsellors tell women that abortion is about equivalent in terms of pain and risks 'to having a tooth pulled'. If this were true Patty concluded that she must be crazy to feel the way she did. Her sense of feeling crazy and weird was intensified by the fact that none of her friends was able to accept her emotions as valid or legitimate. Their disapproving looks convinced her that she had to bury her crazy emotions deeper and deeper. Sadly, burying negative emotions to please others simply prolonged her suffering. Patty's experience is typical of millions. Most women seeking abortions do not anticipate or understand the potential severity of the psychological problems they may later face. The false expectation that abortion can simply turn back the clock leaves women totally unprepared for what may follow. The tragedy of this false expectation was well described by one woman's letter to the editor in which she wrote:

> I am angry. I am angry at Gloria Steinem and every woman who ever had an abortion and didn't tell me about this kind of pain. There is a conspiracy among the sisterhood not to tell each other about the guilt and self-hatred and terror. Having an abortion is not like having a wart removed or your nails done or your hair cut, and anyone who tells you [otherwise] is a liar or worse.[19]

and Dr Burke comments:

> As a society, we don't understand abortion. We debate it. We pass laws about it. We argue about it as a moral and political issue. But we don't understand it as a life-changing experience. In the latter regard, grief after an abortion is neither expected nor permitted in our society.[20]

In another publication, Melinda Tankard Reist writes:

> Two hundred and fifty women responded to small advertisements in women's magazines and letters to the editor in newspapers. In the end I could only use eighteen stories in the body of the book. A number of women commented on how the small heading on the advertisement 'Abortion Grief', in itself had given them permission to open up their grief. They had been stunned by the

profundity and complexity of their feelings, thinking they were alone in their grief, that something must be wrong with them for feeling so anguished.[21]

The natural response to this apparently inexplicable behaviour is for the mother to see her doctor. In the majority of cases the GP prescribed a course of antidepressants, meaning that she was treated for the anxiety and depression, without it being linked to the root cause. In addition, some were offered grief and bereavement counselling through the NHS which undoubtedly helped; however it proved inadequate and showed that there was a need for alternative, or better still a complimentary approach.

A psychiatrist, Professor Philip Ney, writes:

> Harming and killing children causes deep, almost irreparable harm in families. The harm is always reciprocal. Damage done to children always affects those who harm them, for we are all bound together in the bundle of life. One cannot hurt without being hurt. One cannot kill another without killing something inside oneself. Because the family unit is the basic component of society, when the family is hurt, society is damaged and civilisation begins to crumble. When the smallest and most innocent humans are mistreated there is no basis for a civilised society.[22]

When considering abortion, there is always a conflict between the head and the heart which means abortion will never be in the same league as having a tooth or an appendix removed as is claimed by promoters of abortion. Explaining this dichotomy can help a mother to understand the source of her pain for the first time, preparing the way for post-abortion recovery. The wound inflicted by abortion on a mother's soul is so deep that only Jesus Christ can heal it—this is the foundation on which the whole healing process stands.

The Journey to Healing and Wholeness—Only One Healer—Jesus Christ

Pope Francis gave an interview in September 2013 and was asked 'What does the Church need most at this historic moment? Do we need reforms? What are your wishes for the Church in the coming years? What kind of Church do you dream of?' The Pope replied:

> I see clearly that the thing the Church needs most today is the ability to heal wounds and to warm the hearts of the faithful; it needs nearness, proximity. I see the Church as a field hospital after battle. It is useless to ask a seriously injured person if he has high cholesterol and about the level of his blood sugars. You have to heal his wounds. Then we can begin to talk about everything else. Heal the wounds, heal the wounds… and you have to start from the ground up.[23]

In 1995 Pope John Paul II wrote:

> I would now like to say a special word to mothers who have had an abortion. The Church is aware of the many factors which may have influenced your decision, and she does not doubt that in many cases it was a painful and even shattering decision. The wound in your heart may not have yet healed. Certainly, what happened was and remains terribly wrong. But do not give in to discouragement and do not lose hope. Try rather, to understand what happened and face it honestly. If you have not already done so, give yourselves over with humility and trust to repentance. The Father of mercies is ready to give you His forgiveness and peace in the Sacrament of Reconciliation. Moreover, you are able to entrust, with hope, your infant to the same Father and His mercy. With the friendly and expert help and advice of other people, and as a result of your own painful experience, you can be among the most eloquent defenders of everyone's right to life. Through your commitment to life, whether by accepting the birth of other children or by welcoming and caring for those most in need of someone to be close to them, you will become promoters of a new way of looking at human life.[24]

So how can the church provide 'the friendly and expert help and advice from other people' that Pope John Paul II is referring to, and who will administer it? As a post abortion counsellor, I would highly recommend *The Journey, A Road to Post-Abortion Recovery* which is an excellent post-abortion counselling programme produced by Care Confidential.

The journey to wholeness begins with the first contact by the mother seeking help. It is important to recognise that she is someone who has most likely spent a significant period of time unable to grieve openly for the loss of her baby. She will have had to employ a host of defence mechanisms to deal with her unresolved feelings of sadness and loss whilst trying to reconcile the guilt and regret she feels for making the decision which lead to the death of her baby. This is important. Her baby did not simply die in the passive sense, for example through illness or accident;

her baby was killed and it is this terrible reality which she needs to embrace in order to be reconciled and healed. In her very delicate, damaged and vulnerable state she needs to be given hope and reassurance of total confidentiality and a safe place to express her feelings without any judgement or criticism. Mothers are then gently led through the ten-step journey to meet the real and only healer Jesus Christ who will help them to realise who they have lost.

THE JOURNEY

a road to post - abortion recovery

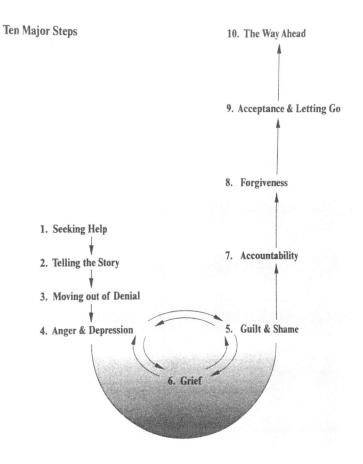

Ten Major Steps

10. The Way Ahead

9. Acceptance & Letting Go

8. Forgiveness

1. Seeking Help

2. Telling the Story

7. Accountability

3. Moving out of Denial

4. Anger & Depression   5. Guilt & Shame

6. Grief

Healing comes from God through the suffering of Christ on the Cross 'through His wounds we are healed' (Is 53:5). This has been developed in relation to inner healing in chapters 6 and 7 of a recent book.[25] Many of the members of the various health care professions are unaware of the part played by God as they use knowledge, skills and experience (Si 38:1-14). Others outside these professions can only say that God may choose to involve them occasionally, or in some cases in a more regular way, in the healing ministry through the gifts and power of the Holy Spirit. There is only one healer–Jesus Christ.

In another book we read:

> God has built into everyone a natural recovery process. If it were not so, humanity would have died from disease or despair long ago. The counsellor's job is to create those conditions where that natural healing process is most likely to occur. The surgeon, by careful suturing, brings together the edges of the wound, but he doesn't make the skin grow. Healing is always a mystery. We acknowledge that, at best, we are partners in what God is doing. Therefore He should get all the credit.[26]

In addition to the natural healing and growing process evident in all life God, upon request, can and will intervene in the way He knows to be best in the lives of individuals. Those who are seeking God's guidance and help and those who are supported in prayer, heal more quickly and more completely. An example of how Christ can bring wonderful healing is given in Chapter 13 in the long testimony written by a lady who had had three abortions by the age of nineteen.

Forgiveness of Self and Others

At some point in the journey to wholeness, usually around step seven, 'Accountability' many post-abortive mothers typically claim: 'I feel as if I am being punished' and when the counsellor uses this to ask 'by whom?,' they almost always reply 'by God!' A Scripture reading that has proved helpful to change her perception of seeing God as a stern and punishing judge, to a loving and forgiving Father, is that of the parable of the Prodigal Son. This as an opportunity of grace and prepares her for the next step of 'Forgiveness'. Forgiveness of self and of others is the gateway to freedom from the pain of abortion.

Larry Crabb, a Christian psychologist wrote:

> Meaningful forgiveness requires full awareness of the extent of the offence... therefore we have to face the pain of relational failure if we are to forgive. It is giving up the desire to get even.[27]

Letter writing can be a helpful way of expressing forgiveness. Many mothers choose to write to God asking forgiveness as well as asking for forgiveness from their aborted babies (See appendices 1 & 2). Once written, and read aloud, some find it helpful to light a candle, burn the letters and place them in a plant pot or garden area beneath a white rose bush or other plant in order to say a 'good' goodbye to their babies and also to serve as a living memory of their lost baby.

The Response of a Surviving Twin

LiveActionNews reporter Nancy Flanders wrote:[28]

> Everyday thousands of unborn humans are killed through abortion. They will never meet their mother. And they will never get the chance to tell the abortionist who killed them that he is forgiven. It isn't every day that a person survives an attempt on her life, but surviving an abortion isn't as uncommon or impossible as people think. People who survive abortion are often full of questions and pain. Knowing that their own mother tried to have them killed is a heavy weight to carry throughout their lives. And knowing that the person who tried to kill them is probably out there killing other children on a daily basis just adds to that pain. That's why one abortion survivor took matters into her own hands, tracking down the abortionist who tried to kill her, and telling him exactly how she feels. The abortionist had succeeded in killing Claire's twin brother but he had missed her. Claire was born just a couple of weeks later, premature and frail. She was placed for adoption, fought for her life, and endured physical therapy to adjust her hips, legs and feet.

Claire wrote:

> In 1988, my birth mother placed herself in your care to perform her abortion... her 20-week abortion. She was assured that the abortion would fix her problem and that her life would return to normal, but it didn't. When she returned to see you, she was informed that the abortion had been successful, in part, but she was still pregnant as she had actually been pregnant with twins but had been misinformed. Due to the botched abortion, I was born two and a half months premature with many lifelong complications.

> I spent 21 years of my life wondering if I had a sibling that was missing. I felt it in my heart. My birth mother confirmed my questions when she told me about her abortion when I met her. Realizing that you have lived your entire life without your twin is a harsh reality. However, the hardest part for me is realizing that you took my daddy's only son from him. His life would have been even fuller and more joyful had he had his son who would carry on his family name and do the things he loves with him—hunt and fish. Because of the selfishness that abortion has brought to us today, our family will remain incomplete and I mourn the amazing adventures my daddy is missing with my brother.

She speaks of her daughter, who wouldn't exist if the attempt on her life had been successful. She talks about how abortion isn't just something that affects the woman who is having the abortion, but it alters entire families, generations, and communities. Then she does something that no one, especially Dr Patel, was expecting. She offers him her forgiveness.

> Dr Patel, I write not only to shed light on the reality of the severe aftermath that can happen when abortions are performed, but also to express my forgiveness to you for what happened. I have lived a full life and been well-loved in my 26 years of life despite my circumstances…In the same way I have been forgiven by God for many things, I choose to forgive you. I forgive you for performing the abortion in 1988 and for the enormous impact it has had on my birth mother and me.

Claire finishes her heartfelt letter by telling Dr Patel that she will be praying for him. She prays that he will remember her face when he is going to perform an abortion. And she tells him that should he leave the abortion industry, many people would be there to support him.[29]

Post-Abortion Survivor Syndrome (PASS)

Psychiatrist, Philip Ney writes:

> Clinical observations indicated that those psychiatric patients who survived when a preborn sibling died were adversely affected by being allowed to live. It seemed that being a survivor of a pregnancy loss, particularly abortion, contributed to psychiatric illnesses. The symptom that most closely associated with the 'total number of abortions in my mother's first pregnancy' was 'I feel I don't deserve to be alive.

and he concluded:

there is a reasonably definable syndrome of symptoms in patients associated with the abortion of their sibling, which we have termed, Post Abortion Survivor Syndrome…Observations of psychiatric patients led me to believe that some people were deeply affected by surviving when someone near and dear to them, usually a sibling, died from a pregnancy loss. The symptoms appeared to be most pronounced if the loss was as a result of an abortion.[30]

Professor Ney has given various examples to illustrate this, amongst which was the following case which had occurred thirty years earlier:

An eight year old girl, referred to me for evaluation forced me to consider the impact of being a pregnancy loss survivor. The mother, who brought this, her only child, was worried because she was not sleeping well, was irritable, could not concentrate, frequently burst into tears, and often seemed to be preoccupied. This all began with a recurrent nightmare. The child clearly described her very frightening dream to me. With three siblings, she had gone to play in a bank of sand. They tunnelled into the sand and her three siblings had crawled in. The sand had collapsed and buried them alive. She could tell me very little about these children, except that she was absolutely convinced that they were her brothers and sisters. Later, the mother told me she had three early miscarriages that her daughter could never have known about. It seemed that somehow the little girl knew or suspected the deaths of her siblings and was now worried something might happen to her. When I voiced these thoughts, the child indicated she felt she was being understood. With her mother's reassurance and an unconditional commitment to love and protect her, the child's fears and her symptoms rapidly subsided. Having been alerted to the effects in children surviving a pregnancy loss, I found others who knew or guessed they had lost a sibling by stillbirth, miscarriage, or abortion. When I questioned their parents it appeared that these children had a surprisingly accurate knowledge of their mother's pregnancy outcome.[31]

Because a mother has had an earlier abortion which has not yet been fully grieved, forgiven and healed, she may not be able to bond fully with a baby conceived later, perhaps some years on. Also the mother may experience depression in the later stages of pregnancy as well as after the birth, and may become listless and not eat properly, so that the baby in the womb is not properly nourished. After birth the baby may be affected and even experience eating disorders years later. Abortion results in more post-partum depression and therefore less bonding, less touching and less breast feeding.

There was a particularly moving experience of the beginning of healing in the weakened bonding of one child and his mother who had had an abortion some years earlier. One day the four-year old became desperate in searching for a ball. Seeing how distraught her son was, the mother joined him on the floor searching for it. They both became very anxious and cried and held each other for some hours and then slept. This began a healing of the bonding and relationship through their shared experience of anxiety, longing and searching.

It should be noted that one of the earliest arguments was that aborting unwanted children would diminish the incidents of child abuse. Statistics show precisely the opposite, that is with more frequent abortions all kinds of child abuse have increased.[32]

Because each new generation learns how to be parents largely influenced by their own bonding and relationship with parents up to the age of about seven (see Chapter 2), then patterns of damage can echo down the generations of a family (see Chapter 7), so that there can be unknown and unrecognised effects of abortions occurring many years later.

Impact of Abortion on Others

Arina Grossu, Family Research Council's Director of the Center for Human Dignity, gave the following comments at the Shockwaves of Abortion press conference:

> The wounds inflicted by abortion on so many people are compounded by its wound on our national soul. By helping individuals heal from their abortion wounds, we hope that the nation as a whole can recover from the shockwaves of abortion.[33]

Abortion is generally presented as a woman's issue and the thoughts and feelings of men are frequently ignored or sidelined. However abortion has a profound effect on men as well as on women, and an ever-increasing number of men are seeking help after a child of theirs has been aborted. As well as fathers, other family members may also suffer after an abortion. ARCH website quotes from fathers include.[34]

> I didn't defend the death of my daughter. I let her die and I died the same day. Scott

If only someone had told me the truth about the possible consequences. Chris

Catholic Philly News in Philadelphia reported on a conference for
counsellors to learn how to help women and men heal after abortion.
Abortion often has tremendous physiological and psychological damage
on the fathers, as well as the mothers. Speakers recently discussed the
important but often forgotten need for counselling post-abortive fathers
during a Project Rachel orientation day at the Philadelphia Archdiocesan
Pastoral Centre. The need for communal healing after an abortion was
the message of Victoria Thorn, founder of the National Office for Post
Abortion Reconciliation and Healing and Project Rachel. She explained
how abortion affects many individuals in addition to the mother. Other
family members and even friends experience the impact of a woman's
abortion decision. Research has found that abortion often affects the
aborted babies' siblings, too. She wrote:

> Few people ever address the psychological impact. People are
> hurting from this because they have all kinds of emotions around
> this. Some men are walking around being so angry because a
> woman had an abortion and didn't tell them. If you throw a stone
> into a pond, the waters don't remain still. At the point it breaks
> the surface, the water is disrupted by a small wave that continues
> rising ring after ring, expanding ever outward. While the point of
> impact may seem relatively small, the ensuing waves reach out in
> greater size, disturbing previously peaceful waters. This illustration
> reminds me of abortion's effect. The point of impact may start
> small. We're told it's just a choice between a woman and her
> doctor. Yet, the consequences spread to the baby's father, other
> family members and potentially siblings—both older and younger.[35]

Abortion's Forgotten Victims

LifeNews.com reported that: in a recent Agony Aunt column of 'Dear
Abby,' a mother wrote with concern for her daughter. Out of spite, her
ex-husband told their teenage daughter that her mother had a past abortion.
Now, she worries about how this may be impacting their daughter. Rather
than offer counsel or advice, Abby's response was, 'The fact that you aborted
a child before your daughter's birth has nothing to do with her.' Meanwhile,
this young girl may be left with questions, fears and insecurities, knowing
she was chosen to live, while her sibling was killed, merely for being

inconvenient. What do siblings feel? One of the most prominent researchers in the field of abortion's effect on siblings is Dr Philip Ney. He says that a common post-abortion symptom they experience is existential survivor's guilt. There's a sense that 'I don't deserve to be alive.' An internal struggle takes place with the knowledge that they lived because they were 'wanted,' while their siblings were not. Symptoms can manifest as depression, anxiety, shame, guilt, self-injury, low self-esteem and dissociation. Unfortunately, abortion isn't widely acknowledged as a trauma, which means that diagnosis and healing can be overlooked.[36]

The pain felt by siblings is very real. Recently, a pro-life television program, Facing Life Head-On produced an episode dedicated to sibling survivors. 28 year old Renee was devastated when she learned that her mother had an abortion nearly 20 years ago. She kept the abortion a secret for 11 years before finally confessing it to her children. Renee recalls the shock and grief she felt that night. Her immediate response was to comfort her mother. She felt sorry for the pain she had endured all those years. Her mother revealed that the child was a boy she had named Joey. Somehow that knowledge gave Renee something to cling to. After finding out, she still had a deep sadness as she grieved the loss of her brother. 'Why was I okay to keep, but my brother wasn't?' she asked herself. She struggled with forgiveness and moving on. Part of her healing process has been to reach out to other surviving siblings for connection and support. Part of Renee's healing was found through a retreat for siblings, conducted by an organization called Lumina. Her outreach continues through a Surviving Sibling blog.[37] She said,

> For the first time in my life I was in the presence of other siblings who could totally relate to my pain and issues. It gave me the confidence to keep sharing my story in the hope that others can also receive the healing and connections I was blessed by.

Some post-abortion survivors are resorting to using social media to talk about their own feelings following the loss of an aborted sibling brother or sister; grandson or granddaughter; nephew or niece.

Helping sibling survivors of abortion is a relatively new concept, so it can be difficult to find the help and resources needed to heal. With over 56 million unborn babies lost to abortion in the USA alone since 1973, it means there's an entire generation of missing brothers and sisters. It's a need that's largely unmet and is going to continue to grow. We need to break through the painful silence. With each step, we can shatter the cycle, and instead, create a ripple effect of healing.

The support group and blog on Facebook mentioned above writes 'If anyone wants to share their testimonies on here, we can arrange it. As with the following two it can be anonymous':

> Okay so this is the story of my sister and her abortion. She is my identical twin. We were about 18 when my sister was first pregnant. Unfortunately she had a miscarriage and they were devastated. A few months later I was at work, when I felt my stomach jump into my throat and I had this horrible feeling that something was very wrong. I began calling people I loved, starting with my twin sister and she said she was fine. I continued to call loved ones and all seemed fine. A year later I was visiting my sister and her husband and she started to cry. I asked her why she was crying and she told me she didn't want to tell me because I would hate her. I said I wouldn't hate her no matter what she did because I love her. She then told me 'you remember when you called me and others worried that something was wrong' and I said yes. She then told me 'well I got pregnant again and was scared and had an abortion' then I was crying too. She told me that the first time she went to the abortion clinic she walked out and couldn't do it, but her husband kept bothering her so she eventually went through with it. I was very mad at him and eventually confronted him about it. He also has regretted it. Well that's my sad story of the niece or nephew I never got a chance to know.

> At the age of 12, my vision of my mum shattered. As she was driving me to a Bible club at our church, she brought up in conversation that she'd had an abortion at the age of 18, before she was with my dad. She gave me a brief bit of info on the abortion, including the fact that she had been told it was a boy by the nurse. I sat silent in the car, and had no idea how to respond to her. I spent the rest of my teen years feeling incredibly angry at my mum. I felt like she had betrayed me. My mother is still a loving mum, despite the fact that she aborted my baby brother. My heart hurts to see, however, that a piece of my mum died with my brother. She's broken and she will never get the piece back that left her on that fateful day. I hope my mum's story can prevent others from enduring that heartache. Her story can echo through the ages as a reminder that abortion is a terribly tragic act, and something that can never be undone. And there are whole families

like mine, quietly protecting these wounded women, while we grieve the loss of a family member as well. My prayer is that one day I will be able to speak openly about my family's abortion journey. Until then, I will speak anonymously with this important story. When we speak up, there is power there![38]

Georgette Forney is the co- founder of Silent No More Awareness and President of Anglicans for Life in the USA and has personal experience of abortion. In an interview in London she had this to say:

We know that abortion is bad for women; we know that emotionally, physically, and spiritually abortion doesn't solve our problems it just creates different ones. The problems can vary, everything from eating disorders to depression to drug and alcohol abuse, relationship problems, all of those issues are common to women throughout the world because you see when we have abortions we in essence go against our very nature.

When an abortion takes place many people are impacted. Nobody is wounded in isolation and nobody heals in isolation. The effects of abortion on the baby are clear and we are becoming more aware of how the mother is wounded by this loss. However, both the pro-life movement and the wider society would benefit from a deeper awareness of the multifaceted wounds experienced by many groups of people within and beyond the family of the aborted child. It is no exaggeration to say that we are all affected and we all need healing.

… abortion is not experienced as an isolated autonomous decision of female empowerment… In fact a host of people are often intimately involved and quite influential in a woman's decision to abort. Though often disconnected from each other, all those involved in the abortion decision and procedure remain deeply connected, emotionally and spiritually, to the child that dies in the womb.

… For the grandparents, family and friends, health care professionals, counsellors and others closely involved in the child's death, there is the strong need to deny or quickly dismiss the mother's and father's pain after an abortion and have life return to normal.[39]

The Society of Centurions

The ethics of healthcare professionals who take part in abortions are compromised, and society as a whole is harmed by the toleration of violence against the unborn baby. Fr Frank Pavone, National Director, Priests for Life in the USA writes:[40]

> Since 1996, under the leadership of Dr Philip Ney, a practicing child and family psychiatrist, the Society of Centurions has existed to provide a path to healing and a mutually encouraging fellowship of those who have used their professional skills to kill children by abortion, but now have ceased to do so. Like the Centurion who, upon taking part in the death of Jesus, repented and declared, 'Surely, this was an innocent man,' so the Centurions of today, having partaken in the deaths of unborn children, have repented and declared, 'Surely, these were innocent lives.' These individuals have been profoundly wounded, and need deep healing. They need a helping hand to walk the difficult path of re-humanising the children they killed by re-humanising themselves. The Society of Centurions provides this path to healing through a powerful rehabilitation program that gathers and guides such former abortion providers. Priests for Life is playing a key role in announcing and fostering this healing. We invite those who are in the abortion industry to come out. And let's pray for all these men and women, that the peace of Christ may be theirs.

They call themselves the Society of Centurions. They are former providers of abortion who have abandoned that practice and now embrace the sanctity of life. Their number includes physicians, nurses, paramedical personnel, technicians, receptionists, and security personnel. The Centurions form an international society, and a United States branch, the *Society of Centurions of America*, has recently been formed. Some Centurions speak publicly of their journey into the abortion industry, and how by grace they were rescued from it. But that is not the focus of the Society. The focus, rather, is their own personal healing. Periodically, Centurions from around the world come together, and under the expert guidance of Dr Philip Ney, walk the long and painful road toward healing. Dr Ney has written a fascinating book, *The Centurion's Pathway*, describing this road.[41] He explains how the wounds of personal abuse often pave the way for a person to abuse others by practicing abortion. He also describes how former providers need to personalize each of the children they have destroyed. Some, for example, will name and even make illustrations of each of the children they were responsible for aborting. My friend Joan Appleton, who was once the head nurse of an abortion facility in Falls Church, VA and now is on the staff of Pro-life Action Ministries in the Twin Cities, coordinates the Society of Centurions of America. She has recently written an account of her own journey, called *Raising Cecilia*.

The Centurions' brochure puts it beautifully:

> The Centurion who stood at the foot of the cross of Christ suddenly became horrified at the crucifixion he was ordered to carry out. When Christ died, this Centurion dropped his sword and fell to his knees exclaiming, 'Surely, this was an innocent man!' Those of us who have participated in the killing of unborn children are the Centurions of today. We have dropped our swords against the unborn child. Now we must recognize the depth of our guilt and deal with the ramifications…To revitalize our humanity we need to forgive and be forgiven, to reconcile and be healed.

May it be so, Amen!

My Vision

I have a dream! I dream of a large Catholic residential centre in England, set in beautiful grounds and surrounded by the natural wonder of nature. In this place arrives a mother suffering greatly from Post Abortion Trauma (PAT), or a surviving sibling who needs to share their pain and loss, or an abortionist who needs forgiveness and healing. They are all warmly welcomed and invited to begin a hard but totally necessary journey to wholeness, healing and well-being. God speed the realisation of this beautiful dream. I dedicate this chapter to the 'wounded mothers' who have taught me so much during counselling sessions, and to Jesus who has never disappointed me in all my work with them.

Appendix 1 Letter of a Mother to Her Aborted Child

Dear Annie

I don't know how to begin. If you were here, I know that I'd hold you so tight and I wouldn't ever let you go. And I'd cry and you'd cry and we wouldn't need words, would we? But you're not here, and it's my fault. I wish I could go back in time and change things, but I can't, and I can't bring you back.

I was scared, Annie, real scared. You must have sensed it because they say that a baby in the womb does sense its mother's emotions. You were so very young, helpless and tiny. I let you down, and I'm so sorry. I was afraid I wasn't ready for you. I knew your father, but I didn't know you.

I was afraid I'd hurt him and spoil all our chances of a nice, safe, secure life. I was confused and very weak. My heart told me how much I wanted you, and that it would all be OK but I didn't listen to it. I wanted you, Annie. I really wanted you. I want you to believe that. I'm just sorry I didn't follow my heart instead of my head. We can't be together in this life because of what I did, but we will be together one day in a better one. Will you wait for me? Will you forgive me and pray for me?

What I'm going through now, Annie is very painful. But I find some comfort in knowing that you are safe with God. There are very special people there with you—three of your grandparents. Ask them to pray for me, Annie, and for your father, too. Help us to forgive each other and ourselves. Help us to have faith. Forgive me. Forgive my fear and my ignorance. Forgive my lack of faith and trust in God. When I go to visit grandma's grave from now on, I'm going to put flowers there for you, too. I always put lilac for grandma. I have a feeling you would like pink: When you see them, let them remind you of my love, and let our tears mix with the rain to keep them alive year after year, as a symbol of our love.

Goodbye, for now, my daughter.

Until we meet again, Your loving Mum

Appendix 2 Letter of the Same Mother to God

Dear God

I've reached a point in my life now where I need you more than ever before. Because now, Lord, I've lost my little girl; and on top of the terrible grief that under normal circumstances a parent would grieve for a child, I have to live with the truth that it was I who took my child's life. I know you love me because you even loved those who took the life of your own son, Jesus. And I need to believe in your forgiveness and in my child's forgiveness before I can ever come to forgive myself. Help me to feel that forgiveness, Lord, so that I may become a whole person again. I'm ripped apart, hating a part of myself that I can never get rid of. I have to bring that part of me back if I'm ever to feel whole again. Keep us all in your care and help us heal. And, most of all, Lord, take care of our children. We have placed them in your loving arms. Let Mary, the mother of us all, care for them until we are reunited with them. Assure our children of how much we love and miss them.

Thank you.

Cathy

Acknowledgements

I acknowledge with great gratitude the help of my dear friends Maurice Ward and Alan Guile without whom I could not have written this chapter.

Material from: *The Journey 'A Road to Post-Abortion Recovery'* used with the kind permission of CARE Confidential.

Material from: *Hope Alive 'Post-Abortion and Abuse Treatment Training Manual for Therapists' Second Edition 1993* used with the kind permission of Philip G. Ney MD, FRCP(C) RPsych, Marie A. Peters, MD.

Notes

[1]   Department of Health, National Statistics, *Abortion Statistics, England and Wales 2015*, May 2016 https://www.gov.uk.

[2]   G. Sedgh et al, Guttmacher Institute, New York, USA, *Induced Abortion Worldwide, Global Incidence and trends*, Jan 2012. https://www.guttmacher.org.

[3]   P. Saunders, *'Lies, damned lies and statistics' from the Alan Guttmacher Institute*, Dec 2012, http://pjsaunders.blogspot.co.uk.

[4]   K. J. Gray, *Abortion is good for everyone, it's science*, August 2015, http://wonkette.com.

[5]   https://www.gov.uk/government/organisations/department-of-health/series/abortion-statistics

[6]   *Ibid*, (section 1(1) (a)).

[7]   RCOG, *Unplanned Pregnancy* 1972, UK, www.bmj.com/content/bmj/303/ 6803/598.full.pdf.

[8]   Academy of Medical Royal Colleges by the National Collaborating Centre for Mental Health, *Induced abortion and mental health*, 2011.

[9]   *I went to the GP when I was pregnant* www.spuc.org.uk.

[10] https://www.gov.uk/government/organisations/department-of-health/ series/abortion-statistics p. 17

[11] E. Sakiz, Chairman, Roussell-Uclaf, *As Abortifacient procedures go RU486 is not at all easy to use*, Aug 1990 https://www.spuc.org.uk/education/abortion/ru486.

[12] R. Hausknecht, Medical Director, Danco, *'it [RU486] is not safer than a surgical abortion'* https://www.spuc.org.uk/education/abortion/ru486.

[13] *Nicole Appleton, Natalie Appleton, Together* (Michael Joseph, 2002).

[14] Abortion Recovery Care and Helpline, www.archtrust.org.uk.

[15] *RCOG Care of Women Requesting Abortion*, Evidence-based Clinical Guideline Number 7, revised edition, November 2011.

[16] W. Hern, *Abortion Practice* (Boulder, CO: Alpenglo Graphics, (2nd Edition) 1990), p. 101.

[17] www.archtrust.org.uk.

[18] T. Burke, D. C. Reardon, *Forbidden Grief, The Unspoken Pain of Abortion* (Springfield,

IL: Acorn Books, 2007).

19   *Ibid.*

20   *Ibid.*

21   M. T. Reist, *Giving Sorrow Words, Women's stories of grief after abortion*, (Sydney: Duffy & Snellgrove, 2000).

22   P. G. Ney, *Deeply Damaged* (Victoria, Canada: Pioneer Publishing, 1993).

23   Pope Francis, A Big Heart Open To God, interview with Antonio Spadaro, in *America Magazine* (30 September 2013).

24   *Pope John Paul II, Evangelium Vitae*, 99.

25   A. Guile, *Journey into Wholeness,—Prayer for Inner Healing—An Essential Ministry of the Church* (Leominster: Gracewing, 2013).

26   P. G. Ney, M. A. Peters, *Hope Alive, Post-Abortion & Abuse Treatment* (Victoria, Canada: Pioneer Publishing, 1993).

27   L. J. Crabb, *Understanding People* (New York: Harper Collins, 1987).

28   C. Culwell, *Abortion survivor's, heartbreaking letter to the abortionist* (Washington DC, 2014) on http://www.claireculwell.com.

29   *Ibid.*

30   P. G. Ney, C. K. Sheils, M. Gajowy, *Post-Abortion Survivor Syndrome: Signs and Symptoms Revisited*, 2012.

31   *Ibid.*

32   Ney, *Deeply Damaged.*

33   A. O. Grossu, Center for Human Dignity, Family Research Council/shockwaves http://www.frc.org/newsroom/frcjoins-silent-nomoreawarenessshockwaves.

34   Forgotten Fathers, www.archtrust.org.uk.

35   A. Edmonds, *Healing after Abortion Conference* 2016, Archdiocese of Philadelphia, USA on http://catholicphilly.com.

36   B. Mattes, *Abortion's Forgotten Victims*, 2014, on www.lifenews.com.

37   Facing Life Now, season 7, *Sibling Survivors*, on http://www.facinglife.tv/episode/sibling-survivors.

38   *Abortion Hurts Siblings and Others*, https://www.facebook.com/ AbortionHurtsSib-lingsAndOthers.

39   G. Forney, *President of Anglicans for Life and co-founder of Silent No More Awareness*, http://anglicansforlife.org/issues/after-abortion.

40   F. Pavone, Priests for Life, *The Society of Centurions*, on http://www.priestsforlife.org/centurions.

41   P. G. Ney, M. A. Peters, The Centurion's Pathway—a Description of the Difficult Transition for Ex-Abortion Providers or Facilitators, (Victoria, Canada: Pioneer Publishing, Second Edition 1993). See www.societyofcenturionsinternational.com.

9

Healing Children and Teenagers

Alan Guile and Kathleen Green

Pope Francis poses the questions that this chapter addresses when he writes in Amoris Laetitia, *'The questions I would put to parents are these: "Do we seek to understand 'where' our children really are in their journey? Where is their soul, do we really know? And above all, do we want to know"'? This chapter begins with a* cri de coeur: *children need adults who are prepared to give time to listen to them, especially those children who are suffering deep emotional pain. Jesus loves these children and they must be helped to know him. If this can be done whilst they are still children, their subsequent life and choices could be much more positive and happy. This cry was written by a lady whose testimony in chapter 13 tells of sexual abuse by several people and of three abortions before she was twenty. The present chapter looks at some ways in which it has been possible to overcome the difficulties of finding safe and sensitive ways to help children to receive some healing ministry.*

Part 1 (Alan)

Introduction

While considering whether or not to include this paper at all, some old files were being cleared to make way for the material for this work. Out fell a piece of paper from many years ago. It is now reproduced in full with minor spelling and grammatical corrections.

> To whom it might concern
>
> I am writing this in the interest of children because I feel there are children who are crying out, and all they need is someone to take time and stop, look and listen to them. It could mean the world to them, knowing someone is interested enough to stop and take an interest in them and set aside a little time for them and also pray with them. I feel this is important. They need to feel they can turn to someone and to know Jesus through people and to turn to

Jesus through prayer. It is important to learn, while they are young that they are important and worth being heard and helped. It is important while they are young that they know Jesus can help and is always with them, and to learn the importance of prayer. I believe schools can be a great help by noticing if a child isn't their usual self, and try and get to know why by having someone available to be able to spend time with them and to pray with the children also.

This was written by a lady whose testimony is in Chapter 13. She had been sexually abused from the age of seven and a half by people both inside and outside her family circle. Before the age of twenty she had already had three abortions. She came for prayer ministry nearly thirty years ago and gradually received deep healing, and became able to live a happy life with her family.

This *cri de coeur*, expressed so passionately by someone who had endured great suffering over many years, drives and informs what is written here. It should also prompt us to pray for the Lord to guide the Church as He shows us further ways to bring His healing to hurting children, whilst they are still children so that they make better choices later on in their lives.

This plea and the source from which it came suggests that however difficult it may be to find safe and sensitive ways in which to try and help a child who is ready for someone whom they trust to listen and pray, this area is too important to omit from the present consideration of ways in which Christ is trying to teach us how to work with Him for His beloved suffering people.

This brief attempt to review the care that is needed and the limitations of our present awareness of how the Lord wants to bring healing and peace as early as possible into life, may serve to bring some more information to light, and to highlight the need for the Church to examine this area more seriously in the future.

Many people of various backgrounds have revealed acute sadness resulting from painful situations in early childhood. After listening to their expressions of suffering, the next step has been to jointly invite Jesus Christ to comfort and heal their troubled memories. The prayer has extended to asking the Lord to change those memories into ones for which they might be grateful to Him. This has afforded many insights into the brokenness and trauma of these childhood situations. It is sometimes aided by the Holy Spirit's gift of knowledge, before going on to pray for other aspects in which healing is needed.

Some of the Factors Involved in a Person Being Ready for Ministry as a Child.

Ideally one might wish to be able to pray for Jesus to heal the wounds in a very young person arising from the three key areas.

a) damaged patterns in past generations

b) time in the womb and at birth

c) babyhood and childhood up to about seven years of age

This could preferably be done before they reach the age when the early damaged roots will, in some cases, influence them to make relationships which later turn out to be very painful or disastrous. This could help to avoid further damage in any resulting children of their own as well as helping them in all the rest of their life.

There have only been a small number of times that a parent has brought a child to my home for prayer ministry in the last 32 years. It is not made any easier by the parents sometimes playing a very significant role in the need of the child for healing, so that in effect they may seem to be more a part of the problem than of the solution. In practice there are potentially many obstacles and difficulties in early ministry being possible. Some of them are:

- The overriding need to avoid any listening or prayer situation placing the child or young person at the slightest risk of hurt, pressure or abuse.

- The willingness of the young person to take part at all.

- The permission of parents or guardians being given and in most cases actually requesting help for the child.

- The establishment of trust between the young person and the one or two people who are there to listen, affirm and be ready to pray with him or her.

- In many people much of the hurts they experience in childhood remain buried in their unconscious or subconscious mind. This is because of the natural defence mechanisms which can enable them to survive childhood experiences and traumas, and they may not be ready to deal with these until later in adulthood.

- In addition to or as part of the natural defence of pain repression, there can be a denial within the child of how bad things are. For instance, the security of a child is threatened if there is evidence of disharmony, raised voices, anger and even violence between the parents. The child may not want to admit how bad this is even to himself or herself. Children may delude themselves into supposing that their parents are better, more loving and more settled than they really are.

- Children can be confused by feeling guilty if they do face and acknowledge disharmony between parents. Many adults reveal that as a child they had felt that somehow it was their fault that there were rows between their parents. One said: 'If it hadn't been for me things would have or might have been alright.'

- Children are likely to feel it was their fault if someone abuses them in some serious way.

- The lack of a healthy sense of self-esteem and self-worth is reinforced by the above and some only become ready for the Lord to heal the roots of poor self-esteem as adults.

- Fear can play a large part in a child's life. It can arise in different ways.

- Fear planted by an abuser of some reprisal if the child reveals the truth.

- Fear that my family unit will break up if I speak to anyone and that will make me feel guilty and responsible for subsequent suffering of my parents and siblings. Where will we children be sent?

- Fear that no one will believe me if I speak out and then I will be in a worse situation.

- Fear can come from many other childhood experiences.

A middle-aged lady who came to us over thirty years ago from a far-away city was unable to sleep despite the intervention of doctors. It transpired, when we listened and prayed, that during her childhood her father had been out drinking most nights and her ailing mother had retired early leaving the youngster to wait for her father's return. She would be dreading his language and violent temper. If there had been a sympathetic adult to whom the child could have offloaded her anxiety and stress and perhaps prayed with her, her life might have been very different. She was healed of the sleeplessness after prayer.

This was just one example of a child being placed in a situation in which he or she is forced to assume inappropriate responsibilities which properly shared would have been carried by a parent. In many cases the eldest child, often a girl was obliged to take on responsibility for younger siblings because of dysfunctional family relationships and living conditions. This role reversal in childhood can have a profoundly harmful effect upon later adult situations and relationships, which could have been alleviated if the child had been able to speak of the pressures placed upon him or her and had received help and prayer.

Within some families where dysfunction exists, the conflict between two much damaged parents leads to neither of them being able to fulfil their maternal or paternal role. The pattern emerges where one child , perhaps the one who has been forced to try to hold things together as far as they are able, becomes treated by the rest of the family as a scapegoat. They are unable to deal with their own emotional traumas or work through and acknowledge the pain nor grow to any real maturity. The other family members blame everything on this child. This behaviour within a family can persist unchecked for decades (see Appendix 1).

The victim may be the only one in the family who ends up with any real faith in Christ and perhaps becomes united with Him through suffering. This may well provide God with the way into bringing grace to others in the family and outside it many years later. If the child was ready to speak about the pain then how sad if there was no one available to listen compassionately.

At the heart of much suffering in adult life is the early damage to self-esteem. It is vital to provide someone trustworthy who is ready to listen non-judgementally and sensitively if the child is able and ready to begin to share their pain. The child would then have someone who would prayerfully help build up their sense of self-esteem. So much later damage to them, to marriage partners, to children and later generations might be lessened or even avoided.

Damage to a Child's Self-Esteem

In the very early years of life, a child comes gradually to realise that he/she is separate from his/her mother and indeed the rest of the world. It is then that the journey of personal discovery begins. Other peoples' attitudes and judgements towards the child become important; in fact how any of us are treated by others plays a large part in how we form the notion of who we are, our identity, and how we evaluate our performance within that identity which forms our self-esteem. Ideally we would receive only positive and nurturing signals and treatment from the main influences of our parents, particularly in our early life, as well as from siblings and other family members. Hopefully this would continue in later years from teachers and other children but sometimes these people do further damage. We would thrive in our self-esteem if we were constantly being told 'I love you unconditionally' and received treatment wholly in accord with that, coupled with separate encouraging comments of 'Well done'. The restoration of a person's healthy self-esteem has already been extensively discussed.[1]

Sometimes the two statements appear to the child to be coupled together:

'I love you when you have performed some task well', or

'I love you when you behave yourself and don't let me down in front of others.'

This can lead to an adult who is unconsciously and constantly seeking restlessly to earn the approval of others. This can continue until the Lord intervenes. Until that time the lie is built that

'I shall only be loved and fully wanted when I perform to the satisfaction of others.'

Self-worth thus then depends on satisfying the expectations and needs of others, not in the fact that I am a beloved child of God.

'Performance orientation', as this adult condition is sometimes called when particularly acute, can be highly damaging and can lead to anger, frustration and other pain.[2] It can be healed in adulthood, but how much better if it could be healed in childhood. Children often learn, even from well-meaning parents to become people who are at the mercy of internal drives and compulsions. These take the form of doing 'good' things because 'I ought' or 'I should' or 'I must'. This is not the freedom of God who never puts on pressure but gently invites us to ask for the power of His Spirit to continue Christ's mission of love. Sadly, many children have very painful experiences of life and can become adults with little or no healthy self-esteem. Anything which can be done to build up a child's self-esteem can play a part in that child growing up into a more fulfilling and happier adult life.

Prayer for Inner Healing

Prayer for inner healing begins before conception (Jr 1:5, Ep 1:4) when each one of us were in 'God's mind', our true self, completely whole, just as we will eventually be, when by God's grace we are ready to be welcomed into Heaven. We can pray for Jesus to heal every kind of damage, whether from genetic influences or damaged patterns of behaviour in earlier generations or evil influences or from disturbing experiences triggering flaws in our own or our parents' reactions. This applies to all our lives but most especially to time in the womb and the first seven years of life where the key roots of damage lie. Through His wounds, Jesus can be invited to draw out any pain in our own wounds into His suffering on the Cross. He can then be asked to give us the grace with which to forgive-when we are ready for this. Thus He is gradually restoring us to our real, true selves, in a journey through life and purgatory towards our destination of the presence of our Heavenly Father. Some of this can be prayed privately if it is judged to be in the best interests of a particular child. I frequently suggest such prayers for children and grandchildren might take place whilst they are asleep, perhaps taking time on different days to pray through each year of their life.

It is important for children to learn as early as possible that each has 'always' been known to God and is totally, unconditionally loved by Him. They also need to understand that each person is unique, with gifts that no one else has and which God needs to use to help others. Children can learn Scriptures which speak of this love of God for each one and His solemn promise that He could never abandon one of His children.

If the opportunity does present itself where prayer for inner healing may be possible with a child, then the child may be prayed with silently for some aspects, if it is discerned that this will be in the interests of the child.

At the present time information is only to hand on three ways of helping children and young people in a safe environment, though there may well be many others. The first two examples which are reviewed briefly have enabled some young people to be helped towards healing. Then in part 2, a first-hand account is given of working with children within school premises.

The Maltfriscans

In the late 1970s, Fr Leonard May, parish priest of Maltby, who was attending meetings in our home, told us how he had a few days earlier walked into a home where a row between a teenager and his mother was in progress. He was inspired by the Holy Spirit to invite the youngster and his friends, a punk rock group, to provide music for a Mass at the parish prayer group. His obedience to that inspiration led over the years to the formation of the Maltfriscans, a community who live by the Maltfriscan rule and has given rise to a number of vocations to the priesthood. Among their activities are national youth events for age 15 and upwards and other events for Young Maltfriscans aged 11 to 16 years.

Young People Beginning Experience (YPBE)

The following account was provided by a lady who for years played a leading part in this ministry in her diocese.

YPBE is a peer-support ministry for young people aged about 11–20 who have an absent parent due to death, separation or divorce. The young people are taken on a residential weekend where in a safe place they are enabled to get in touch with the feelings they are experiencing as a result of their loss. They are taken through a specific programme based on the five stages of grief. The programme is led by young people who have suffered a similar loss. The adults are there in a supporting role. There is a follow-on programme and after this participants are invited to train as team members and they then go on to help new participants. The following statements are written by young team members saying in their own words how YPBE helped them:

Girl 15 years old:

> YPBE helped me a lot, they allowed me to cry, they gave me understanding. They didn't tell me how I should be feeling, they listened to me.

Girl 18 years old:

> Without YPBE I would have been unable to deal with my deepest thoughts and feelings, being able to share these with peers who were in a similar position helped the most.

Boy 15 years old:

> YPBE has been a great help to me as I hadn't mourned for my dad properly. The process helped me to open up not only to myself but to others as well. I was able to express my feelings and found I wasn't on my own and that I wouldn't be judged by what I said. The sacrament of Reconciliation helped me the most as I was able to try and let go.

Boy 18 years old:

> When I started going to YPBE my self-esteem was extremely low but after listening to the team talks and hearing that I had lots of similar feelings and experiences, I opened up and started to share how I felt. I learned that I am lovable and capable. I was made to feel so loved and valued by everyone there. In short YPBE changed my life.

Girl 17 years old:

> YPBE has done a lot for me over the six years I attended from the age of eleven after my dad died when I was nine; the main factor being building my confidence, of talking about my loss with others as long as I trusted them. Teaching me there are no right or wrong feelings when suffering a loss and that I wasn't alone, meeting lots of new friends for life along the way.

Girl 19 years old:

> YPBE helped me come to terms with the loss of a loved one and through this I was able to gain confidence in myself and help other young people. YPBE was a unique experience that will never be forgotten and the coping methods I learned will no doubt continue to help me many years into the future.

From these statements from young people it will be clear that when they came to YPBE their self-esteem and confidence were very low and they felt very alone in their situation. The programme and follow-on work helped them all to move forward with better self-esteem and more confidence able to face their future lives and relationships.

Part 2 (Kathleen)

Areas of Loss in Children

The lady quoted at the beginning of this chapter wrote:

> I feel that there are children who are crying out, and all they need
> is someone to take time to stop, look and listen to them.

Some schools and hospices do endeavour to provide help for children who need spiritual and emotional intervention particularly in the area of loss as mentioned in Chapter 12. The loss of a close relative such as a mother, father, sibling, grandparent, particularly if there is little said about the dying process and the death and when the child is not allowed to go to the funeral, and the grieving process is impeded, can be a major and potentially catastrophic event in a child's life. The child needs sympathetic intervention to deal with highly confusing circumstances. This is because by the very nature of his/her youthfulness, coping mechanisms will rarely be in place. One needs only to think about being bereaved as an adult to realise how much more frightening it must be for a child. The loss does not need to include an actual physical death. There are the losses suffered as the result of divorce or separation. These can include:

- Loss of the original family nucleus.

- Deprivation of presence of one of the parents.

- Loss of siblings when they chose which parent to live with or the family is broken up or put into care.

- Loss of financial stability when one household necessarily becomes two.

- Loss of family role, for example when parents re-marry and households mix, children must somehow come to terms with and even to hold their own with step siblings with all the resulting tensions.

- Loss of attention previously given by parents(s) to the child. The partner who is left by the spouse may be too distressed initially because of their own grief, to give full attention to the grief of the child. If one parent has as new partner then their time with the child of the original marriage will necessarily be curtailed to some degree.

- Loss of stability. Whatever the initial cause of the break-up, things may go on changing. The partner remaining with the child may also form a new relationship so more changes will ensue. New home, new babies may follow. Conflict can occur within stepfamilies. Plain sailing is not guaranteed in first families so is often even less evident in second or even third couplings.

When the child is in the middle of this ever-changing scenario, where does he/she go for help? Often they feel unable to share their troubles with their parents because of a sense of loyalty to both. They don't want to upset mum or dad and they feel constricted by all the new personalities in their lives so who can they to? This is where the following kind of ministry to children can play a very important role.

Programmes Based Within a School Environment

Programmes for children in such situations have been and are undertaken in some schools to offer a listening ear and to provide a Christ-centred faith backdrop where children can explore their feelings.

One such programme which has been running nationally in a number of dioceses, continued for around ten years in the Hexham & Newcastle Diocese with strong support from the bishop at that time and only stopped for lack of committed facilitators. It was based mainly in primary schools with at least one teacher involved, who was assisted by other selected and trained people. A letter went out to all parents outlining a new way of helping their children and inviting them to a meeting. The teacher who was involved also held a whole-school assembly where the children learnt about it.

Those children who chose to come to the programme came because he or she spoke to their parents and asked to go, or because a parent who had come to the meeting felt that a child would benefit. Since the teacher was known and trusted by the parents, a good relationship existed. The teacher even visited homes to explain and answer questions. This not only helped parents to choose to send their child, but often a parent would open up about their own pain. The parents were encouraged to avoid questioning the child about any details of the course, whilst still finding out if the child was happy with it. The parents respected this.

Adults involved in such a course need to be empathetic to the children and might themselves have come from a place of childhood pain after the loss of a close family member through death or divorce. In some programmes all the adults themselves had experience of loss. The idea of the wounded healer springs to mind in this instance. The listening can be done within the school with small groups of children as one-to-one connection can be a little too intense particularly for the very young. The children can be helped to explore their feelings and to realise, that whatever has happened, it was <u>not</u> their fault. Prayers can be said during the meetings. However, the focus is best placed on the children working things out verbally for themselves.

In the case of the experience in one Hexham & Newcastle school, as the children heard first one and then another child begin to talk about their feelings, even the ones who had found it very difficult at first to speak, gained confidence and trust so that they could begin to express their own pain. The growing friendship and trust among the children even led some to seek out others or the teacher involved in places like the playground. Because they were aware that the other person understood, they wanted to spend time in their company. A recent quote from an adult who attended such a programme years ago was 'I realised that there were other kids like me, whereas before I had felt alone and quite isolated.' (Dr S. aged 32)

Alongside this the adult listens, encourages and tries to show each child unconditional warmth and acceptance. There was real dedication of the adults who themselves prayed regularly for the children under their care, both when they met for planning and discussion and in their own personal prayer. In some instances simple prayer services were held which also involved parents and at times the parish priest.

One of the adults in such a healing group commented: 'Our love was God-inspired—we were acting as the hands and heart of God.'

The last words must surely belong to children who attended one of these groups so what follows is what was written at the time in their own words and in some cases their own unique spelling:

> Thank you for organising (the group). It has cheered me up a lot and I am not so bad tempered. I am glad (the group) is here and I have someone to talk to. I am also glad that I will be able to come for another term. (A, aged 11)

> Thank you for helping get through all my worries. (D, aged 7)

> (The Group) is now a special part of my life and I would love to help other children get over their problems. I know this sounds

corny but I think you are the best in the school and you will probably get a lot of satisfaction. I look forward to coming again. (Yours sincerely, a Ryan Giggs Fan.)

I really appreciate it for if it hadn't been for you I wouldn't be feeling happier. (L, aged 10)

Later comments included:

It gave me a lot of understanding about how things could be alright after a divorce. It helped me to come to terms with it … it seemed grown up that I could be taken seriously and was allowed to open up. Overall it was a pleasant experience that helped me grow as a person. (P, now aged 22)

It was massively helpful and it helped me to realise that I had a lot to be thankful for. (Dr S, now aged 32)

Notes

[1]   J. McManus, *The Inside Job—A Spirituality of True Self Esteem* (Chawton: Redemptorist Press, 2004).

[2]   A. Guile, *Journey into Wholeness: Prayer for Inner Healing—An Essential Ministry of the Church* (Leominster: Gracewing 2013), pp. 116–7.

10

Healing In and Through Marriage

Brian and Maureen Devine

Pope Francis has put the health of the Christian family at the very centre of the Church's pastoral care. He conducted a worldwide consultation on the family, held two Synods of Bishops to discuss the challenges facing families today, and published his much acclaimed Apostolic Exhortation, The Joy of Love. *In this chapter a couple with 40 years' experience of married life keep our focus on healing within the family as they share their experience of ministering to married couples especially in the Marriage Encounter Movement.*

Pope Francis, in an interview with Fr Spadaro in 2013, said 'I see clearly that the thing the Church needs most today is the ability to heal wounds and warm the hearts of the faithful... I see the Church as a field hospital after battle... Heal the wounds, heal the wounds and you have to begin from the ground up'.

Our Own Journey of Healing

Our journey of being healed and of becoming wounded healers began on a Marriage Encounter weekend back in 1977. Our eyes were opened on that weekend to the notion of a living, loving God, not the one that we had grown up with in the Catholic Church, the one who was always out to see what wrong we would do next. It was a Catholic Marriage Encounter weekend, so it was an interesting juxtaposition of the fear that we knew, and had been raised on, and the love that we heard expressed so simply and so beautifully in the lived experiences of the three couples and the priest presenting the weekend. Although we were not aware of it until much of the weekend was over, very many people had prayed for us throughout that weekend. These were people whom we had never met and for the most part never will, but married couples who were prepared to give of themselves in prayer so that we might experience the love and blessing of God and His Church on and in our marriage. We did. It had a profound effect on us. We had been married for ten years, had five young children, a business to run, and a variety of meetings to attend. It stopped us in our tracks. It caused us to re-evaluate our lives and it gave us back to each other. We went on to that weekend believing that we were a happily married couple, just going away for some 'us' time, and we left it knowing that our love mattered. It mattered to ourselves. It was something that we needed to work at, to nurture and to cherish, to not take for granted. It mattered also to our children; how we loved one another would have the greatest bearing on who they were and how they would grow up.

Learning to Open up God and to Others

In time, we learned that our love mattered to our Church, to its mission of seeking out the lost souls. We believed it would also matter to the world in which we lived. We were asked if we would take the next step to get involved in being a part of presenting the weekends in the future, obviously the presenting team could see the life and the light that was coming from us. We said 'yes' to the next step simply because we knew that we had been shown a new way to live our lives and we wanted to give something back. Little did we know what that initial 'yes' would mean, where this journey would take us, but we went one step at a time. We did our 'training' and we became one of the presenting teams of the weekend and our eyes were opened. We had both been brought up in loving, Catholic family homes but they had not prepared us for the open expressions of love and the vulnerability which some couples and priests were prepared to give and to live in the name of Jesus. We knew God the Father, watching over us, kindly but rigorous in asserting 'thou shalt not'. We soon met with Jesus, His Son who, through their Spirit, sought to teach us how to 'love one another as He had loved us'. Those early days were full of encounters that had the power to surprise and to shock us. We are an attraction of opposites, one of us was very shy and the other quite outspoken, but we were both called to something more, to shed the shyness and the gabble, bit by bit, and to open ourselves to something new, to whatever God might be asking of us. One day when we were a part of the presenting team on a weekend, a lady asked if she could have a quiet word with Maureen, shy Maureen found this quite a challenge but I went to her room, and she told me a little about herself. She was a mother of six grown up children, and she wept bitterly as she said how she had always been given to understand that she was not meant to enjoy the sexual relationship with her husband but to endure it for his sake. She was the first of many we heard of from that now bygone age where Catholic women 'endured' what was the God-given joy of married love, where 'doing their duty' was the amount of education they had been given and the wonder, beauty, joy and sacredness of married love had never been taught to them. How far that all was from what Scripture and the Catechism have to say about married love: 'Each of the two sexes is an image of the power and tenderness of God, with equal dignity though in a different way. The union of man and woman in marriage is a way of imitating in the flesh the Creator's generosity and fecundity' (2335). Who was teaching such a message and to whom?

In our time working with the dedicated couples and priests of the Marriage Encounter movement, we came across many other heart-breaking stories, powerful stories of how true love overcame the shame and pain that had been handed down to people; it was to prepare us well for a later stage of our lives. We also came across some heroic couples, ones who were giving their lives going out to bring to others the good news of marriage. They were spending their own money, often travelling through the night, to reach out to couples in far-flung places, giving of themselves unconditionally, agapeic love. Through all of these situations, our Lord was planting in us the seeds of compassion and knowledge of His healing power and love. We poured our all into this movement for five years, including becoming its national leadership, and then moved on as we experienced the Spirit calling and guiding us elsewhere.

We sought to put into practice all that we had learned and grown in for ourselves during that five year period. First we turned a part of our offices, then later our home, into a Christian Centre. We cooked and cleaned and welcomed groups of couples to stay over at the weekends so that they would have a place to come to review and refresh their own marriages. We sought to pass on to them what we had received (cf 1 Co 11:23). We were blessed with two more children and although life obviously had its challenges, we sought to stay faithful to all that had been given to us.

Spiritual Direction

In our late forties we decided that with all these people that God was sending to our home, it would be a good idea if we actually took some 'proper' training and so we went on an eighteen-month course for spiritual directors. It was an ecumenical course advertised in our diocesan news-paper. From both the standpoint of our own faith journey and our relationships with other Christians, it was another turning point for us. We enjoyed the course very much and Brian stayed on to become a part of the leadership of the next one, and subsequent ones. A new ministry had begun for us. As spiritual directors we have met with people from a variety of backgrounds and levels of education, including those who have never finished their schooling, to the other end of the spectrum, those with a variety of letters after their names. It was a part of a steep learning curve for us. Now, with over fifteen years in this ministry, we have come to realise that the impact of their very early years on those we see is significant (see appendix). The Jesuits used to say 'give me the boy up to the age of seven and I'll show you the man.' For them it was all to do with the 'conditioning' experienced in the early years. From the time we were given our diplomas as spiritual directors, people started to come our way. The shyness for Maureen was now receding into the background as confidence in what our Lord could and would do was growing. For Brian, the same confidence was growing as he learned to let go of being the man that could always come up with an answer. Most of the people that came to see us were one-to-one situations, occasionally we would offer to see a couple together. Sometimes people came because they were attending a Christian studies course and it was recommended to them to do so. Other times, someone came because word of mouth had suggested that to come to our home they would find a listening ear and a temporary place of shelter. We thought of it as a sacred space for such people and all the time we knew that to keep our hearts and minds open to what our Lord was asking of us, we needed to be making sure that we had times put aside to listen to Him and to speak with Him. The busier we got, the more time we needed for prayer. Some very interesting and challenging people came our way, but always the Lord went ahead and helped us to learn how to listen, what questions to ask, when to just be still.

Learning All the Time

She came first to one of us, then to the other, Deborah, 'the girl behind the curtain'. We gave her that name, not to her face of course, but to help each other understand the realities of what we were listening to in her life. It was where so much of her childhood was spent; her alcoholic parents hid her there in the pub each night. An alcoholic herself, she was in and out of various relationships and had a teenage daughter with whom she was now experiencing difficulties. She truly could not understand her own contribution to the girl's problems; after all she only ever wanted her to be happy. She has been dry for seven years now, which she always attributes to us, and which we always attribute to God and her own choices. It was soon abundantly clear to us that she could not live by the same standards or set of ideals as a nun we had met who we so admired for all her marvellous works. Our awareness that we are all a product of our early years 'training', or lack of it, and of our DNA, was increasing all the time. We learned, through the blessing of being visited by such people, not to judge but to stop and to pray and to ask and to listen to what our Lord might be saying to us at such times. It is through getting to know other people's life experiences that God has been able to break through our prejudices, self-righteousness and ignorance, to teach us how He wants us to welcome them into our home in His name, to enable His healing touch to bring new life and hope.

Complexities of Widely Varying Experiences

Susan and Jack came to see us. They were a good couple, each seeking to do what the Lord was asking of them, but how was it that the Lord was giving them such different messages? Here were two Christians, both church-attending, taking their children with them, but the home, instead of being a safe haven, a sanctuary, was a place where there was constant conflict, sometimes with violence, regularly with harsh words. 'Come, let's talk this over', we would say. Week in, week out, they came along pouring out their own inadequacies, defensiveness and frailty, and it became abundantly clear that what had happened in Susan's childhood held the key to their relationship difficulties now. It was a situation of childhood sexual abuse. This is not to say that Jack is a saint but, although aware of her history, he had not been able to tune into who Susan really was as a person as he himself was not 'programmed' to understand or empathise. Susan had already had many hours of counselling and the neighbour who had abused her had been taken to court and convicted, but where did it leave the two of them? Week after week they came, and our sessions were topped and tailed by prayer together, within which we explored the reality of the previous week in their lives.

Healing Through Couples Listening to One Another

Time went by and gradually, through the sharing and listening, we learned to detect simple patterns and possible 'action plans' for them, where each would benefit from something the other would carry out. We asked them to formulate the thought we had into a question which they might ask each other every day throughout the next week. These ideas are so simple, but so often what Jesus asked someone to do was also so simple. One example we came up with, was related to when Susan thought Jack got too easily impatient and angry with her when things were not working out the way he wanted or expected. One week his question to her was to ask at the end of each day, 'Where do you think I could have been more patient with you today?' He made the commitment to listen to her answer each day without interruption, not to disagree or defend but to try and to see how it was for her, to step into her shoes. Her question to him was to say, 'When do you think I could have been more supportive of you today?' He often felt like he was on his own, running the business, trying to get the children to school, and many other tasks, which simply were not part of Susan's mind set, as it did not happen in her own childhood. These are just simple examples of a short part of the journey with one couple. She eventually ended up training to be a midwife, and his business started to flourish. We do not keep contact with them, so our prayer is that they are still flourishing. We met them out and about a few years later, which is when we discovered those last two aspects, and life had a new meaning for them and their family. They were one of the first couples that we started this kind of approach with. They were held in our prayer on a daily basis, our times with them began and finished with simple prayer which always recognised Jesus as the healer with and amongst us, He who could do all things if we would only seek to listen to Him and follow His invitation. In such a safe zone, this couple were able to start to listen to each other. Eventually they started to pray together and gradually to allow God to lead, guide, and help them to make the necessary decisions. This mattered particularly regarding their own children who had started absenting themselves from school and generally carrying on the patterns of Susan's own childhood. Their sense of helplessness diminished when they found that they could manage this situation as a couple, side by side, walking together in faith, trusting in Jesus and in His healing love for them. We learned to listen to the voice of God as we listened to them, God speaking through the Scriptures and through His people. The Scriptures have such wonderful things to say about married love but since so many people only hear them when they go to a weekly Mass, unless the priests speak about the wonder, beauty and sacredness of marital love, the only message that really gets heard is the world's one.

God's Word Speaks of Marriage and its Meaning

Scripture shows us that Christian marriage is a blessed and beautiful part of God's creative love (Gn 1:27, 2:24), that God determined humanity's fundamental factor as being an image of Himself: relationship. We learn that human sexuality's characteristic feature is relational: male and female. Jesus illustrated, through his own life, total and unconditional giving. His message proclaimed the meaning and purpose of love as well as the relational character of the Trinity, in speaking of His Father (Mk 14:36) and the sending of the Holy Spirit (Jn 16:13-15). Gospel accounts show Jesus affirming marriage's fundamental role in his Father's plan and its importance to Him. It was at a wedding that Jesus performed His first miracle (Jn 2:1-12). John's Gospel unfolds the mystery of Jesus as the sacrament of encounter with God. He stresses only one commandment: to love one another (Jn 13:34, 15:17). The Love between Father and Son is the essential Spirit of John's Gospel; it is fundamentally relational, Trinitarian, communal and personal. He considers the 'fruitfulness' of all relationship as emanating from the relationship of Jesus with His Father (Jn 15:1-17). Entering into the love of the Trinity is what bears fruit and brings life in all its fullness (Jn 10:10). That the Spirit of the love between Jesus and the Father calls for the be-love-ed to love one another, is just one example of its relevance to marriage. Saint Paul understood all this well. He elevated the significance of marriage, calling it a mystery. In his letter to the Ephesians (5:21-33), he concluded that the Christ-Church relationship is a paradigm of the husband wife relationship, in that the wholeness of the union of the spouses symbolises and reflects the total commitment of Christ to his body, the Church. The parallels are there: a mutual relationship (21), sacrificial (25), a call to purity, holiness and perfection (26-27), that requires ongoing nourishment and a sense of one's own goodness in and as the Body of Christ (28-29). Considering the attitudes and culture of that period, the equality within marital relations in the Churches founded by Paul was extraordinary. His theology on marriage might have been influenced by his relationship with Priscilla and Aquila, who knows? He proclaims the dynamic life-giving and unifying principle and potential of marriage. 'Christian marriage', he said, 'should be lived in the Lord' (1 Co 7:39). The New Testament message manifests how the union of husband and wife is such that behind its human 'face' is a spiritual reality filling it with deep significance, meaning and purpose. Finally, the author of the Apocalypse sees marriage in the stirring symbolism of the marriage of the Lamb and His Bride (Rev 19:7).

Marriage: A Reality Check

It is no wonder then that marriage, properly understood and lived in that awareness, is full of grace. The reality however, is that such an understanding of marriage is not common place and, generally speaking, preparation for marriage does not incorporate such a teaching or vision of its spiritual and temporal power and potential.[1] For the majority of Catholics, reference to the Bible is largely limited to the Mass, which means that learning about the beauty, breadth, and life-giving healing properties and potential of marriage, is reliant on the priest and his preaching on the subject. One of the difficulties here is that the Catholic Church, whilst speaking of marriage as a sacrament, has over the centuries almost exclusively focused on procreation as its purpose. However, the Fathers of Vatican II did accord marriage a much more person-centred relational perspective. It was a paradigm shift in how marriage as a sacrament should be viewed; suggesting moral truth has more to do with the human person and wholeness of their life, rather than a duty to obey laws. They spoke of marriage as a 'covenanted' rather than 'contractual' relationship. Indeed, the whole theological thrust of Vatican II opened the door to promoting the primacy of the couple's relationship as sacramental, based on mutuality, total commitment and as uniquely signifying God as Love and Persons in relationship. How much that door was closed again by *Humane Vitae* remains hotly debated. Priests and theologians have discussed ever since how to discern and communicate the Church's teaching on many aspects of marriage, particularly sexuality. Indeed, and unfortunately, the tendency is to avoid the issue or vaguely cover all possibilities.

Appendix 1

Healing of Bitter Roots in Marriage

Alan Guile

Over thirty years' experience of listening to and praying with couples whose marriage is under strain or in grave danger of breaking altogether, has reinforced awareness of the vital importance of the scriptural principles outlined in this appendix. It can be like a light switching on in the darkness when a couple are helped to reflect and share together about these and they begin to realise the root causes of their deepest problems. It is the roots before the age of about seven which need to be healed if people are to become really free and more whole and united in marriage.[2]

If a man, whilst still a child, has consciously or unconsciously perceived his mother in such ways as (a) dominating or (b) fat and slovenly, then he will have formed unconsciously a bitter-root expectation and judgement that the most significant woman in his later life, his wife, will be (a) tending to rule his life or (b) careless about her weight and her habits. He is likely to be drawn towards a woman who, as time goes by, fulfils his negative expectations more and more. In case (a) she is likely to have perceived her father as weak and ineffective, thus causing her mother to take all the decisions. In case (b) she is likely to have had a father who made her feel as a child that she could never please and satisfy him, so that she formed an expectation that her husband would tend to become more and more critical of her weight, appearance and performance. The resulting unhappiness and insecurity can lead her to comfort eating and to become less able to take good care of herself and the home.

Patterns of these kinds become revealed, time and time again, as one listens to a couple who are struggling in their marriage, or to a person whose marriage or relationship with a partner forms part of the lack of peace which caused them to seek prayer ministry.

There are two aspects to this negative spiral. There is bitter-root expectation, where we have repeated negative experiences as a child and we form, perhaps quite unconsciously, the expectation that we will continue to be treated in similar ways as an adult. Frequently, during prayer ministry, the Lord reveals such a pattern to a person. This expectation leads us to put a psychological pressure on others to fulfil this expectation. We do not know at the time that we are conveying this by non-verbal communication, such as facial expressions, tone of voice etc. It should be noted that we do not exert irresistible pressure on others to behave in a particular way—God has given us all free will—nevertheless people are more likely to be influenced by our negative expectations, and act accordingly, if they have made bitter judgements in the past.

Indeed, far more powerful than this expectation is bitter-root judgement, where we, as a child, unwittingly and seemingly justifiably in many cases, broke a commandment 'honour your father and your mother, as the Lord your God commanded you; that your days may be prolonged, and that it may go well with you' (Dt 5:16). When this commandment, which God intended to multiply blessings on us, is repeated, in Ephesians 6:2, it says that this is the first commandment with a promise. Because none of us has completely perfect parents, we will almost certainly have made some judgements of our parents (and others) whilst a child. 'Do not judge, or you will too be judged. For in the same way as you judge others, you will be judged, and with the measure you use, it will be measured to you.' (Mt 7:1-2)

Because we have all, in some cases quite unconsciously, sinned in this way, we come under another of God's laws, 'Do not be deceived: God cannot be mocked. A man reaps what he sows' (Ga 6:7). We always reap far more than we sow. In an extensive examination of how in prayer we can invite Christ to heal all these vital early roots which can cause so much damage later in life, in marriage and other areas of our life, the author describes how an apparently innocuous perception of his father as weak, led to over 30 years of difficult professional life with male authority figures![3]

Thus these bitter roots, which are our own sinful reactions to what others did to us or failed to do to nurture us, need to be repented of by the adult. In prayer we can then invite Jesus into the wounded memories so that through His Precious Blood He draws out the pain of the child into His suffering on the Cross. Then the adult is in a new place to pray daily and perhaps for a long time for the child within to forgive those who hurt them, and for themselves. We need to be healed of such things as enmity, grudges, hatred, anger and many others, which have allowed some forms of bitterness to become rooted in our hearts. 'See to it that no one misses out on God's grace, that no bitterness springing up causes trouble and thus contaminates many' (Heb 12:15).

If we do not bring these things in prayer to Christ then the damage can go down the generations, because discord in our marriage inevitably causes insecurities and potentially a vast variety of hurts in our children, who can then, if unhealed, continue the cycle. This is so significant that it is of vital importance in the healing of marriage relationships and of the wellbeing of the whole family. Indeed, inviting Christ to reveal and heal these early roots and wounds could even be considered an essential element of marriage preparation, thereby providing a healthy foundation from the earliest days of a couple's life together.

Appendix 2

Engagement with Marriage and Family Life in the Formation of Priests

Alan Guile

Couples may turn to priests at many stages, for example when needing marriage preparation from a team in the parish, or later on in connection with children, or at times of strain in the marriage. The priest's own family life and background may play a part together with his priestly formation, in the effectiveness of his interaction with the couples and families in his care, particularly when the latter are under great stress.

Pope Francis has drawn attention in *Amoris Laetitia* to that aspect of his own family background and early experiences which is personal to each priest. The Pope calls for seminarians to include a wider engagement with marriage and family life, and he writes:

> Their training does not always allow them to explore their own psychological and affective background and experiences. Some come from troubled families, with absent parents and a lack of emotional stability. There is need to ensure that the formation process can enable them to attain the maturity and psychological balance needed for their future ministry.[4]

It is heartening that the Rector of Oscott College where human formation has been strong since Pope St John Paul II wrote *Pastores Dabo Vobis* (see chapter 5), immediately responded to this call of Pope Francis.[5]

The same kinds of early roots and wounds discussed above in relation to partners in a marriage and in chapter 2, will need healing in candidates applying for the priesthood and in the seminarians. It is a further reminder of the connections between the sacraments of Holy Orders and Matrimony.[6]

Notes

1   B. & M. Devine, 'What Marriage is about', in *The Tablet* vol. 268 no. 9078 (2014), p. 16.

2   A. Guile, *Journey into Wholeness: Prayer for Inner Healing—An Essential Ministry of the Church* (Leominster: Gracewing, 2013), pp. 83–4.

3   *Ibid.*

4   Pope Francis, *Amoris Laetitia*, 203.

5   D. Oakley, 'Grounded in Reality' in *The Tablet* 270/9149 (2016), p. 13.

6   *Catechism of the Catholic Church*, 1534–5.

11

Healing the Bereaved, Divorced and Separated

Alan Guile

Pope Francis in his Apostolic Exhortation, Amoris Laetitia, speaks about the Church's responsibility for those who have suffered divorce and the breakup of their families. He writes, 'The Synod Fathers noted that special discernment is indispensable for the pastoral care of those who are separated, divorced or abandoned'.[1] In this chapter Alan describes how one particular approach has brought together men and women who have lost a spouse through death, divorce or separation: they have the opportunity to listen to each other's stories; they grow in compassion for one another; their prayer for one another can begin to bring deeper and deeper inner healing. This happens as they have a series of evening meetings, working through a structured programme, and then spend one or more weekends together in a retreat centre. This is followed by a variety of ways in which ongoing support and friendship are offered and developed. Testimony is woven into this outline of the process.

Introduction—Beginning Experience (BE)

Beginning Experience was started in the USA in 1974 by a nun and her friend whose divorced husband had just died. They discussed the need to do something to help people who are grieving the loss of a loved one through death, divorce or separation and so Beginning Experience was born.

In 1984 a group of people came over from the USA at the invitation of Fr Luke Magee CP, Rector of Minsteracres Monastery and Retreat Centre. Sixty people attended the first weekend, which was open to any denomination. They listened to talks from the American team, shared in groups and cried a lot, each relating to their own pain. At the end of the weekend everyone was happy and joyful and so different from when they had arrived. Friendships were made and everyone went home beginning to let go of their past, but keeping the memories they wanted to remember. It was a powerful and awe-inspiring weekend and a lot of healing went on.

After the weekend was over, some of the participants were asked to stay behind and to form a team. The American team stayed for a few days to train them so that the Hexham & Newcastle team was formed, and helped many people for twenty five years until sadly it disbanded a few years ago for lack of committed team members. It had however helped to establish teams elsewhere in England, Scotland and Northern Ireland.

Fr Luke asked my wife and myself to take part in that first weekend. We declined saying that it would not be helpful to those deeply suffering the loss of a spouse, to have with them a couple who had been married for over thirty years. Intriguingly it turned out that before the weekend, a substantial number of those who attended it, had already come to our home for prayer ministry in the weeks before it, completely unknown to one another and quite independently.

The Aims

The Beginning Experience offers an opportunity to:

a) find support and direction in resolving the grief that accompanies the ending of a marriage through death or permanent separation.

b) deal constructively with guilt and experience the reconciling power of God through sacramental ministry.

c) experience the care and compassion of the Church through the non-judgemental witness and ministry of the team and others.

d) discover their own inner strengths and gifts by re-evaluating their lives, so that they can face the future with hope.

e) learn to trust self, to trust God, to accept God's forgiveness, to forgive oneself, others and in a sense 'forgive' God (for anything bad for which we perhaps in childhood and later on mistakenly held Him responsible), and to learn to accept acceptance.

f) see relationships and problems in a different light and become free to reach out and care for others and to learn to trust and love again.

It is clear that it aims towards the transformation and healing of deeply wounded people so that as they co-operate with Christ working in them and through them, they become free to love and serve others. This is at the heart of the passion, death and resurrection of Jesus who lives, suffers, dies and is resurrected in each person. The process of encountering oneself, letting go and reaching out, as people are invited to healing and transformation is a fundamental life-long process which can form a basis for day-to-day living. As early as 1994 it was estimated that more than 200,000 people around the world had experienced the transforming and freeing event and process of Beginning Experience.

The Team

From this first weekend and subsequent training, a team was formed in the North East which as time went on grew to as many as twenty five women and men. After a while they would meet every Sunday to pray and worship and listen to God together. In this way a great love, unity and trust grew in them. From the team it was then possible to draw facilitators who would help newcomers and give talks, sharing their experiences with newcomers at BE weekends at Minsteracres, which at one stage were three a year. Some of the team were available to travel to other parts of England, Scotland and Northern Ireland when groups there asked for help. Every other year there was a conference in England, with some attending the conference in the USA in the intervening year.

They realised that although some people who contacted them for help were ready to attend a BE weekend, there were others who would be better helped by offering a series of support meetings first. Some of these people included ones where the loss of a spouse was too recent. There were no hard and fast rules because individuals vary so much, but often if the loss was within the previous year, the person might need more time to work through such things as denial. These support evenings also provided people who were needing help, with the opportunity to discern whether they were ready for a BE weekend.

Support Meetings

There were nine sessions, held once a week or fortnight, for two hours in an evening.

Session 1

Getting to know the group:

Newcomers were welcomed and thanked for having the courage to do something about their grief. It was stressed that each one is special and has their own grief, while having a similar pattern of pain and loss to others, and that they deserve to have this time aside for themselves. It was explained that the group was for those who had suffered the loss of a spouse (or in some cases another significant loss), and was not a social or singles group. Instead the group was God-centred with a positive thrust, dealing with the past in order to heal the pain of loss, but concentrating on the present and the future. Everything was confidential.

The format was welcome, any introductions, prayers, personal experience talk, questions and reflection time, small group sharing, announcements and closing prayer.

They entered into agreement that sharing is essential; that support needs to be expressed; that we need to help others to explore and develop ideas and feelings with no accusation, ridicule, forcing of viewpoints, or becoming defensive; that each one should just speak for herself or himself; that they should stick to the point; that they are not therapists or judges; that if at all possible they should not miss a meeting; that confidentiality was strictly kept.

Session 2

The purpose of this session was to help participants to identify, understand and cope with their feelings of being alone and single, their loneliness and stress, as they:

- a) faced the reality of their loss, and began to understand the adjustment process involved in being alone,

- b) learned the importance of distinguishing between being alone and loneliness,

- c) identified causes of stress including their own anger, rejection or guilt.

They were helped to change irrational and self-defeating ideas about being alone and the difference between this and loneliness, and to learn to cope better with being alone and with the stresses in their life.

Session 3

This aimed to help towards identifying, understanding and coping with the feelings of grief, looking at

a) the importance of dealing with memories

b) understanding the process of loss, grieving and healing

c) that feelings are part of us—they are neither right nor wrong.

The five stages of grief were explained leading to looking at the process of going through grief, experiencing wild mood swings, identifying feelings and behaviour at different stages, and getting in touch with feelings through writing and verbalising. They moved on to memory in the process of healing, getting in touch with the real facts, remembering and touching the past, the store of impressions, facts and feelings, and the role of remembering, writing, reflecting and talking about the feelings in particular.

Session 4

The purpose here was to help people to gain confidence and trust in themselves, through

a) identifying their feelings about themselves,

b) helping them to identify the fears and anxieties that had been blocking their growth and self-trust,

c) offering them 'tools' to develop self-confidence and trust.

It was stressed that feelings are not right or wrong and that we are most ourselves in our feelings in our heart rather than in our head. Though fear and anxiety are normal feelings to have while going through adjusting to single life, they need not be crippling, because we have inner resources provided by God to avoid staying in a death situation and to opt for life. Each of us is totally loved by God and created for a special service. The differences between being passive, aggressive and assertive with others were explained, together with reviewing activities in which one has engaged and the values acted upon.

Session 5

This was intended to help them to accept and adjust to changes in relationships and social activities after becoming single again, exploring

a)   how relationships have changed

b)   accepting the reality of changes

c)   realising the importance of making new friends and activities.

A number of aspects and attitudes in this were explored.

Session 6

This aimed to help people to deepen their relationship with God and church through

a)   identifying their current feelings about God and church

b)   helping them deepen their faith and grow in their relationship with God

c)   helping them to identify and understand their role and place in the Church.

This could involve dealing with such reactions as bargaining with God, blaming Him and being angry with Him, examining our concept of God and our feelings and attitudes towards Him. Mistaken ideas about the Church might need examining and correcting. Differences between real and unreal guilt needed to be pointed out, and the shoulds, oughts and musts of unreal guilt should be discarded. The need to own and admit our real guilt, sins and failings should lead us to seek God's pardon, learning that God never rejects us but welcomes us back. This should lead on to examining our role in the Church and how God needs us to minister to others who are hurting because they have suffered a similar loss.

Session 7

This was devoted to showing that single-parent families can be healthy, happy and nurturing through

a)   helping participants to deal with guilty feelings

b)   helping them to adjust the amount and quality of time they spend with their children

c)   helping them identify problem areas with their children so as to assist them towards positive changes.

Parents whose children were still relatively young were able to share about how aspects of parental practice may affect children, and to review their own experiences, attitudes, spoken words and behaviour with their own children.

Session 8

This dealt with the memory of the deceased spouse by helping them to identify attitudes and behaviour towards him or her. Any feelings about responsibility for the death of the spouse, and the reality of their not being there any longer needed to be identified towards becoming free to have a new full life. There was a prayer service helping them to deal with the memory of the deceased.

Session 9

This aimed to help towards realising that the grief process can be a process of growth through

a)   restating the stages of growth and emphasising that it is an ongoing process

b)   helping with the examination of growth which has already taken place and looking at further goals

c)   stressing the importance of reaching out to others.

There was then a prayer service focussed on God bringing growth through loss.

BE Weekends

There was welcome and encouragement to everyone that they were so committed that they had taken the step to come away for a weekend, because they really wanted God's help to become free to move on in their life and to begin to help others who were going through some similar suffering. The introduction helped them to find the right orientation and focus so that they could receive as much help as possible from God through prayer and through sharing with one another. They were helped to get in touch with why they came and look at what they hoped to receive from being at the weekend. They would each go away alone to their room with some of their questions and 'hot pen' as they wrote from the heart rather than the head about their feelings.

During a weekend members of the team would give talks on nine topics in which they shared in depth from their own suffering, and experience of how God had been and still was healing them. This was to encourage others to get in touch with their own painful experiences and feelings, and share them in a small group which would meet together between one talk and the next, so that there could be loving and prayerful support for God to bring peace and healing at each stage to each individual. Through the love shown by others who were listening and responding with acceptance, understanding and compassion, and through prayer ministry there would be many tears but a growing peace and even joy as God was at work bringing deep healing. One of the team gave an introductory talk to help people to settle in, to begin to feel relaxed and to be really hopeful with expectant faith about the experiences which would unfold as the weekend progressed. There were four team members for each talk. Two were speakers. The other two were to support them, as perhaps very emotionally they shared deep painful experiences. There was a balance of experiences by having picked, through prayer beforehand, the two speakers to represent two very different and even contrasting experiences of life and marriage. Every small group had a balance between bereaved and divorced/separated. If for that weekend their numbers were not about equal, a facilitator would take one group separately, so the other groups had about equal numbers.

The pattern of God working through the sharing, love and prayer will be illustrated here by drawing from the rest of the talks given at various different weekends, not all within a single weekend by one of the leaders. Because of the prayerful balance just noted, the other team member speaking on the same subject would always have had some unhappy marriage experience, which contrasted with the very happy marriage of the lady whose remarks are quoted here. Also the people composing a small group will have had very different life experiences so that everyone could feel supported and comforted, both in small group and in any whole group sharing, by knowing that there were others with not dissimilar pain who really understood what they were going through.

The second talk was entitled Encounter with Self. The speaker said that as she looked back on her life she had previously wondered why she had acted as she had done at the time. Now however having gone a long way on the journey within herself, she realised that her reactions had come about because she never felt any love as a child, only rejection. She had looked back and wondered whether her parents ever really loved her because they never showed her love. Now however she realised that this perception of rejection does not mean that there was no love in the home. Very often there is some kind of love but what is missing are things which are important—affection, touch and spoken words which build up and affirm. If these are not there, as in her case, then the symptoms of rejection are experienced.

Because she had not felt wanted and loved by parents she felt worthless and as she grew older she felt inadequate, inferior and insecure. Even at school, the headmistress, a nun, would ridicule her at every chance she got even in front of the whole class, saying often, 'You're not like your sister.' Because of the rejection she rebelled in her teens and showed much anger. Her father would beat her with a belt and shout at her to cry but she wouldn't. After some very disturbed years she met her husband and God began to heal her through his acceptance and love.

The third talk in weekends which this lady gave was on Symptoms of Spiritual Death. Her husband had died after years of very happy marriage. She explained that when grief is unresolved it can become very destructive because we tend to bury it, unaware that unresolved grief can make us fearful, angry and anxious and can lead to many physical illnesses. Through discovering and identifying areas of pain we can by God's grace be healed and set free. Resolved grief is life-giving and sets us free again. Grief after loss is normal if we allow ourselves to move through all of the stages and reach acceptance, but if we become stuck in one of the stages we experience symptoms of spiritual death.

She spoke of how a doctor had let her husband down by inaction following symptoms which began to develop at Christmas. The doctor made light of them and didn't check, but by Easter he had been diagnosed with cancer, and only lived three months. There was not only anger with the doctor but with God and with her husband for leaving her to face family problems alone.

She explained how her experience with BE had helped her to come back to life again. Recently she has said that the years with BE are, with her marriage, the happiest experiences of her life.

The fourth talk was on Trusting Ourselves and Others. This particular lady never gave that talk but the most important element in trusting others is getting to know them as they reveal more of themselves so we can establish real friendship, in the awareness that we will not be betrayed or rejected or hurt. The area of trusting ourselves is one where we most of us need great help from God to be healed of many childhood experiences which have made it very difficult or even impossible for years, to love and accept ourselves and therefore to trust God's creation of goodness and worth within each one of us.

The fifth talk was on Trusting God. She said that although she had been a practising Catholic all her life, going 'through all the motions,' it was only ten years earlier that she had her first real encounter with God. She invited Him into her heart and fell in love with Him. She learned to listen to His voice and the Bible came more alive. She became aware that she really was a temple of the Holy Spirit. God transformed her work as a nurse from merely a job, to a ministry to help sick people.

She said that her faith and trust in God has enabled her to get through many trials and crosses. Even though at times she was angry with God or strayed away, He was always there to forgive her and welcome her back knowing that she was loved unconditionally. She was able to write down her feelings in a prayer journal through her lowest ebb when and after her husband died when he was still quite young. She was able, despite all her distress to pray that the Father's will might be done. As her husband neared death he radiated a peace and beauty that can only come from God, and people would come to pray and experience this. He was able to receive Holy Communion each day, and died with his family around him.

For a while after this she couldn't pray anymore and felt she didn't want to, but she knew that God understood. Then she was able to cry and to ask God to forgive her and she could thank Him for helping her through her loss. Today, around twenty five years after the death of her husband, she is one the most amazing women of deep prayer that most of us are ever likely to meet.

The sixth talk was called A Confronting Look at Guilt. After explaining the difference between realistic guilt and unrealistic or false guilt, she reflected on how her husband went downhill after his diagnosis and became very quiet, angry and depressed as he went through stages of grief. She blamed herself for not being able to give him the hope he needed to carry on, but later she realised that this was false guilt. She even felt guilty that she had prayed 'Your will be done', because perhaps if she had not said that prayer God might have healed him. More unrealistic guilt. She spoke of the power of the sacrament of Reconciliation.

At some BE weekend there were five or more priests available for confessions and they would speak of the great experience of wonderful graces being poured out. Sometimes a priest would take part in the whole weekend and share how in his case he was 'married' to God and the Church.

The seventh talk was a Gentle Closing Towards a New Beginning. She said that they were now at the most important time of the weekend, coming to the stage of acceptance which was not resignation but an acceptance which leaves each person in peace and freedom to move on in life. She found that writing a closing letter to her husband, though hard, was part of facing reality and closing the door gently but firmly so there was no going back. She felt that closing the door gently on the past or closing it as far as we could at this stage of our journey, through writing the letter was the climax of the weekend. Even people whose marriage had ended painfully found that there was healing in being able to find words for a closing letter to the one who was no longer there and may have inflicted great hurt on them.

The eighth talk was on Reaching Out. She witnessed that saying yes when asked if she would come on a BE weekend, was the turning point of her life. She realised that these other people were suffering like she was but that they had the courage to help others like herself. This led to acceptance that can bring joy which can be shared by helping others, caring, listening, having a compassionate heart. Through BE the Lord has been setting her free and she felt then and still feels today years later, a new person. If her husband had lived she might never have found this new creation which she had not realised existed. This lady not only went on to become one of the leaders in BE but has been greatly used by God for years in many ways, leading worship and intercession, leading a prayer group and a Mothers Prayers Group, and praying with many people for inner healing.

The closing talk reviewed the stages through which they had been journeying through the weekend.

People were offered questions to which they might like to write their own answers, about how they felt able to move on in new ways and with more hope and confidence in themselves and in God, using the much greater inward strength they had just discovered.

Ongoing Support

There were a variety of ways in which ongoing support and friendship were offered and developed. There was an opportunity to come back together for a Saturday; there was a facilitator in contact with everyone; they could attend further BE weekends and some did a training weekend and attended a team meeting every other Sunday as preparation for being part of the team. Others remained in informal contact with one another and formed lifelong friendships.

There was ample evidence that people who had arrived broken and cut off from others received courage and deeper faith in God to face new challenges and to be ready to reach out to others.

Ann, whose story is told in Appendix 1, wrote:

> BE was the main turning point in my life. For the first time in my life I had people listening to me, not talking down to me or rejecting me. Thanks to God's guidance in BE I gained strength to face the world. BE has given me hope and encouragement as God shows me a totally new way of life. It was a moving experience of hurts and joys, discovering myself as a valued person who was able to share her life journey with others who also had experienced divorce. I also discovered God's unconditional and total love for me with hope for a better future, leaving the past behind. It was wonderful to share and continue afterwards with trusted friends through the life-long process following my time in BE.

The Present Position

Sadly, a few years ago, there were insufficient numbers of committed team members in the Hexham & Newcastle Diocese for BE to continue there, but it is still active in Scotland and in Kent.

It had also led to a ministry to teenagers who had suffered loss which became Young People's BE and this did continue in the Diocese until 2013 and is referred to in Chapter 9.

Acknowledgements

I give very grateful thanks to the lady who lent me her notes and to Fr Jeroen, Rector of Minsteracres, for providing further information.

Notes

1   Pope Francis, *Amoris Laetitia*, 242.

12

Healing the Dying and the Surviving Family

Healing the dying may sound like a contradiction in terms to those who see healing only as physical recovery. Sharon Wilson in this chapter brings out a much deeper meaning of God's gift of healing: the healing of the person's relationship with self, with family and, most of all with God. This healing brings immense inner peace to the dying person and great consolation to their family. Sharon begins by sharing how her own experiences of a damaged childhood and family led her as a child into a deepening relationship with and dependence upon Christ, which has formed the basis for the work which she now does. She knows that God abandons no-one and is very close to the dying person even if he or she is totally unaware of that healing presence. She also includes in her chapter a testimony of a lady who had moving experiences of praying with dying patients in a hospital and a hospice.

Christ is Healing Our Wounds in Many Areas of Suffering. What are We Doing Now and Where is the Lord Calling Upon Us to Do More?

I believe that the Lord is always inviting us to ask that question. I am currently working in a Hospice employed as a qualified Counsellor. My role is to work with the dying patient, to help ease that journey. I also work alongside patients who have recently been diagnosed and those who have been given the devastating news that there are no further treatments, a shock to both patient and families. To do this I build up a trusting relationship so that any barriers of communication are broken down. This helps those dying patients to talk about and to work with the hurts and the pain they have experienced and are feeling now.

I think it is important to write about my own broken childhood and how Jesus carried me through tough times and because I placed all my trust in Him He has brought me to where I am today. I will always be thankful to Him and every day I feel very privileged to be on this journey.

Childhood and Damaged Family

At age six I became a pupil of St Joseph's School and I remember the very first time I walked into St Joseph's Church. Prior to this I had not stepped foot into any church and this was a very magical moment. I felt I belonged, there was something here but I remember not knowing what or what any of the church was about. This was the beginning of my journey and has led me to where I am and what I am doing today.

When I was one year old my brother's twin sister who was three at the time died during an epileptic fit. I was far too young to know what was happening but later in my life I came to understand the impact this actually did have on my broken family.

I was the youngest of five children. My mother experienced multiple miscarriages and a full-term still-born boy. My eldest sister lived and was brought up by my grandparents; my other sister suffered with grand-mal epilepsy from the age of two years and continues to do so at the age of 55. My brother suffered greatly because of his twin dying and in late teenage years became an alcoholic. He has recently been dry for three years. Prior to this he tried on many occasions to take his own life, and still today self-harms.

At the time I thought my childhood was normal because nobody ever talked about what happens behind closed doors. My family was broken and only as an adult and employed as a professional bereavement and loss counsellor can I see how damaged my family is. I found comfort in attending Mass every Sunday and I still remember to this day skipping and feeling excited about going to Church. I went to Church on my own though my parents never attended and my sister came if she was well.

My dad enjoyed his drink but most of the time it turned him into a monster. He would often become aggressive and violent, both mentally and physically towards my mother, my brother and me, but somehow this became the norm behind our closed door. I would often as a young child talk to Jesus, and write notes to Him and place them under my pillow, and I would often fall asleep praying asking Jesus to take me because I knew I wanted to be with Him. To this day I still remember how it felt to want to be with Jesus, to *really* be with Jesus. I remember thinking when I woke up that Jesus didn't want me yet. Often when I was younger as part of my punishment my dad would hide my shoes so that I could not attend church; which really upset me because I needed to get to church. This was my magical place.

Effects on My Family of Our Dealing with Death

Both my parents have now sadly passed away and I know the brokenness within my family was because of the loss of their beautiful baby daughter who was only three years old at the time. There was a lot of anger and unanswered questions. I believe my brother took the brunt of my dad's anger because in his eyes his daughter was perfect and my brother was not living up to his expectations and was often told that he should have been the one that died, and this moulded him into the person he is today and the reason why he turned to alcohol. My sister's death was a taboo subject and was never talked about. The only time I heard her name was when my dad had been drinking and he turned his anger onto my brother. Somewhere amongst all of this anger, the grief my parents must have felt after the death of their full-term still-born son must have been so great, but was never spoken about especially whilst my dad was still alive.

The brokenness and pain of both my parents must have been horrendous and I definitely knew that my dad had no place for God. Sometimes we had conversations and he would often say that he knew the Bible but did not want to talk about it. My dad was angry with God and blamed God for his loss and this anger turned towards me because my dad knew I had Jesus in my life. I knew that no matter what happened I would never let go or give up on the relationship I had formed with Jesus. As an adult and experiencing the loss of grandparents, parents, and other family members I could see how this impacted on the dynamics within a family and somehow came to understand why things happened.

Work in a Hospice

My training brought me to work within a Hospice setting, a place where patients come to die, or come for respite and a place for symptom control. They all experience questions and the anxieties those questions can bring. Especially questions like, "What will happen to me when I die? Will it be painful? Will it be peaceful? What will happen to those I leave behind? When patients are reaching end of life it is no wonder they question life and death. It brings them to look at the life they have led, the legacy they will leave, and any hurts that need to be addressed. They question God, and they ask why God has done this to me, to my family and friends, and they question themselves.

I have often spent the last few weeks with a patient who is dying and for whom God has no place. They frequently say that God has done nothing for me so why should I turn to Him now. When I encourage them to talk about death, and what they believe happens when one dies, they often say they don't know; maybe we just go to sleep. As days go by and they are closer to death, they reach out and want to talk about God, and it has been known that they have asked for a chaplain whereas days before they have refused to see one. I find it fascinating that people closer to death somehow reach out to a God they don't know or have never known.

I have come across patients who have been diagnosed and have belief and trust in God. This in my experience has led to a spiritual peaceful death because they have already made their peace with God. They already have that relationship with God. One lady I saw was so inspirational to me. One day she attended the Hospice and was so distressed, and I was asked to spend some time with her. She had just received the news that there was no more treatment; chemotherapy was no longer an option. She was taken aback by this news and was in a state of shock. She talked about the impact this would have on her family and how she could possibly tell them in order to prepare them. We sat for quite some time and our conversation turned towards her belief in God and what her religion meant to her and what God meant to her, and how God had been good to her during her life. We talked about being in a relationship with God and that we can feel angry with Him from time to time and it was alright for her to feel angry towards Him now. I talked about my relationship with God being the same as the relationship between a husband and wife and that sometimes we do fall out but God understands our hurts and feelings. Towards the end of this session, this lady said she felt an overwhelming peace; she really found it difficult to describe what that feeling was like. She said it was like a weight lifted off her shoulders and she was ready to go home and face the family. Before this lady left she looked at me and said that the work I was doing was a gift from God and I should never stop. This confirmed to me that I am still on this journey and still working closely with God.

This lady went home to talk with her family and not long after our meeting eventually came into the Hospice. She introduced me as the lady she saw after being told that treatment had stopped and with God's help was able to talk with her family. The family could not thank me enough, because of the openness and honesty the barrier wall of communication had been broken down. This lady died not long after and was not scared to die because she knew she was meeting her maker. I believe that God is really present with the dying patient.

Children

A young bereaved child I worked with in the Hospice for bereavement counselling was living with his adoptive parents, after suffering abuse and neglect from his own parents. This child presented with lots of emotional problems, and I worked with him for quite some time. He was about seven years old. Working with children is different to working with adults, adults question death and God and their beliefs children tend not to. What amazed me about this child was that after finishing our sessions he would always make his way into our chapel and become mesmerised, whereas he was not able to sit still for too long and easily became distracted during our sessions. When entering the chapel I could see his behaviour change, he appeared to me to become settled. After every session this child always visited the chapel. I believe he found this chapel to be 'magical' rather like I found my local church. I believe that God will somehow heal his brokenness. I no longer see this child now but I trust God to work within him and guide him in the right direction.

In some families, when a death takes place many young children are not told what is happening and is some cases are not allowed to go the funeral. All that they may know is that there is much distress and change and activity going on around them which is not explained and this leaves them confused and unhappy. Then there is a gap in the family circle. If this was someone they knew and cared for such as a grandmother, they are left with unresolved grief and regret that they were prevented from saying goodbye at the funeral, and they are not allowed to come to terms with their grief. It can be years later in adulthood that grief and anger surface strongly and they ask for prayer ministry for Jesus to heal their loss and anger that they were excluded from the mourning. If death was 'covered up' when they were children it may be harder for them deal with later on.

The Bereaved

I also work with the bereaved, and feel their pain after losing someone they loved. Depression is a normal stage for the bereaved person to work through, and often you hear them saying that they want to be with that person. They question if there is something after death, where their loved one is now, and when they have talked about thoughts about being with them they will often say who is to say that if I took my own life that they will be waiting for me, because they say that suicide is wrong and this may end up in them not meeting their partner again. A very interesting conclusion for someone who doesn't believe.

Interestingly they talk about God even with quite a few of them who do not believe, we could spend quite a lot of the session talking about Him. If someone totally disbelieves then why would this become our main topic of conversation? I feel there is always that niggle that they hang onto just in case they are wrong, because those that have lost loved ones question their own death and question their own beliefs.

I personally feel that there should be more teaching about healing for past generations. I feel that a lot of hurt is carried through generations and the cycle sometimes is not broken; it is to heal this that Mass for Intergenerational Healing is celebrated regularly in our parish (see Chapter 7). Bereavement is dealt with and openly talked about now and is not a taboo subject like once it was before. A lot of families grew up with the stiff upper lip and were told to just get on with it. These hurts manifest as I witnessed as a young child. I believe if more prayer was available to those people crying out then their brokenness could be healed. The work of Beginning Experience described in Chapter 11 is a wonderful example of how help and healing can be received.

Effect on My Mother After the Death of My Father

It saddens me greatly to talk about the brokenness in my family including the quiet deaths of my own sister and my still-born brother. It saddens me now as an adult to somehow understand to a certain extent the enormity of pain they both went through. It saddens me to think they didn't seek help, or that they thought there was nobody to help them. It saddens me to think that they thought the ways they were dealing with their losses were normal, particularly the anger that manifested inside my dad and the way he released this anger. Was it the right way? For him it was the only way. As a bereavement and loss counsellor, anger is one of the stages people feel and if left unaddressed can manifest into other ways. My parents did not know how to address any of their feelings; they dealt with it in their own way.

My father passed away suddenly after suffering a massive heart attack in the middle of the night, and not long before he died he said sorry to me for not treating me the way he should have. He told me that I had been a wonderful daughter and that he was very proud of me. I found that to be very strange at the time because I had never heard these words from my dad before. He said sorry to me but it saddens me to think that he never got to make peace with God; because he died suddenly he never received the last rites.

My mum became very depressed after the death of my father and this surprised me at that time, because of their relationship I had imagined things to be different for her but she became very isolated. Slowly she did start to talk about how she was forced to give up her first- born daughter to live with her parents, the death of her daughter and the death of her still- born son. She showed me a red ribbon that my sister wore in her hair, she talked a little about what she looked like and where she was buried and why they didn't visit her, she said it was too painful. I realise now that she kept these feelings suppressed all of these years because of my dad. She was never given permission to talk about her losses as my dad took control.

Conclusion

The death of a loved one was and still is in some cases a taboo subject for many families. I have witnessed first-hand the impact this can have on a family whilst they are young and growing up and the impact this can have later in life and how this can have a ripple effect into extending families.

I feel we need more education in our churches about the healing of damage and emotions. We need to be able to share our experiences with other people; we need to know that 'It is ok to talk'. We need more prayer around brokenness within families; we need more prayer for past generations. I also feel that within our churches we need more education around bereavement so people need to know that 'It is ok to talk'. If people do not know how to talk about the death of a loved one or are not given permission to talk about their loss of a loved one they simply will not know what to do with the all the emotions that they will feel. Death has a huge impact on any family and without God the pain can be so unbearable. Chains need to be broken but to do this we need God's help.

Appendix

A Nurse's Testimony

I worked in a hospice for five years on the ward and on day care and prior to going to the hospice; I worked on a chest medical ward which involved nursing the dying. During that time I experienced many graces and blessings; this was not a job to me it was a ministry.

Prior to going to the hospice to work I nursed a Muslim lady who was married to an Englishman. She had cancer of both lungs and was dying. She struggled to breathe so I did meditation with her to try and relax her.

I took her on a journey through woodland and over a field where there was a stream at the end. She was happily walking along when she saw this man coming towards her. It was Jesus but I did not tell her that as she was a Muslim. He began to talk to her and asked her to sit with Him on the bank at the other side, so she took off her socks and shoes and He helped her across to the bank on the other side where they sat down to talk. She began to tell Him all her troubles and anxieties and as she was speaking she could see them all flowing away down the river. They sat for some time and when she was ready to go He helped her over and they said their goodbyes. She did not want to leave Him as there was something special about Him and as she was walking away she kept looking back waving to Him until she could see Him no more.

When we finished the meditation she said she said I met Jesus and I told Him all my problems and she asked me to teach her the Lord's Prayer so I wrote it out for her. This lady was very frightened of dying so I told her it's just like a mother expecting a baby, when she starts her labour the baby goes into the birth canal ready to be born into this world and all the family are waiting with joy for this new life. It's like that when we are dying, we go into the birth canal ready to be born into new life with Christ and all the family who have gone before us are waiting to greet us. The lady said 'but I am not ready to leave yet, I have to get things in order'. I said 'would you mind if I said a prayer with you' so I prayed that the Lord give her the strength and peace that she would be able to get her house in order without struggling for breath. She was transferred to the hospice the following day and two days later the MacMillan nurse came to see me with a message from her that she was sitting outside in the sunshine without oxygen getting her house in order. This was a miracle and grace from Almighty God.

I went to work at the hospice later and received many blessings. One man who was dying and struggling to breathe and also very angry, was asking me to help him die. He was frightened of the process of dying. I asked him if he believed in God and very angrily he said, 'No, He took my wife from me.' I explained that God is always there to help us in our troubles. He does help us even though He may not take the problems away but will always help us through them. Sometimes things do not go the way we want them to, but if we surrender them to God He will come and give us His peace. I encouraged him to ask God for forgiveness for all his past sins and invite Him into his life. He asked, 'Will you do it for me?,' so I said the sinners' prayer with him and invited Jesus into his life. He settled and died the next day.

Another lady who was a Catholic and dying was visited by her sister who was anxious and upset. I asked her if she would like me to say the rosary with her. We both knelt down at the side of the bed and said the rosary and surrendered her to God and she died peacefully that night.

When I was on day care at the hospice I had many opportunities to speak to people about God; sometimes they had not been to church for years. I got permission to speak to the parish priest and they began to receive Holy Communion on a weekly basis and also the Sacrament of the Sick.

One lady who had a brain tumour and was not a Catholic said she would love to go to Lourdes so I contacted the SVP who came up with the money. She went to Lourdes two weeks later and had a great time and took ill when she came back and died three weeks later.

13

Healing Victims of Sexual Abuse

Alan Guile

When wounded people become aware that inner healing of their deep wounds is possible they will seek out a minister and reveal the hurts that rob them of joy. Women who have suffered sexual abuse often bury their pain for years and even a lifetime. Though this chapter was written by a man, help in the writing was given by a lady who was a victim and who contributed insights into how both the emotional life and the spiritual life can be gravely affected for many years until the healing power of Christ is invited in through ongoing prayer ministry which may take a long time. A first-hand testimony of another victim is included.

The Devastating Pain of a Victim

Sexual abuse makes victims not only of the abused person but also in a different way of their loved ones and of the abuser as well. This chapter deals with the primary victim. A Scripture passage can encapsulate some of the depths of human experience of the one who has been abused:

> The enemy has pursued me;
> he has crushed my life to the ground;
> he has made me sit in darkness like those long dead.
> Therefore my spirit faints within me;
> my heart within me is appalled. (Ps 143:3)

This passage describes something of the inner turmoil and confused feelings of a girl or woman who was sexually molested as a child. Her ability to trust has been broken, and if it was an authority figure such as her father who violated her instead of giving her protection and security, then she feels totally betrayed. Her parents or other family did not protect her nor did God, so she feels she was abandoned in her time of need and left to bear her pain alone. The abandonment, betrayal, fear and inability to trust, particularly to trust any authority figure, may lead to false bravado

'I'll take care of myself', and to running away from help, particularly when signs of love and care threaten to penetrate defensive walls. She may well be too fearful and vulnerable to risk trusting again.

> Beware lest there be among you a man or woman or family whose heart turns away this day from the Lord our God; lest there be among you a root bearing poisonous and bitter fruit, one who when he hears the words of this sworn covenant blesses himself in his heart, saying 'I shall be safe though I persist in going my own way.' This would destroy all of you, good and evil alike. (Dt 29:18-19)

Here is another example of the bitter root expectancy and judgement (see Appendix 1 of Chapter 10). There may have been a turning away from God who did not save her—a false belief that I shall be safe if I keep away from others–the bitter root that no one is to be trusted and so since I cannot trust help that is offered and I cannot risk taking down the defensive walls I have built I will cope on my own.

Humanly speaking we might feel hopeless about such a wounded victim even being able to receive the help which she needs so much, but the love and healing power of God can not only bring gradual healing and peace over a period which may last for years but in a wonderful way God then uses some of these same women to give very powerful help to other people. This has happened over the last few years to a number of women who came to my home for prayer and for counselling, where sexual abuse in childhood had been a part of their woundedness.[1] They are wonderful people who are now reaching out to others with great love and compassion. Just as the wounds of Jesus have become wounds of glory, so also our wounds of pain, suffering and sin will be turned into wounds of victory as we become more and more united with Christ, allowing all that is damaged within us to die with Him on the Cross and co-operating with the grace given by the Holy Spirit to forgive and to become a new creation with Christ.

Confusion and Betrayal

There may be a good deal of confusion and sometimes a confusion of identity which will be even worse if she was abused by her father or step-father so that she was forced into usurping her mothers' role as the father related to her in ways that should have belonged only to her mother. Her sense of who she was created to be in her femininity, as a daughter and later as a wife and mother has been damaged at its roots. The father/daughter relationship should have given her affirmation, security and confirmation that she is lovable and desirable as a female in a healthy way which would build up her capacity to relax in the arms of her husband in due course. If her father had been seen by her to treat her mother with respect and affection, then she would have learned to identify herself as one who would one day be respected and cherished by a man. But her sense of dignity and worth have been stolen from her, she has been intruded upon and used and made to feel unclean. In addition to guilt at being forced into taking something of her mother's place if the abuser was father or step-father, she will feel other guilts, real or imagined. She may well feel that in some way she had some responsibility for what happened, that she should perhaps have resisted more, that she didn't tell somebody the very first time it happened. The guilt can become worse if there is family break-up with angers and hurts being expressed.

Yet this betrayal even by a father can be healed and redeemed by Christ. The testimony of a lady who came for ministry over twenty years ago bears this out.[2] Aged eight, she found her mother dead in bed. From the same age till she was sixteen her father sexually abused her, yet through the healing power of Christ she became a wonderful channel of reconciliation to others in later years.

Anger is likely to be present—not just anger against the man who molested her, but against her mother if she was still in the family home, because questions may arise within her such as "Why did she marry such a man? Why did she let this happen? Didn't she realise what was happening? Didn't she care? There may also be anger against God. Some of the anger may not be directed just at one person but be an outburst. Doesn't anybody hear me or care about me?

Many other feelings can be mixed up in the confusion, ambivalence of love/hate, fears, very poor sense of self-worth, self-dislike even self-hatred and self-harm which may be worse if she was driven into a period of promiscuity.

Because of all the confusion of feelings and having been let down, it may seem as if her heart keeps opening to love and help and then closing again, so that particularly if ministry is soon after the events, a great deal of affirming patient love may be needed for a long time. All these aspects, whoever the abuser or abusers were, have been extensively discussed in many ways.[3]

Experience of a Victim

One lady, for whom it was very many years before she was able to speak to anyone about the abuse, and even longer before she reached the point where she could talk through what happened in front of a listener, and then weep, wrote this brief summary of some of the effects upon her:

(a) Human feelings

Mum or dad will punish me
I can never trust any man or woman again
My abuser is stronger than me
They will think that it is my fault
I'm dirty and horrible
I allowed this abuse
They will think I'm mad if I dare to speak

(b) Spiritual aspects

Fear	I will go to hell—God hates me
Mistrust	I can't trust God because He let me down
Anger	Where is God? He had the power to stop it so why didn't He?
Power	God is bigger—He is divine—He is greater than I am—He controls my life He can do anything with me
Stigma	I have sinned sexually—I must go to confession for it happening
Guilt	As well as blaming myself for it happening I feel anger, bitterness that I haven't been able to forgive
Self-injury	I feel this is the ultimate sin when I self-harm

The next words written by this wonderful lady whom the Lord uses to help others were 'Abuse leaves wounds so deep that only the Divine Physician Jesus Christ can heal them'.

Boys too can be sexually abused. US statistics of 1985 were that 1 in 4 girls and 1 in 10 boys had been molested by the age of 18, and that most of the reported cases of incest occurred in 'religious' homes with fathers and stepfathers responsible for about half the cases. However, statistics are not reliable in this area of suffering. Some sources indicate that less than 2% of molestations in the U S are ever reported.[4] Present estimates are about 1 in 4 girls abused by 18 and 1 in 6 boys.

In 32 years of my own prayer ministry, many dozens of women have spoken of their experience of sexual abuse and have received deep healing. A number wrote testimonies of how Jesus brought healing to them! Only two or three men have revealed this, although men were about one third of the 550 people coming for ministry.

Healing the Victim

We come now to the vital question 'How do we pray for the healing of someone who has been the victim of sexual abuse?'

It is not a matter of having a method in which one follows a sequence of steps always in the same order. We need to ask the Holy Spirit to teach us how to pray for this particular person, and to teach us just when she or he is ready for any particular stage of ministry. All that appears in Chapter 2 under the heading 'How are We to Pray for Healing' applies here. Intercessory prayer both with the victim and separately is our most powerful means to help and we and others can be praying for God to prepare the wounded heart to receive His healing and blessing. We might offer the victim words of Scripture which she could pray by herself regularly (preferably daily) and also pray them with her during ministry such as:

> I ask that your mind may be opened to see His light so that you will know what is the hope to which He has called you, how rich are the wonderful blessings He promises His people, and how very great is His power at work in us who believe. (Ep 1:18-19)

> I ask God from the wealth of His glory to give you power through His Spirit to be strong in your inner self. (Ep 3:16)

> I shall pour clean water over you and you will be cleansed. I shall cleanse you of all your defilement and all your idols. I shall give you a new heart and put a new spirit in you. I shall remove the heart of stone from your body and give you a heart of flesh instead. (Ez 36:25-26)

It is important in our intercession to pray as in this last passage for defensive walls of the heart of stone to be gently melted away so that light and love can pour in and be accepted. Our intercession is that she be protected against powers of darkness and that clouds of confusion may lift. Our intercession never guarantees success because the person has free will, but it can block the interference of Satan and keep open the door to God so that she may be able to forgive. There will be no freedom and healing without forgiveness. We cannot accomplish forgiveness by our act of will, but we can choose to forgive and ask the Lord to give us the grace with which to do all the forgiving. It may be wise to ask the victim when we come to pray, to say aloud that she chooses to want to forgive completely.

Likely ingredients in our prayers for the inner healing of this wounded person, all the time remembering that we ask the Holy Spirit to guide us as to their order and timing, may include:

1. Pray that she or he accepts Gods' forgiveness, perhaps aided by someone saying 'In the name of Jesus Christ I declare that you are forgiven and assure you of the forgiveness of God the Father'. Clearly the best way for this to happen is in the sacrament of Reconciliation if she belongs to a church which provides this. We can assure her quite definitely that she is not responsible for what happened asking God to let this message go to her heart and that Jesus lifts all burden of guilt and unworthiness so that she can completely forgive herself.

2. Pray that she will allow the Lord to heal every memory and do all the forgiving which she cannot do but for which she is asking for God's grace, so that she is brought in time into a state of total forgiveness towards the abuser, and towards others such as her mother who she feels might have protected her, and towards God that He 'allows such terrible hurts to occur'. This cannot be rushed; we must wait until she is ready at least to want to forgive. We may need for a while to show unconditional love and accept-ance while she verbalises all her negative feelings in a catharsis of feelings which can help to relieve tension and anxiety. But we need Gods' help to know when it would be counterproductive to continue this any further, because it would just leave her more deeply gripped by these feelings. We may then need to bring her to choose either life or death. (Dt 30:19) It will be death if she holds on to the feelings and is unwilling to choose to forgive. If she fails to forgive the abuser then he could be allowed to destroy or damage her life further. We can pray that the adult chooses to

forgive and that the wounded heart of the child within her is also given the gift of forgiving.

3.   Pray for cleansing—perhaps using such words as 'Lord Jesus we ask you to pour your stream of living water into her and over every part of her being body, soul, and spirit', and to go on doing this until she feels completely clean and made new. This may be part of asking Jesus to heal all those damaged memories, and by touching her wounds with His wounds, to draw the pain progressively from her and take it into His suffering on the Cross. A suitable scripture reading would be:

So let her come near to God with a sincere heart and a sure faith, with a heart that has been purified from a guilty conscience and a body washed with clean water. (Heb 10:22)

4.   Pray for her soul and spirit to be separated and set free from that of the abuser. St Paul wrote:

Do you think I can take parts of Christ's body and join them to a body of a prostitute? Never. As you know, a man who goes with a prostitute is one body with her, since the two become one flesh, but anyone who is joined to the Lord is one spirit with Him. (1Co 6:15-16)

Thus we need to pray in the name of Jesus Christ and with the sword of the Spirit to separate the spirit of the victim from that of the abuser so that each can be free to be bonded to their own spouse alone. We can pray that the victim's spirit will forget this bonding caused by the abuse. Her mind won't forget but the Lord can heal the hurts of the memories if she is willing to co-operate, especially in the whole area of forgiving. We pray to cut her free from every kind of bond with her abuser and to restore to her anything that was lost.

5.   Pray that the healing love of God be poured into every wounded part of her being, so that in the words of St Paul 'she may be rooted and grounded in love', so that her whole being is called into life (like Lazarus—coming out of the tomb). (Ep 3:17)

6.   Pray with the authority of Christ to break any conscious or unconscious inner vows which may bind her, or any lies about herself such as 'I am worthless'. Because the victim has felt abandoned in

her time of need she may have been deluded as a child into thinking that she deserved to be rejected because something bad in her played a part in what happened, so she needs to be assured, not just by our words, but by our actions that we love and accept her and can be trusted to be there to help when needed, and that she will receive tenderness and respect. We need to be there when needed in all the ups and downs, helping and encouraging her to choose life, and praying and helping her to co-operate in the crucifying of old habits and patterns of thinking. This is where the stronghold prayers are vital[5] in her own daily prayers, as well as prayers to cut all forms of binding.

A Testimony

My life as a victim started when I was seven-and-a-half years old, the first abuser a friend's father, then at ten years old a brother up to when I was sixteen, and also a family friend at twelve years old until I left school. As well as being sexually abused I was being physically abused at school. I grew up knowing that something was wrong. I kept myself to myself in my own world, feeling that this must be normal because I didn't know anything else but the things which were going on in my life. As I got older I wanted to get out of what was going on but did not know how to. I felt everything was my fault. I felt guilty and dirty and evil the older I got, and felt that I was the only one it was happening to.

My life as an adult was affected. I didn't trust people. I didn't feel comfortable around people. My expectations were that the only time people wanted anything to do with me was to hurt me. I felt inferior and untouchable. There were times I hurt myself physically. I hated myself. I didn't deserve to be liked or loved and I kept people at arm's length. I wouldn't accept the love and help that were offered as I didn't know how to accept it or allow them into my life.

After going through the process of healing and realising things through finding Jesus in prayer, in Mass and in people, I was able to work through all the pain and I was encouraged to look at everything but doing it all with Jesus. As hard as it was, I was able with God's grace to forgive people, and through forgiving I found a certain amount of peace.

I thought that was the last of it but found I had to face the child in me and love her as I should. I was unable to love and accept and forgive myself. I found that I had put myself back in a prison cell with the door open instead of it being locked as it had been for years, thinking that I didn't have to go through anything else by opening up to what I had done. I thought everything else would heal and go away. I went through a lot of unwell feelings for weeks. I ended up again hurting myself and not eating or sleeping. I hadn't even managed to cook a meal. Housework was difficult. Nothing meant anything, not life—even being a mother meant nothing to me. If it wasn't for the children I know I would have considered taking my life as I had tried to do earlier in my life.. This went on for weeks.

Then Jesus revealed to the people I went to for help and prayer that part of my life I hadn't revealed. I was angry at first and felt betrayed as I thought my life wasn't being allowed to be private, as if different people were getting involved in my life. I realised later that I wasn't in the wrong and that I needed to be free from something and admit it. I was encouraged to go to the sacrament of Reconciliation, and by going to this I started to feel a sense of freedom and the fear that I had had started to disappear. I realised later that I was afraid to mention a few things. I knew while I sat with someone I trusted—I felt safe when I talked to them. As soon as I left their company I would be left to cope on my own. I knew I would have no-one to get comfort from, even though I knew that Jesus is always with us. I didn't want to go through any more pain and everything else that goes with it. I know I needed Jesus in body, not just in spirit. I thought I would get away without talking about some things and I found that I was wrong. I had nowhere to hide or to run away to because what I had hidden was revealed.

Through the freedom from the fear, I found I was able to admit to three abortions, at 15 years, 16 years and 19 years. This was the first time I had used the word 'abortion' instead of calling it 'the thing'. I know now that, as hard and painful as it is going to be, I won't be alone and I am willing to go through with it, knowing that it is with Jesus. Though I know I will have no-one in person in between the meetings to be there for me the way I would want someone to be there, I am hoping I will be able to turn to Jesus and to believe that Jesus and Mary will be there with their arms around me and be satisfied with knowing that.

The other thing that has come out through the above being revealed is not only the sexual abuse going on with a friend of the family, but that he was a photographer and when I started babysitting for his children, I was encouraged to go up to the dark room to be shown about developing. The abuse started and then he started to take photographs of me with no clothes on, and that led to some really awful acts. Then he would talk of Jesus and say that if I love Jesus I would do as I was told (I used to go to church and Sunday school with his wife). He would get me to pray to the evil one. He had candles lit to both Jesus and to a picture of the evil one. He used to draw blood from me. He used to mark my body and his with it. He used to put wax from candles over the lower part of my body and a lot more. When I told him I was pregnant I told him, thinking he has to stop. He broke the cross he kept in the dark room and told me that Jesus doesn't want anyone like me because what was inside me was evil, and that Jesus had allowed everything in my life because all my life is bad, always had been bad and always would be.

Going to the sacrament of Reconciliation and other prayers have freed me from the above and given me the freedom to open up what had kept me the prisoner of the past, and it feels good. I have got the motivation to live in the light and the truth. I know now I can't hide and run away. Opening up to everything has made a difference. I know I deserve more than I had ever thought.

The lady who wrote this testimony began to come to our home for prayer ministry nearly thirty years ago. One day, feeling that we were not getting past some block, we suggested that we go to the Blessed Sacrament Chapel of our church to pray. There it came to me that she had had an abortion. When I asked whether this was true, she became very angry and stormed out. Then she began to return and to make great progress, which included prayerful help in post-abortion counselling over a considerable period from the author of Chapter 8, to whom we had recommended her to go.

She moved to another part of the country many years ago, but wrote to us a number of times. Her first painful marriage had ended and she was now able to work through difficulties in her second marriage, and wrote of how their relationship was getting better and stronger. She wrote happily about her children and of the first grandchild soon to be born, and of how she had become a happier and more contented person and now felt secure in herself.

It was this same lady who wrote the heartfelt plea for children to have someone give them time and affection and listening and bring Jesus into their lives, which is reproduced at the beginning of Chapter 9. She knew from her own bitter experience that if people could be there for children and bring the saving power of Jesus to them in a real way, then they might be spared much suffering in later life.

Acknowledgement

I am grateful to the author of this testimony and to another wonderful lady who was herself sexually abused as a child by several men, for helping me with the wording of this paper.

Notes

1   A. Guile, *Journey into Wholeness: Prayer for Inner Healing – An Essential Ministry of The Church* (Leominster: Gracewing, 2013).

2   *Ibid.*, pp. 125–126.

3   P. Sandford, *Healing Victims of Sexual Abuse* (Tulsa: Victory House Publishers, 1988); L. Heitritter and J. Vought, *Helping Victims of Sexual Abuse*, (Minneapolis: Bethany, 2006).

4   L. Heitritter and J. Vought, *Helping Victims of Sexual Abuse*, (Minneapolis: Bethany, 2006).

5   Guile, *Journey into Wholeness*, pp. 135–143.

14

Healing the Wounds Hidden behind Dissociative Identity Disorder

Alan Guile and Margaret Wright

This chapter discusses how to minister to a person suffering from dissociative identity disorder (DID), formerly known as multiple personality disorder. It begins by outlining how some people may be so severely traumatised in childhood that they learn to escape internally by their minds splitting into separate parts (or 'alters', alternative personalities). The stories are summarised of four women, three of them taken from books in which they wrote these stories and one who wrote for the present work (see Appendix 1 at the end of this book). The damage can be so deep that full healing may take as much as ten years of powerful prayer ministry attending regular sessions, perhaps residentially at times. However they can then be used by God in wonderful ways to bring healing to other sufferers.

Introduction

B y the early 1960s the idea of the child ego state was being talked about as transactional analysis developed. Many people have become aware since then that they themselves, and/or others whom they observed, can suddenly and unexpectedly be triggered into speaking and acting out the emotions of some early childhood experience(s).

More recently it has been realised that for some people who were subjected to many severe early traumas and abuse, their natural defences resulted in their mind being so divided as to compartmentalizing some areas of pain, as if they were other distinct personalities, in order that they could survive and function as best they could. This was at first called multiple personality disorder but is now known as dissociative identity disorder (DID).

Carolyn Bramhall explains more fully as she writes:

> The little child would 'go away' in her mind and perhaps watch from a safe distance....or maybe go right away into a safe world of

her own creation. Another part of her would come out into the real world to take the abuse or trauma. That is what 'dissociation' is all about—a separating of the self from reality. Painful memories are all still there... but the mind itself divides into segments in order to protect her sanity and enable her to carry on a somewhat normal life, completely amnesic to the harmful events.[1]

Thus different present-day triggers can result in a variety of different reactions stemming from a different time and painful experience in early life, each seeming to come from a separate personality or identity.

This condition has been very controversial among Christians and among psychiatrists and psychologists. Dr Rosik, a psychologist who was relatively unaware of the controversial nature of the diagnosis when he began to work with Carolyn Bramhall, writes:

Exposure to DID has a unique ability to threaten our pre-existing views of human consciousness as a unitary entity, and hence it can create very emotional reactions in both the church and psychiatric communities. However in the past fifteen years (from about 1990) dissociation has gained wider acceptance among professionals who work with trauma, where it is understood to be a severe form of post-traumatic stress reaction often associated with disorganized parent-child attachment patterns. Studies that have attempted to validate DID patient accounts of childhood abuse have found high rates of confirmation for "ordinary" traumas and lower rates of verification for ritual abuse accounts. Thus, in my estimation, there is little convincing evidence that DID sufferers are mainly suggest-ible people who are making up false memories for attention.[2]

Dr Rosik also writes that:

The most troublesome and potentially harmful issue concerning the spiritual care of DID patients is that of exorcism or deliverance prayer. The crux of the problem is the significant overlap among the symptoms Christians consider to be related to demonization and the indicators of DID. This has resulted in many persons with DID experiencing harmful expulsion rituals as well-meaning but uninformed ministers attempt to expel a part of the individual's mind.[3] Nevertheless he does not rule out the need for deliverance prayers when conducted in a sensitive and informed manner.[4]

He also describes:

The necessity of both psychological and spiritual care in the treatment of trauma-related disorders in general and DID in particular, with the DID patient's sense of acceptance by and belonging to a larger community.[5]

God has created us with the capacity and ability to psychologically and emotionally defend ourselves and our souls against even the worst of traumas, so that we might survive, recover and rebuild our lives. DID begins in early childhood as a part of this defence as the child learns to dissociate from the painful situation, thus creating a separate identity (or alter) which can come to the surface while the trauma is occurring and then goes away again. Many alters can be created as new traumas and abuse occur over time. The average number of these alters identified at diagnosis is 2–4 but can rise to 13–15 during treatment, and for a very few, has passed 100. Some statistics on the Internet show that the rate of DID among the general population is 0.1–1% but that as many as 7% may have undiagnosed DID. Up to 99% of those diagnosed had overpowering or even life-threatening disturbances before the age of nine.

As life progresses some afflicted people begin to realize that these natural defences, which were so necessary for survival, are no longer helpful but are keeping them away from deeper inner peace in developing relationships with others and with God. They may then seek the help of Christians who can pray for healing. Others, through pain in their adult life and relationships need professional help, perhaps after suicide attempts and may also meet Christians who can bring the help and healing of Christ. One such Christian, Dr Neil Anderson, writes:

When I first came across DID, I saw a mature woman switch before my eyes into a four-year-old girl, as if someone had simply changed the software in a computer. It was an unnerving experience. I suddenly found myself talking to a child in the body of a previously normal woman. Yet the voice, the language, the body language and the emotions were all those of a four-year-old.[6]

Not everyone who has listened to and prayed with someone experiencing some degree of severity of DID, would describe the experience in exactly that way. Individuals and the depth and severity of their traumatic experiences are infinitely variable. However some of the experiences of Christians or professional counsellors, led to them believing that they were witnessing effects of demons. People in some churches tried to get rid of the various identities or personalities, thinking that they were demons. This mistake was reinforced because some victims thought that the different identities sounded like 'voices' in their head.

Thankfully, there are now a number of stories of how people who have suffered long and deeply through the early traumas resulting in DID, have been brought gradually, and with many ups and downs, to a deep peace through the loving ministry of Christians, so that they are now able to help others. Some of these stories are reviewed here in the hope that this will lead to more Holy Spirit-led ministry to many others.

Carolyn's Story

Carolyn, until 1992 known to most people as Julie, appeared to enjoy an unremarkable childhood in a typical, loving family. Outwardly at least, normal life continued as she graduated from Bible College, married, had two children and worked full-time in Christian ministry, unaware that her mind was splintered. She wrote:

> I continued to function with a corporate mind, successfully filtering out all that was unpleasant, fearful, terrible, and ciphering those experiences into separate parts, sending each type of memory, feeling or emotion to the part of me created to hold it. That enabled me to lead a comparatively tranquil internal existence.[7]

She first became aware of internal confusion as she committed her life to Christ, aged 14, praying, 'Dear God I know about You, but God—do you know about me?' Satisfied that He did, generally she put aside these feelings of confusion and delighted in telling others about the love of her life, Jesus! But as the years passed, it became increasingly difficult to ignore the growing sense that she was different from her peers. Although she knew God's love was sufficient, she still craved love from other Christians and felt guilty that her faith must be so weak if she needed this tangible evidence of His love.

In her second year at college, her roommate became spiritually distressed and it fell to Carolyn to care for her. One night she reports seeing a manifestation of what she recognized as an evil spirit around her friend's bed. 'I knew that I knew but didn't know why I knew'. The familiarity of the creature disturbed her and awakened a terror, deep within her, and an audible, crying child—sometimes whimpering, sometimes screaming; but always desperate. At about this time she became to feel uneasy in the company of her parents.

For the remainder of her time at Bible College Carolyn struggled with poor health—physical and emotional—and feeling she did not deserve to eat, developed anorexia. But she tried to maintain a 'normal' front and met John, whom she later married.

They worked together ministering to young people, realising the dream of their college days, but still Carolyn felt unfulfilled. Although she was a successful minister, she also identified as 'a crying, lonely child'. It was at a Vineyard conference, after the Holy Spirit was invited to come in power, that she exhibited urgent wails of gut-wrenching distress. Neither she nor her husband understood what had happened, and what continued to happen at other meetings. She was eventually perceived as an embarrassment and subjected to hours of humiliating deliverance ministry.

Picking up the pieces and trying to continue to lead a normal life, Carolyn moved to the USA with her two young children to continue ministry with her husband. They experienced great financial struggles and whenever she was confronted with difficult situations she would 'check out', physically collapsing, wherever she was.

This heralded an extended period of hospital admissions, therapy and prayer ministry, self-harm, and thoughts of suicide as fragmented memories began to surface. When her husband decided to return to England with their two young children, for some inexplicable reason Carolyn did not feel safe at the thought of going home, so remained in California for a further three years but maintaining contact with the family.

She was in her early thirties, preparing to face life alone in a foreign country when her psychologist, Dr Christopher Rosik, diagnosed her as suffering from Multiple Personality Disorder (MPD) now more commonly known as Dissociative Identity Disorder (DID). He also suspected she had been the victim of satanic ritual abuse (SRA), involving family members, which explained her terror whenever she considered returning to England.

In her later book, *Connecting the Fragments*, Carolyn describes DID:

> Particularly grim childhood experiences lead an abused child to develop unique ways of coping. They have to shield themselves from the full impact of the trauma. Some have been so severely traumatised that they have had to learn to escape by internally 'going away'. In some cases their minds have consequently split

into separate parts (which we call alters, or alternative personalities), and we call this fragmentation dynamic 'dissociation'.[8]

As Carolyn's trust in her psychologist deepened, several alters made
themselves known. Eventually 109 named entities were identified, each
with special responsibility to protect her by coping with a different kind
of abuse, or handling a different overwhelming emotion. Their common
goal was her survival. She had been told she would die if she ever revealed
the dark secret of the abuse, so they collaborated to suppress her memory.

In her book *Am I a Good Girl Yet?*, Carolyn describes her dominant alters:[9]

- **Carolyn** was the strongest alter, a capable adult who cared for all
  the others, especially the children. She presented a calm front to
  the world and eventually became who Carolyn is today, after all
  the other alters became integrated into her.

- **JuJu** was a 5 year-old girl whose function was to carry extreme
  fear. Affectionate and spiritually perceptive, she was spontane-
  ous, communicative and disinhibited once she felt safe and
  eventually stayed 'out' for long periods of time enjoying unthreat-
  ening company.

- **J. C.** was a 14 year-old girl whose function was to carry anger over
  the injustice of abuse. She was a bit of a tomboy, strong-willed
  and volatile. She actively participated in deliverance sessions.

- **Meg** was a 4 year-old girl whose function was to evade perceived
  entrapment. She would choose light, loose-fitting clothes 'just in
  case' and constantly removed footwear, ready to make a bid for
  freedom when threatened. She was constantly fearful and suspi-
  cious and would often disrupt therapy sessions by running away.

- **Stormie** was a 12 year-old girl whose function was to preserve the
  dark secret by getting Carolyn out of England and frustrating
  plans for her to return home. She was uncooperative and disrup-
  tive in therapy sessions, loyal to her role.

The alters generally fell into clusters, each with a different role and
purpose. Most were children but some were adolescents or capable adults.
Most, but not all, were female. One male alter, Elliot, was created to
protect Carolyn from the vulnerability of her gender. As she writes:

> Most of them were aware of me as the host personality and one to
> be protected at all costs, mainly from knowing the truth about the
> abuse. The whole point of the separate parts, separated by walls
> of amnesia, was to keep me from ever knowing what ghastly things
> men and women had chosen to inflict on me.[10]

There were occasions when demons would pose as alters but these were
soon discovered and cast out. Alters are love-starved—these demons did
not respond to the light of God's love, except to reveal their true nature.

Dr Rosik encouraged the parts to communicate with each other and
with him. Once their stories were told and the 'amnesic barriers' breached,
integration could begin, but it was about 10 years before this was
completed. None of the alters was lost, rather they became new components of Carolyn's personality, noticeable each time one became integrated.

Fragmentation is learned behaviour and can be habit-forming. After
3 and a half years of living on her own in California, with some alters
integrating, Carolyn decided to return to England and confront the
memories of the abuse where it occurred but it was another seven years
before she was a fully integrated person.

In that time she slowly re-learned the whole process of becoming a
wife and mother again, meeting resistance from extended family members
who were protective of the husband and children whom she was perceived
to have abandoned.

Meg, Elliot, Stormie and JuJu were among the last alters to become
integrated. Once Elliot was reassured that Carolyn no longer needed
protection, he cooperated. However Carolyn was reluctant to 'say
goodbye' to JuJu, worried that without her she would have to learn to face
fear alone. But she also realised that with Jesus at her side, she would
never really be alone, so eventually it was Carolyn who invited her to
become a real and lasting part of the core 'me'. Minutes after JuJu's
integration I had an urgent need to play.

Today Carolyn is living in England with her husband and heads up
Heart for Truth, a Christian support organisation and wrote more recently:

> Heart for Truth is all about encouraging and equipping Christian
> leaders to recognise the huge, untapped potential of those in our
> churches who are hurting or marginalised. There are so many in
> our churches struggling with issues around trauma, depression,
> mental illness or anxiety. God can use ordinary Christians to give

them the confidence to walk into real freedom which is their birthright in Christ.[11]

Jennifer's Story

Jennifer and her husband were both in leadership in their church fellowship and outwardly did not seem to have any problems. However during a weekend meeting, as she began to speak about something she thought she had already worked through, she was surprised by the intensity of pain which suddenly surfaced and she could not continue to speak. She felt like a helpless little child trying to understand what had happened. Some in the group suggested that she had not forgiven those involved but she knew this was not the case and wrote:

> During the next year similar situations arose with increasing regularity. It was as if a child within was speaking in my place expressing buried pain, fear or anger.[12]

She describes her parents as deeply rejected people who found it difficult to express love and affection for their own children. Her father would become very angry if they upset their mother because she was mentally ill with deep depression and was emotionally very unstable. Although Jennifer did not have major traumatic memories, there were several incidents where she was afraid with no one there to protect or comfort her. She grew up thinking she was a nuisance, stupid, ugly and not worthy of love and that everything was somehow her fault.

Jennifer describes her childhood and teenage years until at 18 she became a Christian and experienced the power of the Holy Spirit. After university she wanted to serve God full-time though she was still struggling with fear and low self-esteem. It was not until later, having given birth to two children, that she first felt an adult herself, and realized how very immature emotionally she had been, relating to adults in the mode of a child. This led her to open up to the pastor of her local church and gradually to trust him enough to share some of her darkest fear and pain. However he began to abuse her. She had become vulnerable to him because one of her child alters related to him through her need for fatherly affection, so that what he did was like a form of child abuse. The pastor compounded this by later implying that Jennifer had given full and free consent to his actions, thus burdening her with feeling that she had played an equal part and had equal responsibility for it. She felt a failure who had let God down and was now worthless to Him.

Later, after she had married, she shared this at a weekend for married couples, but the counsellors and others assumed that she had been a willing participant, thus adding to her feelings of guilt. Some years later during ministry at a healing centre, she began to understand her reactions and was able to forgive herself and receive forgiveness and some healing from God. She realized that as a child she learned to bury pain and separate off memories and even parts of her personality as a way of coping with traumatic events.

After a few years of ups and downs trying to serve God, she shared what was happening with her new pastor and some people in her fellowship. With their help she recognized that one alter needed to feel safe enough to surface and to share things she had kept hidden for so long, and the gentle patience and encouragement of one woman in particular allowed this to happen. She understood that an alter is not a demon but part of the whole person who needs to be accepted, welcomed and listened to, so that she can share the burden which she has been carrying, and that although there may be need for repentance and deliverance, first must come understanding and acceptance.

After several months, various alters were ready to become part of the whole person and no longer separate. If she had been asked previously whether she heard voices in her head she would have denied it because all the voices were hers. Now, however, as each alter that had been identified was also integrated, the intense internal arguing diminished as each one became healed and added their personality to the whole person.

A stage of severe depression then followed as Jennifer felt that a gulf had opened up between herself and God the Father as she became very afraid of His anger. She realised that those things which the alters had been protecting her from were no longer hidden from her. Although she had forgiven the abusive pastor, she was still carrying the fear and guilt from the way that situation had affected her relationship with God. It was now time to face the pain and work through it.

At this time God brought a new pastor into her life who had experience of helping people with DID. Until then, most of the counselling she had received was from women, but while she did not doubt their integrity, the child within her had come to believe that women say what they think you want to hear, or what will keep you quiet. Now, however, another alter needed to hear what a father would say, however difficult it might be for her. This new pastor helped her to see she needed to explore some of the negative emotions that were surfacing, rather than just to push them away, as she embraced the truth of God's word with her mind and spirit, accepting these reactions and looking at where they were coming from. She realised that she had been seeing reactions such as fear and anger as entities that were separate from her and renouncing them as sin, rather than seeing that they were part of herself that needed healing. It was a form of self-rejection. That brought to light another alter arising from a painful experience caused by a headmaster when she was seven. The healing of this opened the way for her to feel safe to share other things which had been buried.

In the next stage, God reminded her of several things that had happened for which she had forgiven people, but now He was focusing her attention on how she had felt at the time. As He brought to mind each scene where she had learned to bury her emotions, she now began to release deep inner pain that she had not known was there. Much of the pain was not over what had taken place, but rather over the love and nurture that had been missing which had left a wound in her heart. As God showed what she had believed about herself in those situations, He replaced the lies with the truth of how He sees her in His love for her.

Next she found that she could not pray about the abusive pastor because each time she tried to do so, she would suddenly become terrified of God's anger. There was a deep insecurity because she believed that God had abandoned her. After several days of crying out she wrote about all this to the new pastor, although fearing that he would reject her, but she was desperate for an answer. As soon as she had the courage to do this, she felt God's presence in a way she had not experienced for a long time. The pastor replied, assuring her that God was not angry with her and would not reject her either. It was only after this that she realised what a deep wound it had caused and how much it had affected her relationship with the Father. The enemy had kept her bound for years by his lies about God's love. A verse which became important was, 'I will give them singleness of heart and action, so that they will always fear me for their own good and the good of their children after them.' (Jer 32:39).

Steve Goss, who has helped many people with DID, commented on Jennifer's story:

It's important to understand however that people are not in bondage to the traumatic event itself but to the lies they have come to believe as a result of that event. For example, those who have been sexually abused often come to believe as a result of their experiences that they are dirty. It's the feeling of dirtiness rather than the event itself which becomes the main problem. The truth is that no child of God is dirty any more—we have been washed completely clean by the blood of Jesus. Their healing comes when they are able to recognise the lie and start to believe the truth. Jennifer's dissociation was designed to protect her from looking at the truth of what actually happened because it was too painful for her to face.[13]

That situation can begin to change when we learn who we are in Christ, that we are loved and accepted unconditionally and are completely safe in God's hands. We can then cease to be a product of our past experiences and become a product of what Christ accomplished on the cross. This, it is said, usually takes several months for people with DID, as they work through the issues and learn to allow God to renew their minds. Experiences of other people outlined in this chapter show that it can sometimes take years.

As with all the God-given mechanisms of burying pain to protect us whilst we are undergoing severe trauma, mainly in childhood and early life, these defences begin to break down during adulthood and reveal problems.

If we are faced with helping someone with deep-rooted problems we need faith that the Gospel really works, a real compassion for the hurting person and some basic biblical principles. Steve Goss continues to explain that it's important to understand that we can't 'fix' anyone... forgive for them, repent for them or have faith for them. We need to support them and encourage them to come to Jesus.

Sarah's Story

Sarah had never had any memory of her first 18 years and spent her life striving to make everything look good on the outside, while keeping hidden what she believed was bad on the inside. She had a good husband and two children but feelings of guilt and self-hatred were eating her up.[14]

At 36, after a serious suicide attempt she was admitted to a psychiatric hospital and kept in a locked ward for 5 months. After other treatments had failed to work, her psychiatrist's best suggestion was ECT. At that

215

point, in 1996, her team rector contacted Ellel Grange and she was invited to attend a ten-day healing retreat. She had become a Christian through attending an infant baptism course.

She had always longed for some expression of love from her mother, but now through prayer ministry she began to accept the truth that her mother had never loved her. Later on she recovered excruciating memories of her father sexually abusing her from age 3 to 18, but it was never having any comfort from her mother that was ultimately the root of the deepest pain in her life.

She returned from the retreat to the psychiatric hospital and was to spend two more months there attending from 9—5, five days a week but they allowed her to begin to make regular trips to Ellel Grange or one of the other centres in the South. During these trips she was at first locked into trying to be 'good' and please her counsellors. Gradually the frozen place within her began to thaw in a hunger for love. Love felt wrong and bad. She felt 'I'm bad, I'm wicked, I'm dirty, I'm vile, I hate myself, I don't deserve to be loved.' She was ashamed of the intensity of the craving to be loved. It felt degrading as an adult to long to be hugged, touched and mothered. She fought against and refused the love God knew she needed and which was pouring out through the Ellel team.

For three years she hid indoors either at home, or at the hospital or in a building at Ellel Grange where she did not mix with others who were staying there, and she felt trapped at the bottom of a deep dark well. When she returned home after a visit she would go straight to her bedroom where she had slept alone for years.

As the prayer ministry continued it seemed to her that she was gradually climbing step by step up the inner wall of the well, and that she had reached a door which had been locked for many years and it was now time to open it. It seemed as though she fell asleep but the team observing her, noticed her posture became that of a traumatised child curled up in the corner of the sofa. It was as if the opening door revealed a lost and terrified child. She began to let out screams and sobs that had needed to be released for years. It wasn't just the pain of her parents' abuse that was locked in this part of her, but the injustice of all that she had missed out as a little child. She had been robbed of normality, the freedom to run and play and be with other children. This was a broken part of her locked in DID carrying the experiences, memory and truth of the first three years of life, and broken off from her by the onset of her father's abuse beginning.

She realised the truth that not only had her mother never wanted or loved her, but had blamed and punished her for her father abusing her. At 3 years of age in the extreme moment of abuse, she had broken away from the 3 year old part which held all the memory, pain and anguish of her parents' depravity and cruelty. She began to have graphic and horrifying flashbacks of abuse, and became physically very unwell. It was difficult to sleep or eat and she felt extremely suicidal.

As the team continued to pray, one by one, six more 'prison doors' were revealed behind which were six more 'parts' or alters:- a baby, two more child parts aged 9 and 12, and three teenager parts aged 16, 17 and 18. Each part held the memories of all that had happened in her life from the time of the previous breaking up till the age she then was. Each part was separate and until God later on began to draw them together, there was no flow of information between one part and another.

At 18 she suffered the most extreme abuse and in this part of herself, she felt so dirty and that the abuse was her fault. She hated herself with a vengeance and was intent on punishing and harming herself and intensely suicidal. When sufficiently recovered physically, the team sensitively called the adult Sarah to account where she had chosen in her heart to go against the will of God, so that with a repentant heart she could realise that she had hurt God and that it is never right to sink into self-pity.

At first she distanced herself from the cruel unjust reality of her life and argued with counsellors that these child parts were not real, convinced that there was nothing wrong with her. The team lovingly confronted her with questions, and she began to understand that she had abandoned herself because in her adult state she had locked away parts of herself as a child and a teenager. At first she did not want to embrace the parts which carried the horrors of a past which she did not want to be hers.

The majority of time spent by the team was with the adult Sarah who needed to relinquish denial and unreality, and embrace the whole truth of her past, so that she could take right responsibility, and trust God for the part, however small, which she herself had taken in choosing to separate from the child parts with the traumas. She realised she needed a change of heart so as to see the fragmented parts with compassion and become able to embrace them, and understand that freedom from fears, obsessions, self-hatred and suicidal tendencies could only come when previously locked doors remained fully open and she began to love and accept herself.

The counsellors also spent time encouraging each broken part to talk about her feelings and receive God's love. It was a battle as she was angry asking, 'Why didn't He help me?' They explained that Jesus was there but unable to overrule her parents' choices. They helped her cooperate with Jesus as He took more and more of her pain into His suffering on the cross.

Fourteen months after her first session at Ellel Grange she was released from psychiatric care into the care of Ellel Ministries. The psychiatrist realised that if the full truth of brokenness had been exposed at the hospital the pain could have easily tipped her over the edge. It was only as God patiently and gently revealed His unconditional love, acceptance and faithfulness that He provided her the strength to face painful realities.

As the fragmented parts received tremendous healing they became ready to be joined together again. There were many aspects and stages in the ongoing process of integration leading to greater wholeness. These included, forgiving herself, dealing with false guilt, forgiveness of parents, self-hatred, uncovering festering wounds, facing up to how she really felt, learning to trust the team and discovering what it really meant to forgive. She had to learn that she couldn't do any of this for herself but had to depend totally on God's power.

She realised that as all the pretence was stripped away God was bringing emotions to life. Inside, where there should have been a solid core of personal self-worth coming from a life built on a foundation of love, there was instead a great chasm of emptiness, with an intense craving for something or someone to fill up this space. As she felt the injustice, pain, loss etc. she was expressing anger, fear and many other emotions, and God showed her that these strong reactions in the present were fuelled by her reactions to the past. As counsellors encouraged her to face painful reality she had a driving compulsion to self-harm. At times she wanted to smash the room or kill someone. The fear of unleashing the pain was even bigger than the pain itself. They helped her to release some of it physically without doing any harm. Over time she learned not to act it out but to tell her counsellors who then helped her to turn to God and instead of running down the well-worn escape paths, to learn how to give the pain to Jesus. They taught her about the powers of evil operating through people and how she could stand against them as they prayed for her to be set free.

She would easily swing from denial to an extreme of self-pity, venting her anger and pain against the counsellors. Eventually they had to confront her saying 'this is sin', which caused her huge fear because it was as if a rug of love had suddenly been pulled from under her. It took time to work through all the resulting confusion as for example she learned the truth of 'If we confess our sins He is faithful and just and will forgive our sins and purify us from all unrighteousness' (1 Jn 1:9) and 'By His wounds we are healed' (Is 53:5).

Even after all this, once she was away from her counsellors her feelings again blocked off and OCD had a strong grip again. There were still real issues blocking the way to full healing in total reliance on God, even though the seven fragmented parts had been rescued and healed and there were no more suicidal urges. Deep down there was still a conviction that she was bad and her inner child would hang on to this and use others to satisfy her selfish insatiable cravings, as she strove to be a 'good person'. She was not yet free to be herself. God needed to reach the inner child so that she could develop and grow emotionally and the fragmented parts could be integrated to the adult Sarah. She realised that she must walk on her own with God and a verse stood out. 'Who is this who is coming up from the wilderness, leaning upon her Beloved' (Sg 8:5).

Eventually it was suggested that she should attend a series of ten weekends at Glyndley Manor, the Ellel centre near her home. After a struggle she agreed which began a new journey learning to build relationships with others.

Just over ten years after Sarah's first visit to Ellel Grange, she revisited the centre and was now finally ready to release to Christ the pain, injustice and anger which had been locked inside. She now wanted to come to God with all that she is, holding nothing back anymore, and she was able to go home learning 'to be' rather than being driven 'to do'. Three months later on her next visit, the joining together of her fragmented parts finally took place. For the first time she had full memory of her life and though she could still feel pain she was no longer afraid because she now knew God as her Abba Father, totally loving and accepting her. Through the training of Glyndley Manor she has become involved in teaching and ministering to others from time to time at the various Ellel Centres.

Ann's Story

Appendix 1 of this book outlines significant events which have taken place during the life of Ann, and how she had been desperately hurt and let down by many people in childhood and in marriage. Over the years Ann has sought out a number of opportunities to receive prayer ministry from different people, and gradually more healing has been taking place, going deeper as time has gone on.

Recently she had the opportunity to read the story of Sarah in her book.[15] It was as if a new window was uncovered to bring more light into areas of darkness, and she was given not only new insights but also fresh encouragement and hope. She had never before heard about parts of oneself becoming cut off from the rest of the person as part of the defence against intolerable pain, but she immediately knew this new information was needed for her to be healed more completely. She realised that, sadly, some people had endured even worse experiences than she herself had done, and could still be healed by Christ, though it might be a very long-drawn-out process with many ups and downs.

She was now aware that she herself had been placed in such pain that parts of her had split off so as to survive. Sarah had no memories before the age of eighteen; those before eight were just darkness and fear, particularly being terrified by her mother. This appears to be the age when the first splitting off occurred, unless there was one at an earlier age, of which she is still not aware. A further split took place at the age of ten. There was so much pain and darkness between eight and ten that Ann was not aware of one single major factor because so much was happening. There was sexual abuse by an uncle; her sister left home without Ann being told why she had gone; her mother was deceitful and cruel and unfaithful to her husband so that the children knew about the boyfriend and were constantly being told, 'Don't tell anyone!' Her father, who Ann discovered later had known about it, kept saying, 'You don't talk to anyone about things?' Thus Ann became terrified of contact with people and cut herself off as much as possible. She froze if people spoke to her and tried to avoid anyone looking directly at her.

The experiences between ten and thirteen brought another split at this latter age. There were many fights between her parents, and many beltings. There was sexual abuse from a local man as well as her uncle. She has a vivid memory of walking to the bus stop as her mother left home and took one sister with her. Ann was desperately afraid of the siblings being parted and pleaded with her father to keep them together. He put the major responsibility for this to happen on Ann assuming duties beyond her age. She was told not to talk to anyone about her mother having left. She struggled to survive at school.

After the first experience of receiving some affirmation from one or two teachers, another split occurred at fifteen, when she faced leaving school with terror. She had no self-confidence or self-worth, had no experience of meeting with or working with other people and had no suitable clothes to wear. Thus in self-defence and fear, she chose to stay at home, where she became a prisoner. She was unpaid, had no rights, was not allowed to have any opinions, criticised, ignored, and had even her most basic needs neglected. She had more and more responsibilities beyond her age piled upon her by all her siblings as well as her father. Her father always ignored any of her attempts to ask for help. Nobody offered to help her, and she was made a scapegoat by the others, which has continued throughout her life. There were regular phone calls to say that her mother had made another attempt to commit suicide.

There was sexual abuse from two of her mother's boyfriends, as well as a friend of her father. She was desperately lonely, rejected, unloved, abandoned, ignored and ridiculed. Ann felt completely flattened, and had no sense of existing. All of this lead to a further splitting off at 19, after which she began to seek some work and life outside the family.

Through all of this dreadful childhood, Ann knew Our Lord was with her and she would talk to Jesus and Our Lady about what was going on at the time. She now realizes that even from being a small child, God was giving her gifts of desiring to protect others of her siblings, so as to stop them from experiencing what she herself was going through. She became a peacemaker and it is now clear that her attempts to exercise these gifts played a significant role in enabling her to survive the pain. As God is progressively healing her, she finds peace in bringing help and healing to others, and her gifts of perceptiveness and sensitivity to where others are in their journey, and to connecting with others, are growing and very valuable to the Body of Christ. There has been real progress in her healing and freedom as she uses her gifts for others since she became aware of being dissociative.

Healing and Integration

In earlier parts of the ministry to a dissociative person, those involved in the ministry may be led by the Holy Spirit in ways which are similar to those whose hurts have not resulted in the personality splitting. As memories and emotions surface, Jesus can be invited to transform memories, and comfort the sufferer, touching their deep wounds and through

His Precious Blood drawing progressively more and more of their pain into His suffering on the cross. When they become ready to do so, they can invite Him to give them the grace with which to forgive others, self and God, where their perception is of being further let down by Him. Through the Scriptures and the actions of the Holy Spirit, their minds, with the damaged thinking, can gradually be renewed and cleansed so that they can come to know who they are in Christ, and can accept and rejoice in the wonder of their own being. As they come to recognise God's gifts and love within them, they frequently desire to do God's will in serving others. As the Holy Spirit works in those people with DID, perhaps over several years, through loving, accepting ministry in the Body of Christ, healing can gradually take place in the various alters. There is a struggle in the recovery of the sufferer as they begin to open more of themselves as with God's grace they allow a safe reduction of defences no longer needed.

Eventually there can be sufficient healing within alters and in the mind of the host personality that integration can begin. This can happen in many different ways and be different for each person, and even for various alters in the one person. The Lord can bring each sufferer to an awareness of when and how it can take place.

It can happen gradually as each alter feels safe and secure and able to release whatever secrets or emotions they have kept hidden from the host personality. It may be conscious and thought out or it may happen spontaneously, but it will only be when the person is comfortable with the alters integrating.

Some people choose to be alone when it happens. Others, knowing that they have become ready to accept and embrace one or more of their parts, and recognising that they can't do it for themselves but depend totally upon Christ, ask others to pray for God to do the work of growing up each fragmented part and unite them into the one person.

Both Carolyn and Sarah write of how some number of alters may choose to integrate together, or into one of the others in preparation for the full integration. Carolyn experienced many varied ways in which her 109 alters integrated, including one who insisted on integrating when Carolyn was under water during a baptism-type prayer where the alter boldly announced that she had now chosen to follow Jesus for the rest of her life. Carolyn had already been baptised but this particular alter had been hidden at that time, so did not feel she had made a personal commitment to Christ. As Carolyn emerged from the water, there was no sign of this alter as a separate entity, although Carolyn immediately became aware of new aspects to her personality.

Whatever ways God develops and deepens the process of healing and integration, all parts are integral to the person, and God enables each to be welcomed, accepted and loved, recognising their own worth and the wonder of being one with the whole person.

Carolyn has written about the post-integration period. The feelings may not be easy to cope with, particularly at first. With any kind of inner healing, there is always challenge in becoming a new person, with all the changes and responsibilities to live a new life in Christ. This challenge is much greater for a dissociative people. Some may experience a deep sense of loss when an alter seems to 'disappear', however, as Carolyn explains:

> The only real loss is the complex way of dealing with life, for in reality, nothing whatever has really been lost. All the components of the alter are still there, their memories, preferences, traits and characteristics will still all be retained even as they are now part of the whole.[16]

One of those helped by Carolyn wrote:

> I went from being DID straight into having to be adult. Most people grow into being an adult and can make mistakes along the way. That didn't happen for me and therefore having to be this adult was daunting and overwhelming. There were things I should have known how to do, or how to be, and there was just a blank space in front of me because I hadn't had the chance to learn whatever it is you learn as a teenager and young adult. So everything became totally overwhelming.[17]

However, as Carolyn observes, although it may only take the person hours or days to learn to embrace the new personality, adjust and discover some of the complex ways of dealing with life, support, encouragement and teaching will still be needed. There may be battles with lies, deeply embedded in the mind. There will be the need for much reassurance and help with handling emotions which previously had been siphoned off to one or more alters, in order to avoid the pain and discomfort associated with them.

But as these wounded people experience greater healing, and as they step out of their self-imposed isolation, it is imperative the Church takes responsibility for her own and becomes that 'field hospital after battle'. As Carolyn urges:

Let's walk boldly on, arm in arm with those who are most wounded, knowing that as we move on together Jesus will be mending the fragmentation of both their shattered minds and our shattered communities.[18]

Notes

[1] C. Bramhall, *Am I a Good Girl Yet?* (Oxford: Monarch Books, 2005).

[2] *Ibid.*; C. H. Rosik, "When Discernment Fails: The case for Outcome Studies on Exorcism", *Journey of Theology and Psychology*, 24, (1997), pp. 354–363; Idem, "Some Effects of World View on the Theory and Treatment of Dissociative Identity Disorder", *Journal of Psychology and Christianity*, 19/2, (2000), pp. 166–180.

[3] Bramhall, *Am I a Good Girl Yet?*

[4] C. H. Rosik, Possession Phenomena in North America: A Case Study with Ethnographic, Psychodynamic, Religious and Clinical Implications, *Journey of Trauma and Dissociation*, 5/1, (2004), pp. 49–76.

[5] Bramhall, *Am I a Good Girl Yet?*; J. G. Freisen, E. J. Wilder, A. Bierling, R. Koepke & M. Poole, *The Life Model: Living from the Heart Jesus Gave You* (Bel Air CA: Shepherd's House, 1999).

[6] E. Mitson (ed), *Songs of Freedom—Stories of Lives Transformed by the Deep Power of Christ* (Oxford: Monarch Books, 2005).

[7] Bramhall, *Am I a Good Girl Yet?*

[8] C. Bramhall, *Connecting the Fragments—Freedom for People with Dissociative Identity Disorder in the Context of the Local Church*, (Bloomington IN: Author House, 2014).

[9] Bramhall, *Am I a Good Girl Yet?*

[10] *Ibid.*

[11] Bramhall, *Connecting the Fragments*. See also http://www.h4t.org.uk/about/heart-for-truth.

[12] Mitson, *Songs of Freedom*

[13] Mitson, *Songs of Freedom*, pp. 153–156.

[14] S. Shaw, *Sarah—From an Abusive Childhood and the Depths of Suicidal Despair to a Life of Hope and Freedom* (Lancaster: Sovereign World, 2009).

[15] *Ibid.*

[16] Bramhall, *Am I a Good Girl Yet?*

[17] Bramhall, *Connecting the Fragments*.

[18] *Ibid.*

15

Healing among Women involved in Prostitution

Sophia Burley

In this chapter Sophia shares with us her experience of a most amazing healing ministry among young women who, through the dreadful circumstances of their lives, felt that the only way they could support their own children or their families back in the countries they came from, was through street prostitution. The stories she relates of the women who accepted her love and support on the streets speak loudly to us of the unconditional love and mercy of God, who remains faithful to his children, and who sees not the prostitute but his beloved daughter. Sophia shows us how to see as God sees. We also get a glimpse of why Jesus was able to say to the Scribes and Pharisees who saw themselves as the sinless ones: 'The tax collectors and the prostitutes are making their way into the kingdom of God before you'. (Mt 21:31)

The Call

In January 2009 God sowed a vision in my heart to minister to women involved in prostitution under the name of Women on the Frontline Ministries with a covenant scripture based on Matthew 22: 37–39.

By faith I stepped out. I knew deep within me that I wanted to be a person who would go beyond the four walls of the church to share the love of Jesus Christ. I knew I was a hands-on practical type of person but never would have thought the vision and passion within me would be to minister to women involved in street-based prostitution.

Early Experiences

My initial thought was 'God, what do I know about women in this industry?' 'What could I do?' Are you sure?' But anyway, by faith a group of us went out on the streets to known areas of activity usually called red-light districts. Our first time of going out we went with hot drinks and the love of Christ but realised soon after that the women were not really engaging with us. However we continued until the Lord gave us the idea to bring out gift bags. I would decorate these bags by wrapping up gift items in lovely pink tissue, making the bags look pretty. We soon noticed that this opened up conversations and barriers also came down when we said we were Christians. The women shared and we heard many real life stories some of which I will give here.

We walked the streets usually from the hours of 10pm onwards for a length of time which depended on the number of women we would meet. Over time we engaged with several young women from the ages of approximately 18 years old and upwards. One young lady I can remember was a mother and a grandmother. She was educated and had worked in the past but every job she seemed unable to hold onto, and when she tried studying she never seemed to finish. She found working in prostitution the only option and would drink heavily on the nights she went out. She shared that this was the only way she could make money to support her children. It was a secret part of her life. Her mother never knew whilst staying at home looking after her daughter's children that this was what her daughter was up to. We spent several different nights encouraging her, sharing how much God loves her. I believe a seed was sown; however we are not sure what has happened as we have not seen her since on the streets, but are hopeful that she is doing well.

Then one day one of the women called Penny (not her real name), as soon as she saw the gift bag decided that she wanted one and came over to us. I was still a little unsure at this stage if this was really what God called me to do but I now believe Penny confirmed my journey into continuing to minister to women involved in prostitution.

An Example of Conversion to Christ

Penny worked in street prostitution to pay for her drug addiction of heroin. She had experienced extreme physical violence, being strangled until she actually passed out, rape and emotional abuse. After that night when she first met us her life never remained the same. We would meet with Penny and would give her food vouchers, clothing donations and access to shower facilities. She shared about her daughter being taken into care, her hurt and the guilt she so deeply felt.

We spoke to Penny about God and prayed with her. She thought God was angry with her as she felt He had abandoned her many years ago.

Then she learnt about free will and that she had a choice to change her life and she gave her life to Him.

I gave Penny a Bible which she was so keen on reading and thus she came to understand more about God's love. She then went into a Christian rehab centre and came out clean from drugs. Since then which was in 2011, she has completed a diploma in health and social care, and is now working part-time providing help and support to other vulnerable women and she is getting married next year (2016). We still keep in touch and she shares how she once felt there was no hope, just guilt and shame. She says she will always remember how kind we were and especially giving her the gift bag with the products that she consumed very slowly so as not to finish them too quickly, and that we took time to even speak to her on the street and be so caring. She is now full of passion and has a wonderful relationship with God. It's so amazing what God has done in her life.

I later found out that Penny went into care at the age of eleven years old. Her family was dysfunctional. Her stepdad sexually and physically abused her from the age of four. At the age of sixteen years old she tried a reunion with mother which didn't work out and she ended up on her own. Social services gave her a deposit to put on a room. She worked two jobs. But then life changed when she was introduced to drugs by one of the girls she shared a flat with. She lost her flat and jobs. Things then got out of control. This really touched my heart deeply hearing about it. I now feel blessed to be used by God, and that I was obedient and made myself available, which helped to make a difference in her life.

For Many it is Long Struggle

Meeting a lady called Flower (not her real name) aged 27 years whilst on street outreach, was an experience. She asked for help and said that she was from Romania and was hopeful that her young son aged eight at the time was coming over and she wanted help with a home of her own to live. Flower had been addicted to drugs but was now on a methadone prescription. She had been involved in prostitution from a young age. She was sexually abused by an uncle and ran away from home and found herself working as a prostitute. Flower was the first person I had ever met at the time who told me that she had a husband so I was quite shocked by this and had to ask the question 'Are you serious? Does your husband know?' She told me yes he does and he is ok with it. Really!! I realised through conversations over time that the couple saw this as normal behaviour and a way of making some good money, in excess of probably £500 a night!, but at what risk. I had the opportunity to meet with her husband and he showed no signs of control or threatening behaviour towards his wife in my presence but he did say that she had been doing this well before they married. I even found myself, along with a colleague of mine who translated in their language, praying with them both. What I will always remember is the husband saying that he didn't feel ready or even good enough for God to accept him as he is. I did explain to them that was not true.

It took the police giving Flower an anti-social behaviour order to stop her from street prostitution for a while. We tried to help as best as we could but realised she also needed to be serious about wanting to change and make the choice herself to want to change. She just couldn't find alternative employment and found herself back on the streets because she needed the money. We still keep in touch and she knows where I am when she finally makes the decision to exit.

We met China who was addicted to heroin and several nights we met her we gave her a gift bag, offered hot drinks and shared the word of God. On one occasion she actually came to look for me at one of the centres I was at because she was being evicted from her home so I was able to intervene and get her some extension of time to stay and find somewhere else to live. China shared one story with me that I will always remember. She was out one night and a young man came over to her to ask for business. She said she wasn't rude or anything but politely said no. The next thing she knew he came back to her and from behind hit her with a metal pole and broke her leg. But yet China still came out and still works in street prostitution knowing the risk; she explained she has been in it for years. China was not ready to exit this lifestyle but she too knows where we are when she is ready. You eventually get to learn and realise that even though you may want these women to exit and it hurts to see and hear their experiences and you know the dangers, at the end of the day you cannot make the decision to exit for them. You can just be there and God knows when the time is right.

The Testimony of 'Lily'—On-Going Conversion

This story was written by Lily (not her real name) who gave permission for it to be included here.

> My story really started before I can remember. I have been aware
> of pornography from as long as I have memory and don't know

where I was introduced to it. I was born into a Christian family but my parents worked a lot and I spent a lot of time with various babysitters. I have memories of sexual experiences at one or two of these babysitters' houses. I was also sexually assaulted at the age of ten years old. So growing up my attitude to sex and everything surrounding it had two very polar opposites: on one hand I knew what the Bible said about it and that it was intended for marriage only, but on the other hand I had already seen and experienced some of it secretly. I knew I couldn't reveal this to my family and it forced me to keep a part of myself hidden and private from the rest of the world.

I couldn't reconcile the two parts of myself, and as I grew older I increasingly felt that the secret, shameful, hidden part of me was the real me, and the good Christian girl that I played to the rest of the world was just an act. I wanted to be pure and right, but felt that it was inevitable that one day someone would discover who I 'really was', and that everyone would finally know and they would be disgusted. I found it difficult to trust people, and though I tried very hard to make people like me, inside I hated most people and was very angry.

At 19 years old I moved to LA to pursue my dreams of being a singer and dancer. Upon arriving there, I found myself in a city where my 'secret side' could run wild, and I didn't restrain myself. I loved my newfound freedom and indulged in every way I could. I felt that I was finally being myself, and was loving it. However, this feeling didn't last.

I ran out of money a couple of months into my stay there. I stumbled across the path of the wrong kind of men, and soon found myself going on dates with men in exchange for money. The man who was 'helping' me with this new career was an emotionally and sometimes physically abusive guy that I was in a twisted form of relationship with, and he was adamant that I should stay out of the strip clubs, which is where I wanted to go, as he felt that with my personality I would make more money 'solo' in his 'escort agency'. He showed me a classy looking website which supposedly he ran with a business partner, and said he could put me on his books privately. I got a lot of attention from men, which I loved, and found a lot of pride in telling them that if they wanted to spend time with me, they needed to pay for it. I had been sexually victimised, bullied and harassed for as long as I knew, and finally felt in charge of my body. I wasn't having sex with my 'customers', although some wanted to, so I felt like what I was doing was morally fine.

However, at the same time, I had terribly low self-esteem, was beginning to have seasons of highs where I felt on top of the world, and then very low lows where I wanted to end it all. I realised that if I was spending time with a man and having sex, I felt great, but as soon as I was alone the loneliness was crushing. It made it hard to say no. Eventually I was asked by a client I'd had a couple of dates with if I would spend the night with him. As I was discussing what my fees should be if I started down this road with my self-styled escort agent, I felt such a huge pull in my spirit that this was not where I was supposed to be. I didn't want to become a prostitute, but the fact was that I was dealing with what I believe now to be sex addiction and the shame that came along with it. I didn't see why getting paid for what I did in my private time was such a problem.

Ultimately, it was the abuse at this man's hands that caused me to run from him, as he was becoming increasingly aggressive, which the few friends I had at the time noticed, and urged me to leave him. I ended up running straight into the arms of one or two older, richer men whom I knew, and who offered me an attractive alternative to what I was fleeing: they would take care of my monetary needs, as long as I was physically available for them whenever they wanted. This didn't seem like a bad option, so I took it.

I suppose it was easier not to think about whether I was still a prostitute if I was getting paid by only a few, more regular 'clients' that I could think of as boyfriends. It was a safer, more palatable option for someone who was raised in the church, but these men would sometimes treat me as less than a human being, and in their eyes by receiving their money I was basically waiving all rights to say what could and couldn't be done to me.

My heart and life were in shreds. My growing addiction to sex was ruining my career and my friendships as I was unable to be honest with anyone, was full of hate, would drop everything to fulfil the needs of my addiction and was pursuing only those needs. Everything else came much lower on my list of priorities, and I was deep in depression. I couldn't bear to be alone. I had no respect for my body and my health; I took up smoking cigarettes, cigars and weed and would get drunk a lot, which was ruining my voice so I could barely sing. I took increasing risks in my sexual encounters, and I knew in my heart that I was living recklessly because I wanted to die. I would think to myself, 'give it two or three years and soon you'll have got caught up in something that will kill you. It'll be over within the next couple years.' I didn't necessarily WANT to die I just didn't see what use I was for anyone or anything.

One night when I was still escorting I had cried out to God and asked Him to reveal Himself if He was really there. I believed that He existed but never felt any kind of presence in my life, and really needed a miracle. I prayed that prayer, and began going to church on Sundays.

For a couple months I was trying out different churches, looking for God. I tried quite a few and stayed at each one for a few weeks at a time, but at each one I was let down as I never felt any kind of real power or love in any of them. Then a friend who happened to be visiting from the area I had grown up in told me about a church she had been recommended to try, and asked if I would like to go. I of course agreed, but it took me a couple weeks to get there as they had a morning service and I was always tired from partying the night before.

The day I decided to go, I couldn't get in touch with my friend. She said she was going, so I went too, but when I got to the building I couldn't find her anywhere. I was wearing a very short purple dress and huge heels, and the only seats available were at the very front of a very large room. I had to walk past rows and rows of perfect, happy looking young people, and I was very embarrassed by the time I sat down!

When the preacher began to talk, he was preaching on Romans chapter one. I hadn't read my Bible in a long time, and the words he was saying were like someone was holding a megaphone to heaven and God was listing everything I was doing. I felt it was literally written about me. I was so deeply deeply sorry as the preacher listed the ways I had wronged God, and I knew then that God saw everything, even my heart.

I believed in Jesus that day, and accepted Him into my life. I felt that now my life would change, and that I would be able to focus and heal and become a new version of myself. Unfortunately, it took a lot, lot longer to heal than I expected. My addiction didn't disappear, and I continued to wrestle with it for years. I became pregnant and moved back to where my parents lived in order to raise my child as a single parent. I'm ashamed to say that even then my life didn't really change. But that move ended up helping me, as I joined a small church with a pastor's wife who had a real heart for me. She pursued me and loved me until I allowed her in to my life, and she disciplined me and did all she could to drag me away from my sin and towards Jesus. She never stopped praying for me and giving me grace, no matter how many times I failed and made horrible decisions. I thank God that her love and dedication to me truly modelled Jesus' love and dedication to us, and she taught me so much about what true love meant, something I had always longed for and never received.

I learned that I don't need to look or act any particular way to get my God to love me. His love doesn't come with strings, His provision is unconditional, and His conviction is without condemnation. He took my shame, and gave me never ending grace and mercy, as well as friends who allowed me and helped me to slowly heal from the past that had taken everything from me. He took me through a season of a couple years where I had nothing but Him and my son, and though the loneliness felt never ending and achingly painful, I had His love to show me how I was created to be loved.

I am now married and have two children. I have an outlet to dance with fellow Christians in a dance ministry, and am in the middle of writing my first album. I'm no longer enslaved to the sins that held me prisoner from my childhood, and I thank God for His son Jesus who made that possible.

Very Great Needs

It is not surprising that Lily with her early exposure to pornography and developing sexual addiction became involved in prostitution. One study of sexual addiction and Internet pornography listed three levels of sexual 'acting out':- basic behaviours; level 2 behaviours; and offending behaviours. The first of the eight level 2 behaviours was prostitution.[1]

A team of us were involved in outreach in a certain area 'red light district' where there was an increase of women involved in prostitution to the point of the local residents complaining and signing a petition for the women to be removed. Our team went to these streets to meet with the women and the majority were from Eastern Europe, over time we began to gain their trust. We gave out gift bags, chocolates and hot drinks. Many of these women were from 18 years old to approximately the oldest who was about 30 plus. We did ask questions about their reasons for being in this type of work They all seemed to say it was because they needed to provide money to send home to their families and their family were not aware they were working in this industry because they assumed they were waitressing, childminding or working in a shop.

They were so happy when we gave out Bibles to them, saying no-one has ever done that before and were willing for us to pray with them for their needs and for their family. They had not experienced this type of behaviour towards them and soon barriers came down towards having conversations with us as they would tell other women about us along the street.

These were young women who had lost a sense of hope, confidence and self-esteem and saw this as the only way to make a living. We also had reason to believe and were occasionally told that they were being watched and controlled by a pimp. Sometimes that pimp would even be their boyfriend. Those who were being watched were not very open to have conversations.

One lady knew that this type of work was damaging and said that she would need psychological help when she would leave the industry for good, but for now she saw this as the only way she could set up a good life for her and her son and was making more money doing this than an ordinary 9–5 job. We just continued to meet with these women and encourage them and love them. They were even open to receive hugs from us. Even though we may not see the fruit of our labour we know we have sown a seed in the heart of each woman we came into contact with.

I began to realise that these women about whom most of society have already made up their minds, through judgemental attitudes, ignorance and the belief they choose this lifestyle, can most definitely change and anything is possible with God. We were out there to give, in an environment where these women always expect people wanting to take from them.

There is a great need for those who know God to be willing to step out and share what God has done in their life. Everyone has a testimony which we may hear if we go and reach out to these women, with understanding that they have just found themselves in bad situations on their journey in life. These women are somebody's mother, daughter or sister who do not believe there is a way out of their situation, have lost all hope, self-respect, confidence, most of them with feelings of rejection, damaged goods and not good enough for anything else along with the mind-set that this is all they are good for, which is a lie. But a kind word, a smile, a hug, a gift can make all the difference.

One wonderful lady has written[2] about how such an apparently small thing made a very big difference in how she felt about killing herself. She was living in London in squats and in doorways in the Strand. She was an alcoholic and the man she was with had forced her into prostitution and became her pimp. She had reached the point where she felt like killing herself, when at 5am one morning a lady put on the pavement beside her a cup of tea and a sandwich. That helped her to have a little reason to believe that perhaps life could become worth living. This began a process which has brought her some years ago to baptism in a Catholic church with a deep faith, and to a stable marriage with her family around her. She works with other recovering alcoholics and their families, and she accompanies and helps others on their spiritual journey, bringing them for example to prayer and other church meetings. She is a tremendous and lovely inspiration to know. What an encouragement this testimony provides to those who go out night after night in all weathers, sometimes feeling discouraged and wondering if what they are doing is bearing any fruit in the lives of the women whom they encounter as they walk the streets. When God calls us He asks us to trust Him and to keep on praying for anyone He puts on our hearts.

Reflections

I said 'God, what do I know about women in this industry?' 'What could I do?' 'Are you sure?' I realise through my own journey into this ministry that God used me also because my own personal life too was part of a dysfunctional family, with feelings of not really understanding what it is to be loved, experiencing lack of confidence and self-worth, but by God's grace He brought me through to a life of wholeness through His love and healing. So I am able to bring comfort to another who needs comforting, and I am able to share the love of Christ within me to another, who needs to see His love through me. I can come alongside one of these women who is on her own journey of change, and am able to offer them prayer, practical help and support. That's what I can do and I thank God that He saw the potential within me for me in turn to see the potential in others and He was sure.

The situation is desperate. There are a lot of hurting women in the sex industry and women being trafficked into the industry on a daily basis and we are called to disciple the nations. God called us to go, to love our neighbours as ourselves, to heal the broken-hearted and to set the captives free in the name of Jesus Christ.

Notes

[1] M. Brouwer and M. Laaser, 'Sexual Addiction and Internet Pornography' in B. Geary and J. Bryan (eds) *The Christian Handbook of Abuse, Addiction and Difficult Behaviour* (Stowmarket: Kevin Mayhew, 2008), pp. 147–175.

[2] A. Guile, *Journey into Wholeness: Prayer for Inner Healing—an Essential Ministry of the Church* (Leominster: Gracewing, 2013), pp. 127–130.

16

Healing and Evangelisation in Prison

Elizabeth McGurk

When Jesus describes the scene of the Last Judgement he says, 'Then the King will say to those on His right hand, 'Come, you whom my Father has blessed, take as your heritage the kingdom prepared for you since the foundation of the world. For I was hungry and you gave me food, I was thirsty and you gave me drink, a stranger and you made me welcome, in prison and you came to see me'. (Mt 25:34–36). In this inspiring chapter Elizabeth shares with us the story of how she became involved in prison ministry; how she experienced the Lord healing the female prisoners she led in meditation; how, as a result of the obvious help she was bringing to those women, she was appointed a chaplain to the whole prison, so that she now met and prayed with male prisoners as well as female ones. She established a charity to help the women and men after release from prison. She was nationally honoured for her work. Her experience of how God called her into this healing ministry gives a clear testimony to the fact that our Church, as Pope Francis keeps reminding us, is a 'field hospital after battle'. We must heal the wounds.

An Unexpected Call

There are three prisons located in Durham City, yet in the thirty years I had lived in the city I had given very little thought to the prisons or their inmates. If they were in there then they deserved to be; full stop. No thought of prison visiting or of possible miscarriages of justice troubled me, even though I was a practising Christian and had a friend Mavis who taught meditation in H wing in HMP Durham. Mavis is a very special person with extra special gifts.

Then came the day when, while discussing with my son how good it would be to have a meditation group in the parish, the doorbell rang and there was Mavis who instantly said, 'We've prayed for six months for someone to take over the meditation group on H wing and I have just realised it is you'. My response was an appalled and immediate, 'NO, not me.' I also found I had unknowingly moved six feet back from the door.

My son was puzzled at this and reminded me of our discussion before Mavis arrived, but for me the two were completely different; parish yes, prison no. I explained that I would not know what to say to 'people like that', and at this point Mavis asked me to pray about it and this I agreed to do, little knowing how completely my life would change.

Through renewal in the church I had learned of and experienced the power of prayer, but I was sure that as God knew me so well He knew I would be useless in any prison ministry. Over several weeks my thoughts and prayers were restless and confused until the day I walked into my empty parish church and asked, 'Please show me Lord, do I go into the prison or not?' In my mind the words formed 'Why not?' and my answer was the same as that to my friend. I felt held there until I realised my only concern was for myself. I was afraid of what might be asked of me, of what the Lord might ask of me, afraid of my own inadequacies, so full of fears until I eventually said, 'Alright Lord, I will go, and if I am no good I will say so.' It then felt as though a great load was being lifted from me and I was at deep peace.

The Meditation Group

It took some months for my police clearance to come through and I went with Mavis for the first time through the locked and clanging prison gates and locked doors to H wing, the women's wing. Outside of what I learned was the women's chapel, a group of ten women, after welcoming Mavis, greeted me with the words, 'We thought you would never get in!' and they all hugged me. All my previous fears had long evaporated and they were simply other women, extending to me such a warm welcome. I felt I had come home, and in all the years that followed that feeling never changed. That evening, as well as for the last time the following week, Mavis led the meditation before returning with her family to Ireland.

The following Thursday I went in on my own and a prison officer escorted me to the wing, where again the women were waiting at the chapel door to greet me. I felt at peace and at home and knew this as a healing, not something I had accomplished but purely a work of God. Over the previous ten years I had learned to meditate at a centre for prayer at Burn Hall, a Mill Hill Missionary retreat centre on the outskirts of Durham City. The group held in the women's wing of the prison was called The Julian Group, named after Julian of Norwich, a woman mystic of the fourteenth century. It had been running for about four years.

After our greeting we would sit on chairs arranged in a circle in the chapel with breathing and relaxation exercises leading into a meditation on various themes but mostly from a passage in scripture, and always leading into a time of silence. The silence time grew over the months from ten minutes to forty minutes. Evenings were the only free time the women had and it was encouraging to see that they gave this up to spend up to an hour in prayer.

After about two months, one of the young women asked if she could talk to me after our group time. From then on, most evenings, one of the women would stay behind; they appeared to decide among themselves who that would be. Whilst this was a huge step forward, it took me into a dark place for a while as I was being given information on some of the reasons for their detention, and I didn't know how to process it or why it didn't cause me to reject them, although I was grateful for their trust. Going into the prison for me at this time was like going into a place without light. Talking with a very good friend who was also a priest, put me back on the right path, showing me this was a spiritual problem and directing me back to prayer. The light was switched on again.

I am quite certain that the Lord opened up channels of communication between us. From being silently judgemental in many situations, I now learned the truth of the words of St Francis, 'There but for the grace of God go I.' These were times of many tears and much pain but we always prayed together at the end of the talking/listening time and these times were the beginnings of much healing.

Changed Lives

One young woman, who had not spoken since coming into the prison, was the last to leave as the group left the chapel one evening. As she walked through the door I told her that God loved her very much. She stopped and with her back to me shook her head. I said that He did not love what she had done but that His love for her was unchanging. She turned and whispered, 'Not me,' while her tears flowed. She sat down and I talked of the incredible and unchanging love that God has for every one of us, hating the sin but loving the sinner. We ended with prayer, the first of many, which marked a great change in her. She joined in the sharing we had at the end of every meditation and in the joint prayer which followed and the change in her was commented on among the women and staff.

Another lady in the group, because of her lived experience, could never join in our closing prayer which was the Our Father. She had shared her story with me and we had prayed about it but she could not get past this hurdle until the evening before her transfer to another prison. As usual we joined hands around the group and began to pray, 'Our Father...' She was holding my hand and began to shake. She then joined in the prayer with tears running freely, by the end of the prayer we were all crying with happiness for her that such a barrier had been removed. She wrote to me sometime later, care of the chaplaincy to tell me that she was still meditating and continuing to pray the Our Father.

By now the group had grown to thirteen, and our latest member, Cara (real names are not used), came in wringing her hands and saying over and over, 'I am sorry I can't keep quiet'. This proved to be very true and as there was no way I could or would exclude her, I asked the rest of the women to be patient for a while and to pray that our newest member would be helped as we had been. Over the next few weeks our sessions were marked by this lady proclaiming every few minutes how sorry she was. She sat next to me and I lightly touched her arm reassuringly each time, and gradually she began to be still a few minutes more at a time—to the great relief of the whole group—until eventually, she could hold a forty minute silence.

It was quite amazing, particularly as each week when I handed the list of names of the women who would be attending the group to the wing officer, (as the location of all prisoners had to be known at all times) the exclamation was, 'You will never manage with her there, it's impossible for her to stop talking!' They too were astounded at the change in this lady, which spilled over into the rest of her life.

The group also impressed me by their acceptance of the lack of peace in the meetings since Cara joined us. Not that there was ever complete silence; within the chapel yes, but outside the closed door there was constant banging of heavy metal doors, the noise of people running up and down the metal staircases, and always the chatter and shouting of the other women on the wing. The group learned to accept all this and let go.

I have thought of this often when, over the years since, people have commented on the difficulty of finding a quiet place to meditate. Were these women searching for a way to live with what they had done? They were on a journey most are never called to make, a long journey through deep darkness. In that search for and longing for peace, repentance, forgiveness, acceptance from God, they overcame many hindrances. They also knew that many in society would never accept them. Some had committed terrible crimes, but some also came to true repentance. I recall one lady who, when two others were talking over another's crime said 'I should go through the rest of my life with a bag over my head for what I have done'. The discussion stopped.

God did not wait for these women to become pillars of any church or be reintegrated into society before He began to heal them. Many might feel this God we believe in is too lenient—these women were convicted of murder. But that is to forget that repentance is a grace, not something we conjure up from the self, and surely they needed great grace, and in their need He gave it. The healings they experienced were His setting them on the road back, an assurance of His presence, an assurance to them that they were not beyond redemption.

The Call to Chaplaincy

After I had been leading the group every Thursday evening for about two years, the senior prison chaplain who, at that time was always an Anglican, asked me if I would become relief chaplain covering the whole prison. He went on to say that while I was a Roman Catholic, he did not want me to come into chaplaincy via the Church as any incoming Catholic Priest Chaplain would bring in his own relief chaplain. I had no hesitation in agreeing and gave my bishop and a parish priest as referees. My document of appointment duly arrived from the Home Office and I began going in to HMP Durham as a relief chaplain, which initially entailed two full days weekly. However, whenever a chaplain was ill or absent for some reason, I also filled in for them so that often I was in the prison five days a week. I also continued to take the meditation group every Thursday evening.

A prison chaplain is part of a team and does not only see prisoners of his or her own faith, but is there for everyone, of all faiths or none. There are times when we all have to face the results of our actions. For those coping with their imprisonment and deepening awareness of what they have done accentuates separation from those they love and can cause depression, despair and often a seeking for that something more. Each faith has its own service time, and in the absence of the Catholic Priest, I would lead a Service of Word and Holy Communion in the main chapel, which is for male prisoners only, quite large and is always full for services. This would be followed by a service on H wing for the women prisoners.

There is a great need in our prisons and indeed in the Church for more people of deep and living faith, people who know that evangelisation and healing go hand in hand. It is what Jesus taught and we are always called to follow. When she learned that I was working in prison one lady told me I should be ashamed of myself for doing so. I could tell her that I once felt rather like her but that it was Jesus who says we are to go into prisons and indeed to recognise need wherever and in whomsoever we find it. As Pope Francis says, 'We need to be fearlessly open to the working of the Holy Spirit'. When you and I recognise our own poverty of spirit, our deep and constant need of love, healing and consolation, we open ourselves to the healing power of the Holy Spirit, who is God-with-us in the immensity and intimacy of His love.

We must own our own brokenness before we can truly minister to another and this ministry is not only for members of the priesthood, but for laity too. We all have our own gifts and ministry through the sacraments of baptism, confirmation and marriage. Among the male prisoners I found the same pain and needs as the women had, but they did not express it so easily. They would ask for prayer and ask if they could have their mates come into the cell for the prayer time. They would want prayer for a wife, partner, child or family member but it took some time for them to begin asking for prayer for themselves.

Prayer for Souls Not at Rest

Once, one of the men asked if I would pray because he had twice seen a figure 'in a long gown and with what looked like a hood' walk across his cell and disappear through the opposite wall. There are always jokers, but he appeared to be a little uncomfortable, perhaps wondering if he would be believed, but quite clear in what he had seen. The RC chaplain was on holiday so I went along to his cell armed with holy water and prayed for peace for any disturbed spirit and blessed the cell. He and his two friends, who had joined us appeared content.

Some weeks later, he thanked me and said there had been no more sightings. What was most interesting was what the Catholic priest told me when I reported the incident to him upon his return. He took me back to the wing and said that there had been a time when there were no cells there, and that area was a corridor down which those condemned to death walked to the 'long drop', and he showed me fixed to the floor in the corner, the lever which used to operate the trap door of the long drop.

The condemned man would often have been accompanied by a priest or a monk. There is much that cannot always be explained.

A lady on H wing asked if I would pray in her cell, as every night she saw a figure familiar to her at the end of her bed, a figure which instilled great fear in her. She was a very quiet lady and it was obvious that she was very disturbed by this. That afternoon I went along to her cell, and immediately on entering it felt intense cold. After praying and blessing the room, I left her. It was good to see her smiling face some days later and to hear her sleep was now undisturbed and her cell normal and warm. About six months later her conviction was quashed and she returned home.

Prayer Requests

More and more I was being asked to pray with either the men on the main prison wing or the women on H wing. Quite often the requests came from other chaplains who had been asked but for a variety of reasons were unable to do so at that time. If it was the anniversary of a death, the service would often be in the chapel or in a room off the main chapel for the men. They would always have two or three other prisoners with permission to be present and I would invite them to say a prayer or a few words too. These were times when I felt humble and happy to be there, available and trusted with their stories. We all need to listen to one another at a deep level, not coming in with easy answers, but open to receive what the other is sharing so as to discern what is actually needed. I learned that there are many happenings which are not coincidences but 'God incidences'.

I came to consider it a blessing that I had no previous experience of prison or social work and no theoretical knowledge. I did have much experience and involvement in my own church and in ecumenism, a deep faith and belief in the immediacy of God in the here and now through the presence of the Holy Spirit. I also had much experience of listening to and praying with people for inner healing. I knew the joy and pain of nursing a sick husband for years before his death and bringing up a family of five, all of which I consider relevant experience. I went into prison with an open mind, knowing that God wanted me there and that was enough.

The Revolving Door Syndrome

Every morning one of the chaplains on duty is present to interview all prisoners who have come in since the previous day and I soon found the same men returning, sometimes only a week or two after they had been discharged. I learned that this is known as the 'revolving door syndrome'. One quiet man who cleaned the chapel I wished good luck to on the day he was to be discharged, only to greet him again two weeks later when he returned. When I asked him why he said, 'Chaplain, I have been living in a pipe in the park with two blankets and I'm afraid I'm going to be attacked or die of hypothermia this winter so I break a window to be brought back.' When I saw the senior chaplain later that day I told her of this and asked if we could do more to help these people when they were discharged, but was told that at that time if you worked in the prison you were not allowed to be involved in any way on their release.

A short time later when this man, whom I will call Barry, was about to be released, I spoke with the prison housing officer and told him Barry's story. He had been an alcoholic and while he had not been physically violent, he had been verbally abusive when drunk. He now did not drink but of course was well known around the area and many thought he was beyond help. When he had to share a dormitory or room in hostels he would just walk out if an argument or fight began; now no-one would take him in. The housing officer and I spent hours on the telephone that afternoon trying to find him accommodation. The answer was always the same—sorry. Eventually the officer wrote down an address and gave it to me. I took it to the room where Barry was waiting to be discharged. He took the paper, but with no hope. I told him to tell the manager of the care centre that he had changed and to ask for another chance, to stay there no matter what and after a month he would be given his own place. That was the last time I saw him and during the following three years, he did not return to the prison. I have always remembered him and prayed for him. His plight touched me deeply and my longing to do something more for ex-offenders remained.

Move to Another Prison

Three years later the Methodist chaplain asked if I would like to visit HMP and YOI Low Newton, a women's prison and young offenders' institute, in another area of Durham to see a new drug rehabilitation unit. It was a very interesting experiment with new innovative methods and committed staff. When we left my colleague said the senior chaplain had invited us for tea. After a warm welcome Carol the senior chaplain asked if I would be interested in being her relief chaplain, replacing her on her two days off and holidays. I had been about to leave the Durham prison due to health reasons. It is a large prison and even though the prison officers were very helpful and supportive in bringing the prisoners down to the ground floor for me there were still difficulties. HMP Low Newton is mostly ground floor so this was very good news for me. However I pointed out that I was Roman Catholic whilst Carol was Anglican, so it was very unlikely that her bishop and mine would agree to my being her replacement. Carol pointed out that the Anglican Chaplaincy did not have a communion service on Sundays, simply a prayer service, with communion only at Easter, which she or another Anglican chaplain would take. Happily both the bishops agreed to my taking on this role.

It was sad leaving everyone in Durham, especially the meditation group on H wing, which by then I had been leading for seven years. For quite some time I received the occasional letter from some of the women sent to me via the Low Newton chaplaincy. Transferring from one prison to another was not difficult and it was only a three-mile country drive from my home. The prison held approximately 310 women from the age of 17 years, some on remand for many months, others serving short sentences for petty crime, but most in for drug and alcohol-related crimes. Most people think that the majority of offenders are in for drug-related crimes, but this is not so; many more are charged with alcohol-related crimes, yet alcohol is tolerated so much more than drug taking. Why do we go on accepting and tolerating alcohol excesses in all our major towns and cities? True, there are occasional outcries but what is done to help young people especially to see and know the dangers? Could we not have more teaching in our families, schools, colleges and churches on having respect for our own bodies and those of others, teaching them not to be afraid to say 'no'? In our homes and churches do we teach with conviction that we are each a temple of God's Spirit, precious in His eyes, or do we still in many places teach a dry and sterile religion with mainly a list of rules? Let us pray to lose our fears and speak of the ever-present passionate God who loves us enough to die for us in the person of his Son, and over and over, inspires and gives us new life through their shared Spirit. Jesus said we are 'Jewels in His Crown.' We have a new outreach beginning in our diocese entitled Forward Together in Hope. May it ignite the faith within us and fill us with the joy of the Gospel so answering Pope Francis' prayer.

Sitting here writing I am again in the prison, knowing the pain and despair of so many; comforting a heartbroken woman who has just learned that her children are being put up for adoption; praying with another who is violently ill as she goes through 'cold turkey' withdrawal from drugs; on to see another who is scared on seeing me because her father is ill and she thinks I have come to tell her he has died—always the Chaplain's job—she is relieved that that is not the reason, this time. Chaplains are always being asked for Rosary beads and one day I am asked to show a young woman how to pray the rosary. I go along to her cell and in no time there are six other women, all crammed into the small cell while they all learn to pray the Rosary, and a true 'Rosary cell' is formed.

Soon after I joined the Low Newton team the senior chaplain became sick and never returned, so my two days a week became five. It was almost a year before a new senior chaplain was appointed and after about six months she also was absent for some time through illness. It seemed I was more full-time chaplain than the 'relief'. Very often, one or other of the women would ask to pray in the chapel and be listened to. On these occasions, after listening, I would ask if they would like me to pray with them; only a handful in all the years, in both prisons, ever refused.

The 'revolving door syndrome' also applied to many of the women in Low Newton, often returning over and over again, as in all prisons. One day in chapel, as I was talking to a young girl (Marie) who I knew was being discharged the following week, I commented that she must be very happy to be going home. She promptly burst into tears and said, 'No, I'll go back on the drugs and I know I'll steal from anyone to buy them.'

Another time a young girl confided in me how nervous she was about her pending release because her family lived some distance away and there was no-one to meet her at the prison gates. This made me aware of how many of the women were in this situation, they came into to the prison in a closed van either straight from court or having been transferred from another prison and had no idea where they were.

The Volunteer Drivers Scheme

I spoke with a friend in the parish who immediately agreed to collect the girl when she was released and take her to the railway station in Durham. On the day she took her for a coffee and then saw her onto the train. The experience had a profound effect on my friend. I had an idea about setting up an arrangement with volunteer drivers, the idea being that they would collect the women on the day of their release and take them to the bus or railway station. I decided to approach the Governor of HMP YOI Low

Newton who was delighted with my proposal and said how troubled he often felt when women left the prison alone without anyone to meet them. I sought permission from my then parish priest, the late Fr Michael Corbett at St Joseph's RC Church Durham, to speak after a number of services with a view to recruiting volunteer drivers. I would have been happy with six volunteers but when over forty people came forward I knew the Holy Spirit was in this. The Holy Spirit is much more generous and extravagant than we are. This was the beginning of St Joseph's volunteer drivers scheme with parishioners from St Godric's also offering their services.

One of the people who volunteered was Esther Robson also from St Joseph's parish and subsequently we became close friends. Esther was a great support in showing me how to use a computer and worked alongside me in setting up the volunteer driver process and subsequently the Open Gate Project.

The late Bishop Kevin Dunn offered to pay the cost of insuring the drivers and my travelling and telephone expenses. I spoke in churches throughout Hexham and Newcastle Diocese asking for volunteer drivers and mentors. My aim was to draw women from predominantly faith-based communities but the programme itself is for those of all religious backgrounds and those of none. To date the service is still running and over 1,000 women have used the service. There are many lovely stories resulting from this work, one of my favourites being the volunteer who was so concerned about the nervous young woman she had taken to the station that she got onto the train with her in Durham and stayed with her until Darlington.

Shortly after this a new senior chaplain was appointed and six months later I was told I was past retirement age. I was seventy but immediately knew there was something more I had to do. The 'something more' became Open Gate, a Charity supporting women from HMP & YOI Low Newton from custody back into the community.

The Need for Community Support on Discharge

The conversation with Marie had intensified my sense of the great need for something and someone to be out there to support women after discharge from prison. It was only at the point of being told I was past retirement age and needed to leave my work as chaplain that it became clear that the 'something more' would be in the community.

A week after my retirement I made an appointment to speak with Dave Thompson, the then Prison Governor of Low Newton and I shared my thoughts with Dave about the need to provide support for the women before and after discharge into the community. Dave's reply was along the lines of, 'If you could do that it would be great Liz, I see the poor little beggars crossing the yard on the way out and know many of them will be back.' Dave told me to pick up my keys, come in any time and work with Bronia Bronecki who was Head of Resettlement and Carol Prouse who was then Prison Chaplain.

At this time Major Laurie Brown of the Salvation Army came to the prison and spoke of a Community Chaplaincy Project running in several male prisons in the country. Community Chaplains were appointed in these prisons to prepare men for their release back into the community by linking them with religious communities in their area who then provided mentoring support. There was to be a conference at Birmingham Citadel Salvation Hall and Laurie asked me if I would speak about the specific needs of women, our mentoring ideas for what was to become Open Gate and also the unique volunteer driving scheme that I set up and which was by now operating successfully between the Durham Catholic parishes and HMP & YOI Low Newton.

At the conference I spoke about women who were fearful of leaving prison, failed to attend pre-arranged appointments with Probation, Employment and Social Services and so on because of their lack of confidence. To illustrate the need for such support, I highlighted an occasion when I accompanied one lady to register at the doctor's surgery. The surgery was packed and the receptionist called out across the room, 'Was HMP Low Newton your last address?' You can imagine how this affected the lady I was with and how I felt about it.

I talked about women who also faced challenges such as homelessness, domestic violence, drug and alcohol abuse and often had a history of sexual abuse and mental health issues. Many of these women were lone parents whose children had been taken into care. Some suffered from a lack of any basic education, led chaotic lives and had no prospect of employment. A significant number had attempted suicide or self-harmed, had low self-esteem and faced all the difficulties of re-establishing family life and settling back into the community.

A lack of regular positive support, combined with social and peer pressure, resulted in a return to bad habits and re-offending. The Justice

Select Committee following its inquiry into women offenders, concluded that 'prison is an expensive and ineffective way of dealing with many women offenders who do not pose a significant risk of harm to public safety' The average cost of a woman's prison place is about £56,500 per annum. This does not include court costs. To reduce crime and alleviate the fear of crime in our communities is important but the cost in human terms is incalculable. This conference was the beginning of many which we attended across the country over the next four years seeking funding, greater knowledge of the system, potential solutions and ultimately to bring about change in Government thinking and policy and also public perception.

Open Gate

Over the next few years the Open Gate Mentoring Project began to take shape despite encountering many cul-de-sacs, locked doors and stone walls whilst we sought funding. A Management Board was formed and we formally registered as a Charity. Not having any funding at that time I took on the role of Community Chaplain and mentored three women who had been discharged and were in great need. Our first funding of £1,000, to train volunteer mentors and pay their expenses, came from Bishop Ambrose Griffiths of the Diocese of Hexham and Newcastle. He was always very supportive of both chaplaincy work and the proposed work of Open Gate. Bishop Ambrose endorsed my appointment as Community Chaplain to ex-offenders which was reaffirmed by Bishop Kevin Dunn. Ten volunteers began training at a weekend held at Minsteracres Retreat Centre and subsequently became accredited mentors. In addition the Diocese agreed to pay my expenses until we obtained funding.

Esther and I together completed many applications for funding and were delighted to be awarded a large grant from The Northern Rock Foundation to set up the project. Other funding followed from Christ Hospital in Sherburn, The Methodist Church in Carrville, St Joseph's RC Church Durham, Siemens and the Pyke Trust. This meant we were in a position to employ staff but we still didn't have premises from which to work. Since the meeting with the Governor, I had been meeting regularly with Bronia (Head of Resettlement) who later said that she had tried several times to tell me that the project would never happen, but that she was always caught up in my enthusiasm and never quite had the heart to tell me. Before one such meeting Bronia sought advice from the Governor who informed her that he was seeing me that afternoon and he would tell me it was a non-starter. Bronia recalled how later on she had bumped into the Governor and asked him how the meeting had gone. He replied that he had said Open Gate could have a property outside the prison gates for offices. I had only asked him for a room but that it needed to be outside the prison. Open Gate will always be indebted to Dave Thompson for his support.

We subsequently advertised for staff and appointed a Project Manager (Fiona Neasham) and a Project Worker (Alison Wemyss) who are still with us ten years later. The official opening of the Open Gate Project in February 2006 at County Hall, Durham was a huge success, and attracted much interest from the media, other agencies and local churches. It led to a number of wonderful women volunteering to becoming mentors. At this point we still had no-one to replace me as Community Chaplain as we had not secured funding for this role, because many funding bodies were not happy with the faith element. This was crucial as I was about to retire. Fiona and I filled in what we decided would be a final application to Lloyds TSB for funding for a Community Chaplain. It was a great joy to achieve a positive last-minute result and confirmed my strongly held belief in God's support for this project. Rachel Waller was subsequently appointed Community Chaplain and remains with the project today.

The Struggle to Help Marie

In the role of Community Chaplain one of the first women I supported was Marie to whom brief reference has already been made. Marie's case was one which I will always remember and which highlights many of the difficulties which women face 'on the out'. She agreed to have a mentor. In the first instance this was Fiona who met with her regularly for three months before her release. Unfortunately no accommodation was found by prison housing and on discharge Fiona accompanied Marie to Durham City Housing hoping to arrange bed and breakfast but none was available. After six hours of unsuccessfully trying to find a room, a friend of Marie's offered the floor of her flat for the night. The following day Marie failed to meet her mentor as arranged and was arrested later that day. She was drunk and was asking to be returned to HMP YOI Low Newton, distressed and angry that no accommodation had been arranged before her discharge. I informed housing in Low Newton of a contact which I had made in Supported Housing, who later agreed to take in Marie on her future discharge. I then accompanied her to court where she was discharged only after her solicitor informed the court that I was to mentor her. I was in a better position to offer the intensive support she needed. I drove Marie to Supported Housing and to register with a GP. We met regularly and I accompanied her to Jobcentre Plus, Probation interviews and to enrol at college. Whilst completing various forms it was heart-breaking to hear her give Open Gate as her next of kin.

During this time when I was meeting with Marie at least twice a week she spoke of her fears and concerns and her need of help for her addiction. She was receiving excellent support from the key worker in the supported housing I had arranged in Gateshead, but at that time was not receiving any help with her addiction and complicated mental health issues. After a couple of months Marie and I decided that she would contact me regularly or when she needed assistance.

A few months later I telephoned her probation officer and learned she had been evicted from her accommodation and had thrown herself from a rooftop breaking an arm and a leg in several places. She had not contacted me as she expected me to reject her for 'messing up'. It impressed her that I had taken time to discover her whereabouts and would not reject her. She had plaster casts on an arm and a leg and was on crutches for five weeks following three weeks in hospital. As Marie had had no benefits for six weeks I spoke with Jobcentre Plus and found her details had been lost. They asked me to accompany her to a meeting with them and as a result the situation was resolved; they arranged an interim payment until regular payments went into her account. The support-housing arrangement had broken down due to her erratic behaviour and Marie at this time was in hostel accommodation arranged by her probation officer who had shown a very great deal of forbearance.

Shortly after this she was again evicted due to her heavy drinking. No help to tackle her addiction had been found. I drove her to Nightstop where they found a place for her overnight. She was very down and afraid of being homeless again. A bed was found at a night shelter in Darlington and she travelled there each evening but had to leave each morning at 7.30 am. She returned to Gateshead each morning to report to Probation and was on the streets until she returned to Darlington each night. I continued to take her to appointments and to lunch or for a drive which at times helped to relieve the tension and stress. On Christmas Eve she phoned me to say she had been attacked by a woman at the night shelter and would not go back. Probation, Nightstop and other agencies were closed for five days. I phoned the emergency social services for accommodation and all the guest houses but without success. I then gave her money for food and had to leave her on the street. She slept in hospital toilets.

We met on Christmas morning and I provided warm food and clothing and again made calls but no bed was found. I drove Marie to Newcastle where she would more easily find a place to sleep. She slept in the Metro Station. On 26 December, Gateshead emergency services provided bed and breakfast in a hotel in Whitley Bay for two nights. At that time Open Gate had no funds allocated to provide accommodation so I paid for Marie's further nine days stay in the hotel. The hotel then closed following a tragedy and Marie went back to the Darlington shelter until she was interviewed by Supported Housing and was subsequently given a flat. She was interviewed by an agency with a view to receiving help for her addiction; I had pressed for this since her release but there is very little help for alcohol addicts. During these months I had regular meetings and calls with Marie and she says that without the support of Open Gate she felt she wouldn't have survived the experience. I don't know if this was the case but I am quite sure she would have done something resulting in her return to prison which to her stood for an escape back to warmth and safety.

As a result of Marie's case the Open Gate Management Board ring-fenced some of the funding received for non-specific purposes, to fund emergency accommodation in the event that one of our mentees becomes homeless when all agencies are closed. Jobcentre Plus also looked to improve the service to women released from custody and requested Open Gate mentors to accompany mentees to meetings. This case also highlighted that women at high risk of re-offending require the support of more than one mentor.

Eleven Years Later

Eleven years later Open Gate has:

- Raised over one million pounds
- Supported over 500 women
- Over 45 volunteers have provided support
- Over 800 lifts have been provided on release by staff and volunteer drivers
- Achieved ISO, 9001/2008 Accreditation

- Achieved Mentoring and Befriended approved provider standard

- Trained mentors for other agencies

An independent report stated:

> Open Gate's uniqueness lies in the quality of their interactions and the strengths of the relationships they have with women leaving prison. This is made possible because of their organisational values, the quality and dedication of their volunteers and the cumulative experience of their staff in the prison and in the community. They are held in high regard by the prison, probation and voluntary sector organisations alike for the work they do and their approach as an organisation; they are a small and excellent organisation.

The report highlighted a number of important outcomes as a result of the work Open Gate does for the women, volunteers and the community including positive impacts on mental and physical health, resettlement and communicating with the general public about prison and resettlement.

Feedback from Women Who Have Been Helped

There has been positive feedback from many women who have been supported by Open Gate. Some of the many quotes from them include:

- If you hadn't taken me straight to Probation when I got out, I'd have gone straight back to me dealer like I've always done.

- Thanks, I didn't know I could get that benefit.

- I was terrified at the thought of going to hospital appointments on my own, thanks…

- When you're released you have nowhere to go and therefore you end up staying with friends and then you are back in the same vicious circle again.

- Open Gate kept me going and gave me something to hang on to…

- Open Gate helped me build my life back, my confidence, my home, everything… I would not have been able to do it without them.

- I continue to grow in confidence; I have my job, a flat, a great family, good friends and a partner so life is good thanks to the fantastic help and support from Open Gate. I cannot thank them enough.

Since the early days of Open Gate, the project has grown both internally and externally. Women are given details as soon as they arrive in prison through interviews, advertisements, information leaflets and referrals from the chaplaincy team. They can access a twelve-week programme where they look at their life and move forward, developing a personal change plan with Open Gate working closely with Resettlement. Relationships continue to be built up with statutory agencies and there is provision to reunite mother and child whenever possible. Local MPs have provided support, the media continue to be interested and we attend conferences and training courses, networking with a range of services and faith communities.

Reflections

I am constantly reminded of:

> I was hungry and you fed me, thirsty and you gave me a drink; I was a stranger and you received me in your homes, naked and you clothed me; I was sick and your took care of me, in prison and you visited me (Mt 25:35–36).

I pray that the pursuit of this vision continues and in the words of the late Fr Michael Corbett:

> You pursued this dream, not for yourself but to give dignity and respect and a safe rebirth from prison into the fast and indifferent world into which many of these women are emerging.

The Open Gate office has a plaque on the office wall which reads, 'The task before us is not greater than the power behind us'. Living Gospel values and a genuine love for the women has carried us all through. Lucie Russell, Director of Smart Justice, a national crime reduction campaign says:

> We need to question whether custodial punishment of women fits the crime especially when innocent children are being punished too. Surely a cheaper and more effective solution to women's offending would be better drug treatment services, mental health

support and community sentences which enable a woman to keep her home.

Open Gate seeks to play its role in this and our aim is to recruit future peer mentors from those women who have benefited from the scheme themselves and can therefore empathise and understand the complex difficulties facing ex-offenders.

17

The Cenacolo Community: Healing and Liberation for Addicts

Fr Shaun O'Neill

In this chapter Fr Shaun O'Neill shares with us his profound experience of seeing how addicts are healed and liberated from their addictions by living in the Cenacolo community for four months. Though not himself an addict and known to be a priest, he was accepted by them as another person in need of healing and of knowing the love of Jesus on a new and more profound level which was not superficial, safe or comfortable. He writes that these most broken of God's children will evangelise the world in a most profound way, as he himself saw happen when they gave testimonies of God's love and healing to pilgrims and when they went out on mission. He also writes 'this was the most honest and humble way of discovery and truthful healing of self and others that I have ever encountered in my life—surely a most profound way to train seminarians?'

Hope and Providence

The founder of the Cenacolo Communities is Mother Elvira Petrozzi, and the best way to understand her vision is to read how she writes about HOPE and PROVIDENCE, as seen in the first chapter of *Sparks of Light*:

> It is the time for evangelization; it is the time to give witness. I can joyfully announce and give testimony to God's works, because each day I contemplate them with amazement, marvel, consolation, and gratitude.

> I began this adventure on the hillside of Saluzzo (Italy) in an abandoned villa that needed enormous restoration. I did not have any human security, but with the eyes of faith, I could already see everything that exists today, so much hope, joy and life. I remember the day that we arrived. Amidst the vines and the rubble, my gaze caught sight of a small image of Our Lady over the front door lintel. It made my heart exult with joy to see that Mary was already

there in this new Cenacle, waiting for us, welcoming us, and confirming the desires of our hearts!

We began with fervour, trust, and with the beauty of a love that is greater than any difficulty, struggle, fear or failure. Inside me was a strength that was more than human. Even though I still did not know if I was capable of loving, in my heart I felt the courage to believe that we could not fail. I was still not fully aware that God's love had already invaded my will and my weakness, to make me more capable of following Him. For me, it was like re-discovering a more authentic faith, an incarnate faith, a faith that is active, generous and concrete, that gives me the joy of contemplating every day the smiles, the bright eyes, and peace with which our youth experience today. I see the tenacity and the strength that they demonstrate in wanting to live in a community that does not sugar-coat things, but rather proposes a serious and demanding way of life.

We want to love them with a demanding love, believing that young people have within them a precious potential that has yet to be ignited, even though they have failed in the past. We help them to find out who they truly are and to find the real meaning of life, simply by believing in them and journeying with them in hope and with faith in Him who renews us.

I realised that when we do things with love, passion and joy time becomes eternity. We welcome and embrace the youth with their needs today and do not worry about what tomorrow will bring. We want to experience the present moment with them and in the way they do, which is always full of surprises, unexpected events, victories, emotions, pain, struggles, defeats and joy. We want to help each other have a positive attitude towards the gift of life, smiling when life brings tears to our eyes, forgiving when someone rejects us, and beginning again each time with trust without keeping track of offences and criticisms. In this way we obey Jesus who tells us, 'So do not worry about tomorrow; tomorrow will bring worries of its own. Today's trouble is enough for today.' (Mt 6:34)

We are determined to follow this way of life, which I constantly propose to our youth, consecrated, missionaries, families and friends: to live a more intense abandonment to the Will of the Father. We want to overcome the temptation of planning our future or worrying about tomorrow, thus losing the richness of today in which is present all the beauty of Divine Providence, to

Whom we have entrusted ourselves since the very beginning. There is so much to experience every day; therefore we will continue to place our future in the hands of God more than ever, certain of His everlasting faithfulness.[1]

Therefore the vision of Mother Elvira, or Sister as she was then, was to be fully alive in the unconquerable Love of God, so that hope, joy and life itself could bloom and blossom with perfect beauty, regardless of the difficulties and the fear of failure that could all too easily stunt the growth that God had put into eyes of faith, of Mother Elvira. She sees Cenacolo as a School of Life for the Brothers and Sisters who enter, a school that will teach then to see the precious potential within themselves that has yet to be ignited by the flames of Love from the Body of Christ who is Jesus, from the Body of Christ who is their fellow Brothers and Sisters and from the Body of Christ who is themselves. For Mother Elvira difficulties in life and in community life do not mean that things are wrong but rather that they are just that, that they are difficult and tough and hence all the more material with which to grow with in Love through Christ and the Community of Cenacolo. For Mother Elvira, Life is a gift that needs to be unwrapped in love to reveal the beautiful gift beneath—a gift that is called, Beloved Child of God. It is this undying belief in her young people and in God's power that has spurred her on so relentlessly in hope and so trustfully in providence.

From Humble Roots

Mother Elvira Petrozzi had an alcoholic for a father and so was no stranger to the traumatic and devastating effects that addictions can have on individuals and on families. Mother Elvira came from a poor family, being one of seven children, and was effectively illiterate for most of her life. During her time in the convent she was often put down and ridiculed by her sister nuns and superiors in the convent, often being made to do strenuous acts of obedience which amazingly only served her to be more aware of God's awesome love and mercy. Despite her first-hand experience of the chaos of addiction and tough convent rules she is able to give thanks for her father, life and sisters in the convent. She came to a healing in the power of God and had the spiritual courage to step-out over 30 years ago, in 1983, at the age of 50 to bring young people closer to Jesus. For many years before 1983 Sister Elvira had a great concern for the destructive nature of alcohol and drugs that she had witnessed was destroying young people. So in 1983 she was allowed to step out of the convent and leave her Order to begin to help with addicts whom she was to find, or rather who the Lord was to send her, in and around the town of Saluzzo, in northern Italy. Now with 60 houses, some for men, some for women, around the world for those addicts who want to be healed of their 'poverties' through communal living, sharing and reflecting on the Word of God in their lives, adoring the Lord in the Blessed Sacrament, hard physical work and truthfully challenging each other in the community in love and brotherly/sisterly solidarity, the world has found a place of true healing from within oneself, within community and with the Lord.

We All Need Healing

I had only been in Cenacolo for a few minutes and having been given my work clothes we were off, with my Guardian Angel, to start living Cenacolo. Within an hour or so I was feeling guilty for not being in the parish doing some useful work—this feeling of guilt for having left one's family or those who were depending on you was not uncommon—how wrong could a person be, for the really useful work had truly just begun.

We are all in need of healing. Even the addicts realised that their addiction was not the true problem, for this was just the route they had chosen to deal with their true wounds, or poverties as they would call them. I lived fully the life of an addict; eating, sleeping, praying, working, washing, cleaning, confronting, forgiving, journeying, healing and being healed with them all. Yes, they knew I was a priest but for those four months I was merely another person in need of healing, another person in need of knowing the Love of Jesus on a new and more profound level, a level that was not superficial, safe or comfortable.

We were woken at 6 am or 6:15 am depending on the day and then we would be in chapel for 6:30 am ready to pray the rosary at 6:30 am in the presence of the Lord in the Blessed Sacrament. After the rosary the Gospel of the day was read. Each of the Brothers has to take it in turns to share on the Gospel of the day, at least once a month. Choosing a line from the Gospel that helps them to share what has been happening to them in their lives over the last month. The Brothers have to say how they have been feeling within themselves, how their work duties have been going, how their relationships in the house have been developing, how many reactions they have had with each other, what they were, who they were with, and what were the emotions and feelings that they felt they had to deal with at the time, for example anger, pride, fear, superiority, inferiority and whether they had been resolved or not, and finally they had to say what their compromises were over the last month, for example things to do with laziness, food, lack of prayer—the breaking of Community rules. The shear depth of honesty, reflection, expectant forgiveness and support is tangible across the community as one of their Brothers opens up in all humility to their fellow Brothers. Opening up their hopes and fears and struggles; for all the Brothers knew that it is only in being profoundly uncomfortable with our poverty and in the sharing of them with others that real healing is brought about, and no one wants anyone else to slip back into the old way of life that only leads to death. All are challenged to walk The Way, The Truth and The Life who is Jesus Christ and so surrender oneself to Him who can bring about real healing. It is by living with the Fraternal Body of Christ that we are brought into the healing of the Body of Christ in Word and Sacrament. Catholics, other Christians, Buddhists and so on as well as those of no faith are encouraged to place their poverty and reactions with their Brothers into the hands and heart of God, especially through Jesus in the Blessed Sacrament. There is an expectation that God will bring about true and lasting healing.

True Friendship

If one has a reaction with a Brother such as fear, anger, pride and so on, one is expected to go away and reflect in prayer, and often ask another Brother for help with this time of reflection, in order to discern why this reaction came about. A couple of days later one is expected to go back to the Brother and apologise for the reaction that he had towards the other; that is, not to blame the Brother for one's own reaction but merely apologise for the reaction. Why? Because the Brother does not make you angry, fearful, prideful but rather he has merely revealed deep within you what is already there, that is the poverty that you have been battling with that has led you to your addiction, and so this reaction becomes a gift not a burden to be acknowledged. The expectation is that because of each person's reactions with another a more profound friendship blossoms, rather than a friendship ending, and in the power of truth, humbleness, fraternal solidarity, and in the power of Christ, healing comes about, hence amazing things happen in Cenacolo.

'It is the time for evangelization; it is the time to give witness.'[2] Who in their right mind would put 50 addicts together (the number in the house of Lourdes) and allow them to take care of each other? There will normally be one or two Responsibles in each house who have oversight of the running of the house—the Responsibles are themselves addicts. There are no professionals living in the community, no social workers, psychologists, counsellors or therapists of any kind. The addicts are the wounded healers that bring healing through and in the Power of Christ to one another in profound humbleness and honest challenge.

Trust in the Lord

There has to be and there is a real trust in Providence for every meal, cleaning product, building materials and clothes, for if it is not grown in the grounds or offered as a gift to the house it is not bought (twice in Lourdes we ran out of toilet rolls—I truly did thank God for bidets on those occasions!). Hope and prayer have to run high in Cenacolo so that life may run smoothly and it is this living together in the power of Christ's Love that allows all to be well, and it works! An amazing discernment of Spirits and trust is required and yet Mother Elvira entrusts this to the most broken of all laity: addicts. I am sure that it is these most broken of God's children who will evangelise the world in a most profound way, as I have seen happen with themselves and when they give their testimonies to various pilgrims and when they go out on mission—they come back full of energy and praise of God: sounds familiar to when the Lord sent out the 72! There is a complete surrender to, '… the beauty of Divine Providence.'[3]

> I began this adventure on the hillside of Saluzzo in an abandoned villa that needed enormous restoration.'[4] Enormous restoration is the phrase that comes to mind when we think of the needs of the Church and of her children in need of healing—it is the fears, pride, insecurity and so on of the Church in this area of needs which has to be rebuilt, as Christ said to St Francis, 'Rebuild My Church,' but which Church did God mean? The institutional Church—the Body of Christ—and of course the individual Bodies of Christ, you and me. We just need to begin to walk in faith, as Mother Elvira said, 'I did not have any human security, but with the eyes of faith, I could already see everything that exists today, so much hope, joy and life.'[5] It is only in the power of Christ that this can come about, a new expectant faith and a new vision is

required—a courage that is beyond us but not beyond the Spirit, a trust in the broken to bring healing to the broken in the power of the broken Body of Christ on the Cross—there was no pattern on the Cross, only trust and expectant faith in the Father.

'Amidst the vines and the rubble, my gaze caught sight of a small image of Our Lady over the front door lintel. Amidst the rubble of our lives we find God already there taking care of All.'[6] 'With God all shall be well and all manner of things shall be well.'[7] We just accept the invitation to step inside and see what He wants. We do not have to make plans as such, but rather believe that He is the Way: let us be true to the present moment and not worry about the future—let us trust in Sister Providence, even when begging for a listening ear from the Church!

'I see the tenacity and the strength that they (the addicts) demonstrate in wanting to live in a community that does not sugar-coat things, but rather proposes a serious and demanding way of life. We want to love them with a demanding love, believing that young people have within them a precious potential that has yet to be ignited, even though they have failed in the past.'[8]

Hence Mother Elvira is not naive to the struggles and failures that life throws at us, and of the weaknesses of the addicts, but underlying all this is the hoped-for love of Christ to transform all into good, as the Catholic Catechism tells us, 'God can transform a moral evil into good.' What else is the Cross and Resurrection all about if not this? As Cardinal Newman said, 'It is a rule of God's Providence that we should succeed through failure,'—wow! How freeing is that?

The Truth Will Set You Free

In Cenacolo I slept in a dormitory with between ten and twelve Brothers, on bunk-beds, with Brothers who had been fabulously wealthy, had beautiful wives and children, had great skills and talents—top chefs, tradesmen and so on and of course some with more dubious pasts. All the Brothers had a wound that they could not heal by themselves, they had turned to a particular way of life to deal with the pain of that wound, but a way that would ultimately lead to death, and yet there was not one Brother that I would not bring home and live and work with. Why? Because, they had discovered something that the world had not shown them or that the Church had not shown them fully enough, plus, in truth, they had not been willing to see for themselves as well. Yet, now having lived with the broken Body of Christ in a Catholic faith community they had been shown a new way and a new truth and a new life that was Jesus, the Body of Christ Himself; they had been shown a beauty that was themselves—they were discovering that they are, '…God's work of art, created in Christ Jesus for the good works which God has already designated to make up our way of life,' (Ep 2:10), hence we are all made in God's image and likeness to paraphrase Genesis (Gn 1:27). Yes, not all were 'Gospel- or Jesus-greedy', and some of the Brothers left after a few days of community life, but for those who stay for three years as is hoped, then amazing healing and freedom is discovered. Struggles remain on many levels, but the ability to choose one's 'uncomfortable' in the power of prayer and brotherly solidarity allows life to be lived to the full as much as is possible with wounds that are slowly been healed.

The Brothers were always asked to choose their 'uncomfortable', meaning that during their stay in Cenacolo they had to do things that were not normal for them, for example challenging bad behaviour in others and in themselves, choosing to do extra works of charity, penance and so on, so that once they are out in the world they had built up a lifestyle and prayer base that is used to choosing the uncomfortable, that is saying no to old 'friends' who offer them drugs is not comfortable for addicts, but through prayer and healing a resistance is built up.

In the first few weeks as I listened to the Brothers and saw how they shared and acted towards each other I became more uncomfortable with being a priest, for I knew that I did not share with or challenge my brother priests in the way these broken children of God did with each other. Indeed I knew that if I did I would be seen as quite odd and well out of order, and yet these Brothers knew that for them this was the only way into healing. The Brothers would spend many hours with the Blessed Sacrament, and at any time of the day and night, there was always a stream of the Brothers in the chapel, and especially during the early hours; again a real challenge to priestly prayer in the parish!

In the last few weeks of my time in Cenacolo I became quite sad because I knew that during my time at seminary if I had shared in the way and had reactions in the way that the Brothers do in Cenacolo, I would have been asked to leave Seminary. Yet, this was the most honest and humble way of discovery and truthful healing of self and others that I have ever encountered in my life—surely a most profound way to train seminarians. Indeed, when

I first arrived in Cenacolo one of the Brothers said to me, 'Ah, do what you want, no-one will give a ——.' After a few days I realised what he meant, it was not that they did not care what you did but rather they cared so much that they were prepared to allow you to show your true self and your true woundedness so deeply that no matter what you said or did to yourself or to another Brother they would be there for you to help you. No-one would be offended in such a way that reconciliation and healing could not be brought about, just as St Paul reminds us, 'however much sin increased, grace was always greater' (Rm 5:20).

It is in this most honest discernment and challenge in the power of fraternal love and love of Christ that healing comes about in Cenacolo, as the Letter to James reminds us,

> So confess your sins to one another, and pray for one another to be cured... My brothers, if one of you strays from the truth, and another brings him back to it, he may be sure that anyone who can bring back a sinner from his erring ways will be saving his soul from death and covering many a sin (Jm 5:16,19–20).

This is a perfect summary of the Cenacolo spirituality—nothing that a parish, seminary or the Church could not achieve as individuals and as a community of love in Christ. Just as Mother Elvira says,

> We want to help each other have a positive attitude towards the gift of life, smiling when life brings tears to our eyes, forgiving when someone rejects us, and beginning again each time with trust without keeping track of offences and criticisms.[9]

It is then that we know we are on our way to true healing.

Healing Ministry

If addicts can bring about so much healing in each other in the power of Christ then why is there so much fear of the ministry of healing? For me it is two sides of the same coin:

a) Fear that it does work,

b) Fear that it does not work.

If as in a) above God does demonstrate His immeasurable merciful love and healing then this will demand a total surrender of our being to Him, which for most people, and especially priests, is a truly uncomfortable reality demanding great abandonment, surrender and loss of control, and yet it is this very 'letting go and letting God', as the phrase goes, that gives one true freedom. It is this ability to live with one's 'uncomfortable' that Cenacolo can teach us.

If as in b) above God does not appear to 'work' then what does that say about us? Pride becomes the stumbling block. And yet, if one prays something will and does happen, it just may not be seen or 'felt' as we had hoped for or expected—for the Lord has a great vision! As God reminds us through the prophet Isaiah, '...so it is with the word that goes from my mouth: it will not return to me unfulfilled or before having carried out my good pleasure and having achieved what it was sent to do,' (Is 55:11). But, as Cenacolo can teach us, it is not appearances that matter, it is the truth of learning from our failures that set us free, again just as Blessed John Henry Newman was quoted earlier. So let's not worry if it does not appear to work let us just trust that the Lord is working somewhere in the midst of our brokenness and fear.

And yet when Mother Elvira began she too was unaware of her strength in God, but she allowed the fears to be outweighed totally by God's love, as she writes,

> We began with fervour, trust, and with the beauty of a love that is greater than any difficulty, struggle, fear or failure. Inside me was a strength that was more than human. Even though I still did not know if I was capable of loving, in my heart I felt the courage to believe that we could not fail. I was still not fully aware that God's love had already invaded my will and my weakness, to make me more capable of following Him.[10]

So it is not about us, but rather it is about Him and about Him so much that we are able, 'to live a more intense abandonment to the will of the Father,'[11] where there is no failure or fear.

Cenacolo's particular form of healing ministry and its potential for bringing real life in a very concrete way into people's lives cannot be ignored and as Mother Elvira reminds us,

> For me, it was like re-discovering a more authentic faith, an incarnate faith, a faith that is active, generous and concrete, that gives me the joy of contemplating every day the smiles, the bright eyes, and peace with which our youth experience today. I see the tenacity and the strength that they demonstrate in wanting to live

in a community that does not sugar-coat things, but rather proposes a serious and demanding way of life.[12]

What Church would not want this to be an active part of their armoury in the battle against sin, evil and brokenness?

This ministry of prayer for healing is not reserved to the priest of the parish. The whole community joins in prayer for the sick and some members of the community may be gifted with special charisms by the Spirit for praying with people for healing—this is a sentence written by Alan Guile—a sentence that could be applied truly and concretely to a great number of the Brothers in the Cenacolo community that I lived in for four months. A good number of the Brothers had come to point in their lives that they knew the Lord and knew of His healing through abandonment to His will and to surrendering oneself to the care of the Community—the Body of Christ—the Church in action! The addicts ministered to themselves, they were becoming and some had become wounded healers, in the power of God, prayer, Christ crucified, Christ in the Blessed Sacrament and Christ within each other. We have to believe, as Mother Elvira does, that, 'We want to love them with a demanding love, believing that young people have within them a precious potential that has yet to be ignited, even though they have failed in the past. We help them to find out who they truly are and to find the real meaning of life, simply by believing in them and journeying with them in hope and with faith in Him who renews us.'[13] Again, what Church would not want this to be an active part of their armoury in the battle against sin, evil and brokenness?

Parish-Based Ministry

It would be amazing what God might do if there were parishes where the discernment of the gifts of the Spirit occurs in really effective ways. Indeed this should be the norm rather than the exception as we are all part of the Body of Christ and as such we as individuals and as a community should be able to know how the Spirit is acting or not acting within our own communities—the Body of Christ. Unfortunately, I personally do not know any parish that embarks on such a discernment of the gifts of the Holy Spirit. To my knowledge most parish priests and hence parishes are more likely to discern who can help in the day-to-day administration of the parish, and who is good at leading catechetical programs—both of which do actually require a level of giftedness given by the Holy Spirit as we read in Romans and 1 Corinthians.

The questions for our parishes and for individuals are, 'Why have these particular ministries of healing not been fully realised in the parishes for the building up of the community of faith? And what are the barriers that need to be broken?

As suggested, there is much good work going on in parishes, work of the Lord, but I feel that the management of the parish may be the priority for most priests and laity, rather than having a vision for the parish; a vision which is about being in relationship with Christ and the Kingdom of God. A vision that is not lost in institution and spiritual bureaucracy! A lack of vision means a lack of knowledge which in turn leads to ignorance and fear, which in itself leads to a paralysis, which allows one to live out a comfortable relationship with God and parishioners and parish management systems, which may all be good in themselves, but which may not actually bring about a deepening faith in the children of God, who are in need of healing and leadership, just like the Brothers in Cenacolo. As Mother Elvira says,

> We must believe that life does not come by chance. It is not ours; it is a gift from God, born from His Heart that is love. It is a gift that we must begin to unwrap, just like when we are given a beautifully wrapped gift. With curiosity, we tear open the package to find what is on the inside and why it was given to us, a reason that undoubtedly will give us great joy.[14]

There's the problem: we do not beautifully wrap that most precious of gifts—God Himself and His Healing: Jesus Christ—and we certainly do not seem to be curious or joyful about receiving such a present: our communication of the gift of Jesus and the gift of Healing is not wrapped well, nor is it promoted well through the Church as a valuable gift that is on offer for free. We ignore the gift wrapped in 'safe' brown paper, and hence, this rarely leads to a curiosity which in turn would lead us to realise that the present might actually be for me! Do we really believe the gift is either real or for me? Ultimately can I truly believe that such a poorly wrapped gift would give me joy—this lack of curiosity by both Church and individuals is a real problem?

Ultimately there is a lack of awareness of the need for healing in our lives. The Brothers in Cenacolo when they arrive are battling with their addictions, but it does not take them too long to realise that the addictions are not the true problem—a real problem yes, but not the true problem.

Having shared and prayed and been challenged on many levels the Brothers come to realise that their true problem is their woundedness or their poverties as they would call them—but it took the fraternal and broken Body of Christ to help them to see this reality in their lives. We as the Church—institution, broken Body and healing Body—need to help people see their need for the healing of their true and deep wounds that may not be obvious in our daily lives because of other distractions—such as life itself! Ignorance, denial, lack of guidance, lack of challenge, lack of loving care, for as Mother Elvira says, 'I realised that when we do things with love, passion and joy time becomes eternity... it is time for evangelisation; it is time to give witness.[15]

As mentioned above I think that fear of the healing power of God either working or not working is a reality for most priests, and therefore outside of the healing Sacraments little is offered to those around us who are in need of prayer ministry and healing ministry.

A lack of a personal relationship with the Lord as Our Saviour and Healer results in most of us settling for what is comfortable and easy and non-threatening to our status quo in prayer, healing and works of charity—for relationships demand high amounts of input and effort to get them to work well, as well as a letting go of who I see myself as and surrendering to the other, which is quite frightening in itself: but as we have the perfect partner then what is there to be afraid of by letting ourselves be consumed by the other who is God after all!

Is there a power play at work here also, in terms of who has the authority and commissioning to take the Healing of The Lord to others? Priests or laity? Or both? Again Cenacolo can teach us here! All are equal in Cenacolo, yes there may be Responsibles, but they too are in just as much healing and love and support as are the Brothers who have just arrived. I remember being in tears with one of the Brothers, a lad of 20 years old who had more wisdom and love and support and acceptance than I could ever have revealed at that time as a 48 year old priest.

Who can Minister?

Wouldn't it be amazing if our lay ministers who take Holy Communion faithfully to the sick and housebound, and offer great sacramental comfort and healing as well as social interaction, could offer prayer and healing ministry through the charisms and gifts of the Holy Spirit. Again from my perspective, I have rarely if ever reminded the lay ministers to pray directly with the sick and housebound, outside of bidding prayers and prayers of petition. I feel that very few if any lay ministers would have been trained to pray with others for healing. We are told by St Paul in his Letters (1Co 12, Rm 12 and Ep 4) that there are many spiritual gifts which are to be used by the individual and the community for the individual and the community, including the charism of healing. And yet these recognised gifts/charisms are not truly exploited by the Church or parish or priests or laity.

Do priests even realise the gifts of the Lord's healing ministry and His authority that they have at their disposal? Personally I would doubt it. Again it is about fear and a reluctance to get too involved as well as a time issue, hence a need to have a vision of priesthood and parish life that can lead to a certain hierarchy of priorities. After all, the Lord did, 'summon His twelve disciples, and gave them authority over unclean spirits with power to drive them out and to cure all kinds of diseases and illness.' (Mt 10:1) We too as priests through our baptismal ministries of Priest, Prophet and King are called and commissioned to bring others to the power of Jesus: as priest through prayer, as prophet through proclamation and as king through witness and action. We as priests are further commissioned through the power of Ordination or Holy Orders to galvanise the faithful through the authority given us in being Christ for others so we are called to be Priest, Prophet, King and Christ—what a calling and privilege, but do we not all too often down play the power given us as Nelson Mandela said in his inaugural speech upon becoming President of South Africa:

> … Our deepest fear is not that we are inadequate. Our deepest fear is that we are powerful beyond measure. It is our light not our darkness that most frightens us. We ask, who am I to be brilliant, gorgeous, talented, and fabulous? Actually, who are you not to be? Your playing small does not serve the world. There is nothing enlightened about shrinking so that other people won't feel insecure around us. We were born to make manifest the glory of God that is within us. It is not just in some of us, it's in everyone. And as we let our light shine, we unconsciously give other people permission to do the same. And as we are liberated from our own fear, our presence automatically liberates others.

This is the very thing that the Brothers of Cenacolo are led to believe and understand: how does it help anyone or oneself to live a life less than God had imagined for you? Priests are seen and known as the Alter Christus and as the Persona Christi—so within us we have the power and authority of Christ—no wonder we shy away from such 'power beyond measure.'

Into the Light

Do people really understand the need for spiritual healing or have we reached a point where everything is down to medication and an attitude of submission to a decadent and secular culture? How can expectant faith that the Lord always wants to bring about deeper inner healing be raised throughout the Church?

I would say that the majority of people who come to Church do not understand the need for spiritual healing, nor the breadth and depth that is on offer, as St Paul prays in Ephesians 3:14–21. As suggested above it was only when the Brothers entered Cenacolo that they truly began to realise that their real need for healing went far beyond their addictions. It was only when these addicts had truly hit rock bottom that somehow God got them to a place of refuge, security and healing—but, surely we should be able to catch people before this point! Life was too busy for them to realise that they had deeper and more profound hurts to be healed than that of addiction. 'Others are the cause of my problems' would not be an unknown belief and comment, but once an awareness of the need to take personal responsibility for one's actions, reactions and attitudes came about then also, slowly came into focus the road to recovery and healing. The need to be healed from past hurts, abuse and rejections and so on that have led to the reactions and poor choices in life becomes a reality.

It is through community living that the Brothers realise they are in need of healing, and it is when they go out to give testimonies that other people begin to realise that they too are in need of healing. It is as Mother Elvira says, 'It is the time for evangelisation; it is the time to give witness.'[16] If nothing is done then people, as with the addicts, can only submit to a secular way of life that leads to death of the true self, whereas submission to God leads to life and life to the full. As said above, to be consumed by God is surely infinitely more freeing than to be consumed by drugs, alcohol, anger, fear, bitterness, hatred, loathing of self! Mother Elvira says:

> We belong to Someone who wants to take care of us and who wants to discover the true flavour of life, for He knows that only

in this way will we be truly happy. Every life that is without God is false, darkened, insipid and void of warmth and love. This is why the Community was born, so that many lost and lonely youth could find the heart of life. Every day that you spend in Community is a miracle of God's Love.[17]

Appendix 2 at the end of this book gives an extremely moving testimony of one Cenacolo Brother.

It would be beautiful if dioceses were more proactive in encouraging priests and their parishioners to become involved in the ministry of prayer for healing. Bishops could encourage this by offering Pastoral Letters, on a regular basis, that encourage people to reflect on areas of their lives that might be in need of healing, and guiding them to make inroads to recognised groups in the diocese who offer ministry for healing. There is the need for the setting up of recognised ministry teams for healing, who have been fully trained and commissioned, and who are overseen regularly, and which are linked with the diocesan team of exorcists.

Notes

[1]   Mother Elvira Petrozzi, *Sparks of Light* (Saluzzo: Comunita Cenacolo, 2012), pp. 11–12.

[2]   *Ibid.*, p. 11.

[3]   *Ibid.*, p. 12.

[4]   *Ibid.*, p. 11.

[5]   *Ibid.*

[6]   *Ibid.*

[7]   Julian of Norwich, *Revelations of Divine Love*, chapter 27.

[8]   *Ibid.*

[9]   *Ibid.*, p. 12.

[10] *Ibid.*, p. 11.

[11] *Ibid.*, p. 12.

[12] *Ibid.*, p. 11.

[13] *Ibid.*, pp. 11–12.

[14] *Ibid.*, pp. 13–14.

[15] *Ibid.*, pp. 11–12.

[16] *Ibid.*, p. 11.

[17] *Ibid.*, p. 14.

18

The Need for a Catholic Residential Healing Centre in the UK

Alan Guile and Maurice Ward

There is no Catholic residential centre in the UK wholly devoted to the healing ministry whereas there are a number of such centres, some very large, run by other Christians. Around 5000 people a year seek prayer ministry for healing in these residential centres. This chapter makes a case for the setting up of a Catholic centre for healing where people can receive prayer ministry when in need and where men and women can be trained in the art of listening to people of praying with those who are in need of healing of various kinds.

Introduction

Thirty two years ago, one of us and his late wife felt called by God to move to Norton, Stockton-on-Tees. Since then well over 550 people have come to that house to ask for prayer ministry for inner healing. In many cases they have needed to come for months or even years, perhaps at increasing intervals between visits after the first few sessions each of about two hours.

As has been described[1] some of these people have come very long distances and a few of them had to arrange overnight stays in the area so that they could receive prayer ministry from us on more than one day. They have by now included people (some of whom were priests) from Sussex, Shropshire, Cambridgeshire, Lancashire, Northumberland, Nottinghamshire, Leicestershire, Gloucestershire, London, Northern Ireland and two who flew over from Europe to stay in a nearby hotel.

Over recent years there have been considerable developments in inner healing ministry and a realisation that the process can spread over a long time, and that it can be helpful to people to have more than periodic two hour sessions. Some Christians in the UK have recognised for decades that there are troubled people who need to be able to stay for some days in a centre where there are 'trained' people available to listen to them and pray with them. Although there are still many Catholic retreat centres open, none of them is wholly devoted to providing inner healing prayer ministry whenever there is a genuine need, and for as long as the individual needs to stay. At least one Catholic lady had a vision some thirty years ago of being called to establish such a centre but was thwarted when her diocese overbid her offer for a convent which was becoming available.[2]

The need for such a healing centre can sometimes be recognised more clearly by secular bodies than by the Church. For example, among the earliest visitors to Harnhill Manor, a healing centre for the Anglican Church near Cirencester, were a young mother and baby who were sent from a town on the South coast by a social worker. The founder of Harnhill Manor, which within six years of opening had rooms for fourteen guests, writes[3] 'The young mother responded wholeheartedly to the welcome and love she received at Harnhill. She knew little about Jesus but lapped up everything she was told or read about Him. She gladly gave her life to Jesus in the second week. This clearly illustrates the case which has been made[4] for the deep connection between praying for inner healing and evangelisation. Sadly, an awareness that the Church can sometimes lag behind secular professional awareness, has been noted elsewhere[5] in connection with prayer for physical healing.

It should be remembered that to begin prayer ministry for inner healing can be for many people the start of a journey with many ups and downs. Emotions and memories, wholly or partly buried in our natural defence mechanisms begin to be faced and this can be very difficult and painful over a long period and we need ongoing love and care. Even when ministry is available at a residential healing centre it may in certain very deep woundings take as much as ten years for some people, as shown in Chapter 14. As we open ourselves more and more to God we may become more aware that we are in spiritual warfare and in need of protection and support of others. It may be far more difficult for someone who receives initial ministry in a setting away from home if there is no ongoing prayer ministry, support and fellowship in their own parish or surrounding area. All of these means of prayer ministry are needed and are complementary to one another.

Harnhill Manor

In 1984 Canon Arthur Dodds and his wife, who had for some years held healing services within the parish, were invited to lunch in Harnhill Manor, two miles from Cirencester. In his thank-you note a few days later, Arthur wrote 'What a wonderful centre of Christian healing your lovely home would make.'[6] This began a process involving many people, which led to the opening of Harnhill Manor as a Christian healing centre and it is now in its twenty ninth year.

Over the last eight years residential guests have averaged about 540 per year. Though the demand over these recent years seems fairly static, the depth of ministry needed has increased a great deal. The impression of the ministry team is that it has changed as the churches in general have started to offer prayer ministry in their own congregations much more than before, so they at Harnhill are now picking up those who have not been helped by relatively simple ministry.

Some people who turn out to ask for prayer ministry come for personal retreat for a variable number of days to suit themselves. Where people do come to ask specifically for prayer ministry for healing, they offer a choice between a week-end or a stay from Monday to Friday. During the latter there are two public services and some background teaching on faith and on healing and each person can have a prayer ministry session on the Tuesday and Thursday. The story they most often hear is that people report that real healing comes not at the second session, but during the night or at the Service on the Friday morning. The team's main observation is the often remarkable difference in their demeanour from when they arrive and when they leave on Friday. There is a steady trickle of testimonies, some while they are still at Harnhill, and some much later when they are sure that the change is lasting. Those who come range from late 20s to mid 80s and they have seen wonderful changes at both ends of the scale. Almost all the guests come because of personal testimony and recommendations from folk who have personally been to stay themselves.

Crowhurst Rectory

Crowhurst Rectory which opened in 1928 is the oldest Christian healing centre in the country. Residential guests can stay for two days or a maximum of three days and tend towards the older age group. As well as prayer ministry they can attend a daily service which includes teaching. In addition they have family weekends including children though they have ministered only to few children. There are men- only weekends and women- only weekends. Including people attending weekends or coming during the week, some two hundred and fifty people a year receive prayer ministry.

Rev. Steve Clarke reports 'I was a pastor of churches for years but now we achieve more in one weekend than I was able to do in a parish over a whole year'. He had previously worked at Scargill House in Wharfedale and at Burswood. He has seen immense good happen due to guests being resident. As he put it, 'the residential experience is like Jesus going up a mountain for prayer. When a guest comes for ministry two prayer ministers sit quietly praying for discernment of what God the Father is doing or saying. Then they receive words or perhaps pictures and questions to ask, so that there is group discernment.' There are twenty full-time staff and thirty prayer ministers. They have twenty five beds and 250 prayer partners.

Ffald-y-Brenin

In 1999 Roy and Daphne Goodwin were appointed directors of a Christian retreat centre in a valley in west Wales. Roy had long been an evangelist and after a few months there he cried out to God because there had been no one for him to lead to Christ. Then people with no Christian faith, driving or hiking in the area began to arrive feeling compelled to come up their drive. Sometimes the Goodwins would offer to bless them and they would weep, or the Holy Spirit would fall on them as they walked in the grounds or sat in the chapel. As they showed one couple around the husband kept telling filthy stories until they showed them into the chapel. He and his wife fell down and he cried saying to God 'I'm so sorry I didn't know you were real'.

They began to see physical healings taking place, and this led on to praying for inner healing as more broken people were drawn there. Often these were boisterous in their faith and clear in their testimony, but after they had stayed a few days, they would crack open and the truth came out as the Holy Spirit touched them. This breakthrough might happen in the chapel, at the high cross in the grounds or through dreams. Their experiences of many people bear out the inseparable connection between inner healing and deeper evangelisation, and also that some days of residence can lead to a new opening up.

Roy writes[7] of how their earlier response to personal need was to open up counselling conversations leading to prayer, which limited them to seeing only a few people a day and left him and his wife emotionally drained. They began to move away from the counselling and prayer frame work to simply asking people 'Are you willing for God to come and touch any area of your life that is troubling you?' Then they would pray briefly and ask for a word of knowledge, discernment or prophecy. Sometimes they received something, sometimes they didn't. However they find that God is dealing with people in various ways during their stay. They report that so many people are coming and receiving healing that they cannot say how many. Their stay varies between three and seven days with an average of four.

Whitehill Chase

Bishop Morris Maddocks, who was called by the Archbishop of Canterbury to develop the healing ministry, established with his wife The Acorn Christian Foundation in 1983, and Whitehill Chase in Bordon, Hampshire became its home, opening in 1985. They quickly became able to take up to twenty six residential guests and began to offer a service of healing and wholeness each week, together with opportunities for personal prayer for healing. The number of people coming for prayer ministry has definitely increased in the last few years, stretching their practice and prayer ministry resources. More than 300 are coming per year and averaging a stay of two to three days. The ratio of women to men has been about 60/40, mainly in the 40–60 plus age group, though more young people are now coming and provision is being targeted towards them. Some parents bring children in the holidays and they are prayed for as part of the service. Any children's ministry is handled carefully and sensitively but is not the norm.

Green Pastures

Green Pastures near Bournemouth was opened in 1955 and many hundreds of people have gone there since then. Last year about 180 came for personal retreat which gave them the opportunity to ask for prayer ministry if they wished. People usually stay between 3 days and a week. They have noticed that in the recent past they haven't had so many testimonies of miraculous physical healing, which used to be the norm, but these physical healings still do occur. They comment that the

277

emotional and spiritual well-being of the individual is recognised more and more as being just as important. The average age of those coming is over 50 though they are seeking ways of drawing younger people. Women tend to outnumber men slightly. They have noticed the benefit of a longer stay as God is able to work in them and they can receive prayer to work through issues over a number of days. There is a team of four managers who live on site with a chaplain and pastoral team of twelve from a wide variety of denominational backgrounds who give at least a day a month to lead services and to pray with guests.

Holy Rood House

Until 1992 Holy Rood House at Thirsk was occupied by Sisters of the Holy Rood, an Anglican religious community, after which it became an ecumenical centre, with two Anglican priests, Stanley and Elisabeth Baxter as directors. Residential and day guests are offered psychotherapy/counselling and other therapies from a large team of volunteers from around the area, with a wide range of medical, counselling and other professional qualifications, so as to offer a holistic approach to the Christian ministry of healing. They quickly provided overnight accommodation for up to twenty four people so that groups as well as individuals could come.

Ellel Ministries

Peter Horrobin felt a call from God to Christian ministry and to healing in particular for years before he and others were able to purchase Ellel Grange near Lancaster in 1986. Within nine years the full-time team of Ellel ministries had grown to over 140 people running continuous healing retreats and training courses, with over 300 trained associate counsellors in the different centres. In 1991 Glyndley Manor, near Eastbourne was purchased, followed by a centre in Canada and Pierrepont Estate in Surrey, in 1995, and a centre in Hungary was developing.

a) Ellel Grange opened in 1986 and since then 12,000 to 20,000 people have come for prayer ministry. It now has a residential community of about 50 and a volunteer ministry team numbering up to 70 supporters at any one time. In each of the last few years about 1200 have come for prayer ministry, staying two to five days with an average of three. About two thirds have been women and the average age range has been between 20 and 80 years. In addition 1500 people a year attend residential training courses, the majority coming to learn, but many have also received personal healing in the process. They only minister to young people with the express permission and presence of their parents. The pattern of ministry on residential healing retreats provides powerful evidence that a residential stay provides opportunities for more in-depth prayer ministry with longer lasting results. Testimonies received from those who have been on healing retreats are in general outstanding. They have many long-term testimonies of lives transformed. Many Catholics have gone on their courses.

b) Glyndley Manor opened 1 January 1992 and now has about 25 staff on site assisted by about 5 volunteers. There are 25 people who help with teaching and about 55 in the prayer ministry team. In each of the last 2 years some 1200 people have come for healing prayer ministry. Most stay for 3 days, a good number for a week and some for up to 20 days. They are about 65% women and 35% men ranging between 18 and 90, but not many under 25. They do sometimes minister to children if a parent is with them, mostly in the 15 to 17 range. They find many benefits in people staying for some days, time to process what is going on within them and to allow God to speak, gain further understanding through teaching and ministry, and a safe, confidential place away from the stress of everyday life. Some who come for their residential teaching courses find that they need healing. They do receive many testimonies about the benefits.

c) The Pierrepont centre and its estate opened in 1995 and now has 60 residential staff with 150 associate prayer ministers who come in from the local community. About 850 people ask for personal prayer ministry per year, staying for up to three days. The demand has increased in the last five years, with about 70% women, 30% men, and about 70–80% over the age of forty. They have done a small amount of prayer ministry with children but only with the presence and consent of parents. They also have a prayer ministry training school with from 30–80 attending in ten weekends a year, and 2500 people attend their free conferences per year. They often receive testimonies many months or years later, and they range widely from relatively new Christians to church leaders and ministers.

Burrswood

Dorothy Kerin experienced a remarkable physical healing in 1912 for which no medical explanation could be given. This led her to establish her first home of healing in London in 1930 as a registered nursing home. In 1948 she bought Burrswood near Groombridge, Kent, a large country house with a church and large grounds. It is still a nursing home with some people coming for four public healing services a week.

Catholic Retreat Centres

Although none of the existing Catholic retreat centres devotes all of its time and resources to praying for inner healing, there are likely to be people attending courses or private or organised retreats who reveal areas of need and receive prayer ministry from members of the community or others present. The following example of this has been given by the Rector of one of these centres:

At Minsteracres Monastery and Retreat Centre the ministry of healing takes place in several ways. It happens with people who come on retreat either as individuals or as members of a group. In the course of their stay which is usually a couple of nights, but sometimes longer, there are opportunities to speak with a member of the retreat team. Some people use this to share areas in their lives where healing is needed. This happens during most of retreats for parish groups and also during other organised retreats, for example Pentecost or Holy Week. Team members listen and pray with people and often it is connected with the sacrament of Reconciliation. Every year there are around sixty individual retreatants. A number of them ask for spiritual accompaniment during their retreat and at times it is in that context that prayer for healing takes place. It also happens that people call in and ask to see a priest or other member of the team with whom they share their need. This happens on a weekly basis.

Other Organisations and Groups

Christian Healing UK, which began seventeen years ago, is an affiliation to which some of the healing centres and advisors belong. It aims to provide a national forum and voice, and to hold regional meetings to encourage and support those involved in Christian healing ministry. In addition to the residential centres with their resident community and substantial local prayer and other support, the main ones of which have been mentioned above, there are a number of other organisations and groups which hire various centres for courses of prayer ministry for healing.

Conclusions

It would seem from the information obtained that Christian healing centres cover a wide spectrum of emphasis, from total reliance on the power and presence of God to bring healing, to considerable dependence on professional qualifications and experience and the use of therapies alongside prayer. Our emphasis and concern is very much on the first of these two approaches.

It is clear from the number of Christian residential healing centres in the UK and the many years they have been open, that substantial numbers of people are coming to stay for some days in order to receive prayer for inner healing. The numbers per year reported to us from the largest Christian residential healing centres total around 5000. A substantial number of others seek such ministry whilst they are staying at Catholic retreat centres, or when various organisations or churches put on courses or hire centres for courses of prayer for inner healing. It is also clear from their experience that appreciable spiritual benefits and progress in the process of inner healing come to individuals who choose this form of ministry, as compared with having a number of sessions of listening and prayer ministry at intervals of days or weeks. Thus there is a clear need and willingness to travel in many people which is borne out by the people who have travelled hundreds of miles for ministry in one Catholic house, hearing about it simply by word of mouth.

Of course this need of people for a residential centre does not alter the fact that the healing ministry should be a normal part of the everyday life of the Church, present as far as possible in the local area, ideally in every parish. Those who receive some healing at a centre away from home, are likely to need further ministry and support from their own church for some time.

Pope Francis is continuing to call strongly for the Church to bring the healing of Christ to wounded people. He says that there are many wounded people waiting in the aisles of the church for a minister of Christ to heal them from their pains and sorrows and liberate them from the demons that plague them.[8] The Pope said, 'to heal and care for its people is the mission of the Church'. This requires he said, 'healing the wounded hearts, opening doors, freeing people and saying that God is good, forgives all, is our Father who is tender and always waiting for us'.

In the Catholic church this is not going to happen on any scale unless and until the bishops and priests give a very positive lead and help lay people to open themselves to the power and gifts of the Holy Spirit which lie unused and latent within the body of Christ. It is vital that this happens as quickly as possible, because of the depths and extent of the woundedness in some people whom Pope Francis is calling upon the Church to heal. If and when this begins to happen, and if God wants a Catholic residential healing centre, some large property will become available and those people chosen by God will come forward to form its resident community, whilst others in the locality with the right gifts will offer their assistance.

Acknowledgements

We thank the various healing centres for all their help in answering questions and supplying information.

Notes

[1] A Guile *Journey into Wholeness: Prayer for Inner Healing—An Essential Ministry of the Church* (Leominster: Gracewing, 2013), pp. 57–63.

[2] *Ibid.,* pp. 4–5.

[3] A. Dodds, *Desert Harvest* (Cirencester: Collectors Books Ltd, 1993), p. 128.

[4] Guile, *Journey into Wholeness.*

[5] J. McManus, *Healing in the Spirit (*Chawton: Redemptorist Publications Ltd, 2002*),* pp. 5–19.

[6] Dodds, *Desert Harvest.*

[7] R. Goodwin and D. Roberts, *The Grace Outpouring,* (Eastbourne, David C Cook, 2008)

[8] Pope Francis, Morning Homily, 5 February 2015.

19

The Healing Role of Peer Support and Forgiveness Following a Homicide

Barry Mizen

In this chapter Barry, whose sixteen year old son was murdered in 2008, tells the story of that dreadful day and how he, his wife and their other children have handled that grief. He stresses the need for the healing power of peer support. Barry and his wife Margaret have become evangelists, giving talks in churches and in schools and helping many suffering people to begin to cope in new ways with their pain. They experienced Christ walking with them in their pain and now they share that experience with many. Barry writes very movingly about the struggles of forgiveness and the healing power of forgiving.

Introduction

I am a married man, aged 64, and I have lived in South East London all my life. I have been married to Margaret for 38 years and we are the parents of seven sons and two daughters, ranging from 44 to 17 years of age. As with all of us, our lives do not conform to some supposed ideal of perfection, whatever that is, but we do have a deep love and respect for each other. I am forever grateful to the gifts God has given me. The reason we have been invited to contribute this chapter is that our second youngest child was murdered in 2008, and I would like to talk about how we have managed as a family since the loss of our Jimmy. My wife has been a Catholic all her life, I became one in my late thirties following a longing for answers to many questions swirling around in my mind. I didn't find answers as much as more questions. However what I did find has impacted my life since and I believe has enabled us to cope with what would seem the 'uncopeable', the murder of a child.

Grief for me was a very real physical pain. I would feel it in the pit of my stomach, as though I was being folded in half and jammed into a vice that was then wound up. Immediately I would begin asking for Our Lady's intercession, and the pain would ebb away. As the days went by, as soon as I felt a tightening in my stomach I would begin again, and it would ebb away. I very seldom get that now and I miss it; it's a link to Jimmy. Is it an ever-widening gap? Is it another day further away?

Following the murder of my son, at times all the prayer I could muster was:

> 'I believe You Jesus, I love You Jesus, I trust You Jesus; help me Jesus.'

The Death of Jimmy Mizen

Our Jimmy was killed sixteen years and one day after he was born one sunny Saturday in May. He came into this life on a Saturday and he left this life on a Saturday. His killer was a local nineteen year old, well known for his aggressive and violent nature. He had attacked an older brother on a couple of occasions before the fatal attack on our second youngest child.

I was at work mending shoes in my shop. I had given Jimmy, who worked with me, the day off because the day before was his birthday. Following a frantic phone call from my wife to 'get to the baker's quick, Jimmy's been attacked and it looks bad,' I left the shop. I had no idea at the time that it was the beginning of a new path, along which I will continue until my own leaving of this life.

Tossing the shop keys to my employee saying what I had just been told, I raced to my van to drive the five miles to the shops around the corner from my home, all the time with a dreadful sense of foreboding and a constant verbalised plea on my lips, 'Please God let him be alright'.

> Approaching the area, roads heavily congested, an illegal U-turn on a dual carriage, driving along the road to the baker's, lights, ambulances, police cars, tape, many people, I drive my van straight onto the driveway of someone I know who is standing outside her home, surrounded by neighbours, heads peering in the direction of the bakers, concerned, wondering faces. Throwing her the keys, 'it's my son,' I say as I run the last fifty yards.
>
> Margaret my wife, coming towards me, a handprint in blood on her top, a son to one side wearing shorts, the bottom half of his body with bare legs covered in blood, another son sitting on the ground, his back against a tree, head in hands sobbing uncontrollably.
>
> Someone, a paramedic, emerges from the baker's, taking their rubber gloves off; a voice from somewhere saying, 'He's dead!'

Dead?

What am I supposed to do now?

I sit on the kerb, suddenly thinking where's George? My youngest son, dear sweet George, a week away from his ninth birthday. He's in the back of one of the emergency vehicles. I sit next to him and put my arm around him; he's crying. His sister says 'don't worry Jimmy's in Heaven', he stops crying and hasn't cried since.

For anything.

The perpetrator was convicted some ten months later of our Jimmy's murder and was given a life sentence with a minimum tariff of 14 years; the consequence of uncontrolled anger and smashing a glass dish into Jimmy's face and severing vital arteries.

Healing Power of Personal Responsibility

We had a lot of media coverage and as we emerged from The Central Criminal Court, more commonly known as The Old Bailey, there was a phalanx of photographers and journalists. Whilst acknowledging our thanks to the police and thanking God for Jimmy, I also had a chance to share what had been running through my head since our loss. I spoke of our country as one of 'civility, fairness and safety', and how we were rapidly losing that and becoming a country of 'anger, selfishness and fear.' I went on to say 'it doesn't have to be like this', calling for us all to come together so we can change it.

For us the many issues in society and perhaps also in our Faith Communities are our responsibility both as collectively, and perhaps more importantly as individuals. It's not up to someone else to solve these problems. We share our Jimmy's story in many schools, and one of the things we ask the young people is 'who is responsible for the society we live in?' We offer 'Is it the police or government's responsibility?' Whilst agreeing that these bodies have a role to play, the young people realise that the latter cannot do it on their own. When prompted as to what organisation or person is the most influential of all, sooner or later a student will offer 'me'?

And that is it—if we want a more peaceful and compassionate society, what am I going to do?

This also applies to our faith communities—we have to change our focus. It's not the responsibility of our parish priest, our bishop or indeed the Pope to do everything. They have a hugely important role of guidance and leadership, but they cannot do it on their own. We all have a role to play.

What am I going to do?

The Healing Power of The Gospel

As this book is specifically to look at healing in its various ways, I would like to write about the role to which Margaret and I have felt drawn. Perhaps it's our mission in life. We were aware within days that what had happened had to have a meaningful outcome; I had such a sense of God saying to me, 'Barry I am giving you a teaching denied to most. Use it.' My wife spoke in the early days and still believes passionately that she was not meant to have our son Jimmy for longer than 16 years and one day. There are whole libraries full of discussion on this topic of determination, but for the purposes of this chapter let's take my wife's and my understanding for what it is. This is how we are, this is what we believe and think.

I stand in admiration of my wife when she speaks in public about her faith. She says she has a simple faith, she believes with all her heart that she loves God and she knows God loves her, even with all her imperfections, and she doesn't know what else there is to know. Margaret and I share the daily readings, perhaps not as regularly as we could, but for weeks after Jimmy's death the readings, especially the Gospel readings were almost leaping off the page. I had such a sense of God saying, 'Barry this is for you.' Every reading was so relevant to what was happening at the time. There were many other connections which perhaps some would dismiss as coincidence, but so much and so often? I regret that I didn't keep a journal; our sense of God being with us was, and is, profound.

The Healing Role of Peer Support Following a Homicide

Apart from all else we do, whether talks in schools, confirmation groups and all the other activities to which our lives are now dedicated, the most important is helping others who are experiencing a loss of a dear loved one due to homicide. In short, peer support. Norman Cresswell wrote:

> Words are useless in the face of tragedy, as any priest will tell you,
>
> There is no scope for a trite reference to a loving God, a just God,
> a caring God.

He has momentarily been obliterated.

All we can do is to offer a hand, a shoulder, a tear.

All we can do is transfer the Christ in us to the Christ in the one suffering,

And hope against hope that they will meet.

Our younger daughter Samantha, now 29, has Down's Syndrome and after her birth we wanted to meet other people in our area who also had children with Down's Syndrome. We formed the Lewisham Down's Group and met regularly with a core group of five families. We shared experiences, issues of health and education. We all became close friends— we had a common bond that helped us through a difficult time, it helped us manage. We still have those relationships now.

The healing power of peer support which we had experienced when Samantha was born was very much at the front of my mind after our Jimmy's death. We wanted to meet others with a shared experience. Since the start we reached out to a family bereaved two weeks after we lost our Jimmy and continue to the present day; it helps, it heals. Much of our time is spent meeting and talking with others bereaved by homicide. This allows the instant bond between us to help manage a huge change. We cannot change what has happened but we can walk alongside others, even metaphorically, whilst a new path is taken.

Jesus walked and walks side by side with all of us, and that is what we are called to do. Walk side by side with others especially when they are in pain, when they are hurting. If we also have a similar experience of the hurt and pain, then perhaps it's easier. However we can still help others to find healing by just being with them. For us it is to be open to God working through us to heal at the deepest level. In the end it's not we who are doing the healing, we are just the conduit. God brings healing, whether physical or spiritual, and perhaps the greatest sign of that is people praying for their own healing, for full restitution, whether through a physical healing or the healing of their relationship with God.

This is what Christ did. He walked with those who were alone and with those who were vulnerable. I believe He is asking all of us to do the same. We have used different terms when we've been asked what we hope peer support will do. We have tended to say, 'it's helping people manage their loss'; it's assuring them that what they are feeling, whether it's anger, lethargy, physical pain, and more, is perfectly natural and they need not feel as though they are in some way odd. However what we believe is really happening is healing. We have resisted calling peer support healing as many will dismiss it as 'religious' and will not want to listen further. Of course to us it is the very faith that people are reluctant to acknowledge that we believe is actually at work.

Our Common Humanity Brings Healing

St Francis said: 'Preach the Gospel at all times, and when necessary, use words.'

This was most vividly demonstrated to me following our Jimmy's death. Our house had become full of a constantly changing mixture of family, friends, local parish and community. All grief stricken and looking to do something, anything, that could in some way help. Food was brought, (we've never had so many tea bags) the house cleaned, laundry done, our youngest son taken to and from school. This is the love we can show each other; this is also healing. Why is it only in the most terrible of circumstances that our common humanity comes to the surface?

One particular visitor was a former parish priest who had baptised our Jimmy. He stood in front of me and cried. I do not recall what our conversation was, or even if we actually said anything at all. The greatest comfort to me at that time was that he came and he cried. Even now that visit, that reaction from a priest, brings comfort to me. I thought he would offer words of comfort and perhaps he did, I don't remember, I thought he would be the font of all knowledge concerning life and death, I don't remember, but—He came, he cried, and I thank him for it.

The Healing Power of Empathy

Sister Joan Chittister wrote:

> Humanity is about identifying with somebody else's pain, with being there.

> We all know the familiar ache our hearts feel when we see someone who is suffering. Our humanity is the powerful thing that stops us from passing by that person on the road.

> Humanity is the ability to hurt for the others because that's the only fuel that will stop the injustice. You must know people as people, and you must do what they need in the middle of their pain.

Our faith is where we have drawn strength to cope since the loss of our Jimmy. Many people continue to be part of this journey and in various ways have brought healing, whether they know it or not, by allowing God to work through them. I worry when I see others who at the time when they need God the most, turn their backs. For me at the time in my life when I needed God the most He didn't let me down. Healing is to accept we cannot do this by ourselves, but with God we can; in the final analysis what else is there?

If healing is to take place, it won't be us doing it, it will be God. There is nothing demanded of us but to love, and we do this by being there for people and walking the path with them, until they can manage on their own, or are no longer in need. Our faith should enable us and encourage us to put others' needs before our own. There I believe lies the 'Peace beyond all understanding,' promised by Christ. If I am only concerned about my own needs I believe I will always have a sense of disappointment. Healing is our relationship with God, and we can, if we want, help others to connect with God for the first time, or re-connect if contact has been lost or encourage them to continue if they are under extreme challenge. For all I've just written my son is still not with me, although when I receive communion it is also my closest moment to him. Although I manage my life, the path is still one I would rather not be on if it meant my son would not have been murdered.

The Healing Role of Forgiveness

The day following our Jimmy's murder was a Sunday, and as usual we went to the 9am Mass at our parish church. The place was packed, everyone was in tears except us. We found ourselves comforting many people and my shirt was quite literally wet with tears of other people. If any of us look back on our lives we may well notice that through the truly difficult times we managed; God gives us the strength to cope when needed. Our grief didn't start for some time.

Outside the church was a huge gathering of the media: TV, radio, newspapers. We spoke words of empathy for the killer's family; my wife spoke of anger but it was anger that killed our son and she wouldn't go down that route and would not let it destroy our family. When we got home we said to each other 'where did those words come from?' We had never spoken to the media before, and yet we spoke quite clearly and eloquently.

The followings day's headlines read, 'Barry and Margaret forgive the killer of their son.' We were astonished; we said to each other that we never mentioned forgiveness, we only spoke about empathy for the killer's family and that we were not angry. Although we didn't realise it we had spoken words of forgiveness. The common perception of forgiveness would seem to be, 'don't worry about what you did, it doesn't matter, it's not important, it's all forgotten'. We believe this is not forgiveness; when people hurt us it does matter, it's not forgotten. It can impact the rest of our lives. Whatever forgiveness actually is, I believe, as with grief, it is unique to each individual. I thank God that I have never had a desire for revenge. I could not do to my son's killer what he did to my son, and that is my forgiveness. My wife would say she has never felt angry, yes incredibly sad, but not angry.

Many books have been written about forgiveness and they may all make sense academically.

Forgiveness is needed for healing to take place.

If God forgives unconditionally, who am I not too?

Only forgiveness can set us free.

All great stuff, but!

What should I say to the mother whose daughter became addicted to drugs and turned to prostitution to feed the habit and who in the course of her lifestyle became the victim of a serial killer who cut up her body, and disposed of it piece by piece? The only parts recovered for burial was some of her flesh and bones.

What do I say to the young mum whose partner of many years and the father of her young children has been murdered only days before, and who can only speak through huge sobs of grief not knowing how to explain to her children?

What do I say to the mother whose daughter was murdered by her partner, in the hope of gaining financially?

What do I say to the wife whose husband was stabbed over one hundred times in a random attack by a mental health sufferer who had stopped taking his medication, and whose last words to his killer were, 'Why are you doing this to me?'

There are many more, equally as harrowing.

The answer to all is nothing at first. Just listen. Just walk alongside. Just care.

This is part of the peer support we are trying to give. So where to talk about forgiveness? Where will healing come from?

I don't need my son's killer to have anything to do with me forgiving him. It is immaterial whether he wants forgiveness or not, indeed whether he's alive or not. I choose to forgive, and I do it for myself. I was determined after Jimmy's death not to be beaten by what had happened. This is a pragmatic view understood by people who do not have any belief. It is a deliberate decision. This can bring healing. To heal the sick and suffering is to bring the Good News, we just don't have to say that at the beginning.

As I finished writing this, the son of some dear friends has been diagnosed with terminal cancer and has some months to live; he will leave a wife and two small children. However I will continue to pray for a miracle knowing that the only hope is God. Through all the pain and suffering, it is only a belief in God that makes any sense, and so the only prayer I can still utter at times is:

> I believe You Jesus, I love You Jesus, I trust You Jesus; help me Jesus.

The Healing Role of 'For Jimmy'

We were determined that with God's grace we would not be beaten by what happened and that something good would come from it. Margaret speaks of seeking refuge in our bedroom the day Jimmy died due to the huge amounts of people that came to our house. She speaks of getting a clear message from God, 'not to worry, Jimmy is safe in Heaven'. She also made a vow to Jimmy that we will dedicate our lives to working for peace for all our young people. From that has come the charity work that we both do, along with the support of our family; it's called For Jimmy.

Since the charity was founded we have worked tirelessly to create a legacy of peace, in Jimmy's name, which has positively impacted the lives of thousands of young people and helped create safer and more connected communities.

Our mission is to share Jimmy's story to help all our young people fulfill their potential and help build the types of communities we want to live in. Our core work is running a flagship programme in primary and secondary schools in Lewisham and surrounding boroughs. This pro-gramme helps socially and academically at risk young people build stronger relationships with their local community so they feel safe, build resilience, gain confidence and feel valued.

Alongside this Margaret and I continue to share Jimmy's story with thousands of people across the country in Catholic schools, conferences and confirmation groups. The charity runs two community cafés that offer training, work experience and employment opportunities to young people in our local area.

One of our projects is establishing safe havens. Working with schools, local police and communities, we get shops and public buildings to be safe havens, somewhere a young person can find a refuge, where the door can be locked and police or family summoned. The greatest outcome of this is the building of relationships within our communities. Cohesive communities are safe communities.

When our family lost our beloved Jimmy, it changed our lives irrevocably. Since that day we've been determined to make a positive change to our society, this includes trying to change the thinking that ever harsher punishment is the way to lessen the instances of crime and anti-social behaviour. That change will only come when enough of us are prepared to say 'it doesn't have to be like this and what can I do?' That means challenging widely held assumptions and asking big questions about the kind of society we want to be. Jimmy's legacy will not be one of vengeance or fear, but one of hope and peace.

We thank God for the few years we had with our Jimmy, we are proud to be his parents, and we pray that God will guide us and give us the strength to continue the work we are doing. We did say to each other at the beginning that if whatever we do is meant to be then it will happen. We have said from the beginning that we trust God, and at the fifth anniversary I mentioned this to someone, who said, 'Well He hasn't let you down yet,' and I can say as we approach the ninth anniversary in a few months, 'He hasn't let us down.'

Thank you Jesus.

20

Healing and Parish Life

Kathryn Turner

In this chapter Kathryn Turner reflects on the place of healing in the life of the parish. She highlights the fears and the blocks that so often inhibit ministers, both clerical and lay, from even speaking about a healing ministry in the Church. From her experience as head of the Department of Spirituality in the diocese of Hexham and Newcastle she describes the very effective liturgies of Mercy that have been celebrated throughout the diocese in the Year of Mercy. The experience of God's mercy is always a healing experience.

Loss of a Legacy

> *God has appointed in the church first apostles, second prophets, third teachers; then deeds of power, then gifts of healing, forms of assistance, forms of leadership, various kinds of tongues.*

> (1 Co 12:28)

St Paul's letter to the Corinthians and James' letters to his group of early Christians both indicate that one of the most significant parts of the legacy of Jesus' ministry was that of healing. There are, of course, miracles associated with healing recorded in Acts but also the more everyday ministry of the visiting and anointing of the sick.

In later years, monks and nuns provided sanctuary for those who were ill and offered medication and care. This ministry was largely lost in this country with the dissolution of the monasteries during the Reformation and the work of the wise man and, more particularly, the wise woman and their herb lore began to be viewed with suspicion. The fact that prayers would accompany their ministrations may have led to their being associated with superstition or, at worst, witchcraft. As medicine became more scientific, much was gained but, we could argue, a great deal was lost.

One of the key losses was of confidence in the breadth and richness of Christian healing. Rather like the confusions around astronomical and other scientific discoveries, questions were being raised that people in the Church did not feel confident about addressing and so she either became defensive or silent on many of them.

In the eighteenth and nineteenth centuries Orders of religious women were formed, dedicated to the care of the sick and frail and they influenced people like Florence Nightingale with their gentle orderliness and standards of hygiene. These probably did as much in aiding recovery as the rudimentary medication which patients would receive in the hospitals of the day. We might remember that she was not known as the lady with the drugs trolley but the lady with the lamp; the one who brought light into the dark places and nights of sickness, fear and loss.

This is not to minimise the great things that modern medicine offers. Countless lives have been saved by medication and treatments which have been subjected to rigorous scientific testing at least in the developed world, though thankfully increasingly in the developing world. However it has perhaps left those forms of healing which depend heavily on prayer being seen as questionable. How do you prove that something works when it cannot be measured? How do you take out any possible human influence in proving the effectiveness of a 'treatment' that by its nature depends so much on a person of prayer and with the gift of healing being a part of it?

Reclaiming the Gift

One of the great gifts of the Charismatic Renewal was a rediscovery of the gift of healing in the Church. The timing of this coincided also with the renaming of the Sacrament of Extreme Unction as the Sacrament of the Sick. Many Catholics of a certain age will remember situations in which a priest was positively discouraged from visiting a sick person because it was feared that if he did, the person would be convinced that they were dying and lose hope. The fact that some people were anointed and recovered was not entirely missed, but to a greater or lesser extent the legacy of this understanding of the Sacrament as a last resort is still with us, even though St James insisted almost 2000 years ago that anointing was for those who were sick, not just those who were dying.

There is, however, a resurgence of awareness among Catholics that the Sacrament of the Sick has much to offer. Perhaps as modern medication has increased the chances of recovery from illnesses that would previously have been fatal, we have begun to realise that such recovery also needs a spiritual dimension. Some treatments can be as taxing on the human spirit as the illness itself and the prayers and sacraments of the Church are invaluable in the ups and the downs, the challenges, frustrations and fears of dealing with long-term sickness as well as the more obvious acute and 'near death's door' events. While psychiatric treatments have done much to ease the suffering of those living with mental illness, there are deep wounds that also need a spiritual and inner healing.

Perhaps we are in a stage of transition in our understanding of the sacrament and of healing in general. There will always be a place for special graces for the final journey across the threshold from this life to the next but, increasingly we recognise that people need the healing hand of the Lord as they deal with many other situations during their lifetimes that may not kill them but which are nonetheless life-diminishing.

What, though, might get in the way of this being taken up as widely as it might be?

Blocks and Fears

One factor might be the almost impossible task of measuring the effect. Studies have been undertaken to see whether being prayed for has an effect on the recovery of people suffering from a variety of illnesses. Most have been inconclusive—which is, perhaps, not surprising. One problem in determining the effects of prayer might simply be that there is a difference between a *cure* and a *healing*. No prayer can bring back an amputated limb, for example—but may well bring about a fortitude and positivity that enables the person to adjust to their new way of being. Extensive work produced by doctors in the USA since the 1990s seemed to highlight the power of good pastoral care involving prayer and religious practices. (See Chapter 6)

It is also significant that Christian prayer for healing does not treat someone as an *object* to be 'done to' but as a brother or sister who is also a *subject*—part of the 'doing' in their own healing; God will not impose healing on someone who does not want it. (cf Jn 5:6, Jesus and the paralysed man at Beth-zatha pool). It is also true that full cures through prayer and miracle are extremely rare. We only need to look at the great centres of healing such as Lourdes where very few miraculous cures are attested and yet there can be little doubt that countless thousands have found healing there. Whilst not minimising the value of a cure, healing may actually be something much deeper and much stronger; yes, improving physical health and well-being, but giving hope and strength to face some of the worst illnesses and disabilities with dignity and courage.

This very power might be something that causes people to be wary of healing and, to a certain extent, to less restricted use of the Sacrament of the Sick and anointing. Knowing its powerful graces could lead to fears that too easy an access to the Sacrament in particular could trivialise this great gift. Whilst it is true that this might be a risk, it is not one that seems to be particularly prevalent in practice. Very, very few people will repeatedly approach a priest for anointing for a headache or common cold and, where they do, this speaks of some underlying condition which may itself be in need of healing. Long-standing conditions of anxiety or suppressed memory may well manifest in physical illness and it may take repeated administration of the sacrament alongside prayer and, where necessary, counselling to root out the cause. Like someone embarking on a long period of surgery, chemotherapy and radio-therapy who may need periodic anointing to re-gather strength for the next phase, so someone embarking on a long journey to deep inner healing may need the same.

Another issue potentially associated with healing concerns the expectation that might be raised and the fear of the loss of faith if the healing 'does not work'. It is true that severe illness can make people, and perhaps more frequently those around them, desperate. We want the disease or injury to go away, we want to put the clock back to when everything was alright, we want *something* because the doctors have said there is nothing more that can be done. So many things bring people to cry out for healing, almost like a last resort when all else has failed. Their expectations may be unrealistic and there can be a feeling that this anguish is beyond human healing and intervention. This is indeed true. The beauty of our spiritual understanding of healing, as opposed to the work of the medical profession, is that it does not depend on our strength but only on our willingness to co-operate with God in offering His love and healing to this son or daughter and those who care for them. Like Florence Nightingale, we may not be able to bring everyone back to perfect health but in faith we can stand alongside them in their darkness and bring God's light into it.

This also raises something of a challenge for those who are held back from seeking prayer for healing by the teaching of 'offer it up', whereby people can mistakenly assume that all forms of suffering and sickness are automatically redemptive and part of the cross that God has given them to bear, perhaps even to the grave. Whilst it is true that we can always strive to unite our pain with that of Christ[1] (see also the words of Pope Paul VI in his closing address to Vatican II given in the appendix to Chapter 2), it is also right as the Church teaches[2] to pray at the same time for healing so that we allow God to do His will, not what we assume to be His will.

Another, almost contradictory fear is that healing might work. Although this might be what we want, there is also something lurking within us that we are not worthy of such a great grace. Life can change dramatically for someone who has been healed, particularly of a long-standing condition. For some, it might mean a radical change from considerable dependence on others to the need to be more self-sufficient, which can be daunting and naturally takes some adjusting to. There could also be the fear of the expectations of other people following a healing. Not only might the person be expected to be more independent but there might also be a feeling that they should now live a perfect life of witness and thanksgiving to the God who healed them, which few of us could do. Or there might be some conjecture about a great purpose for which God has healed them and an inevitable sense of disappointment if it is simply to live an ordinary life in all its fullness. It has been suggested that the man healed by the Pool after 38 years of waiting was one of the witnesses against Jesus. Perhaps in his question, Jesus was identifying a question-mark over his desire to be healed, and perhaps the transition from sick person waiting for someone to do something for him, to one who was now fully responsible for himself and possibly others, was too much to make.

There can also be a justifiable fear that if someone becomes known as a 'healer', people will lose sight of the Lord who is actually performing the healing. Very few people court this reputation; not many, but enough to raise the fear in some people's minds that it is more about a person's self-aggrandisement than the service of God and God's people. It can also sow a seed of doubt in the mind of someone who has been a minister of healing or feels called to be: am I doing this for God or for myself, and how do I know? It is the greatest of sadnesses when such concerns get in the way of someone responding to the call to pray for healing, especially when they simply withdraw with feelings of perceived unworthiness. It might be said that this is an indication of the importance of healing that the enemy works so hard to prevent people from believing that God really can work through them.

Supporting the Healing Ministry

Where healing ministry is taken seriously, it is important to ensure that there is support and supervision. The latter gives connotations of the person with the badge who walks up and down production lines or around stores but it is less about ensuring that people do the job properly and more about what the word means. It brings together the words *super* means over and *vision* meaning *seeing*. In our context, we are looking to people who watch over those ministering and being ministered to. This may happen during healing prayer, or in a confidential conversation later, but is an important safeguard for all concerned.

The idea of supervising (in our sense) a healing might be a surprise to some but it highlights that healing is very rarely a 'lone wolf' activity. There is a place for a private administering of the Sacrament of the Sick particularly, for example, when the recipient is also seeking Reconciliation. Even here, it is good for a priest to have people praying for him (in general if not for each particular visit) and a supervisor with whom he can share any concerns. Where a priest has a trusted friend or group of friends, this offers a profound spiritual support for more difficult situations. He may, for example, be being called to the bedside of someone his own age (particularly as a young man), or to that of a child, or a particularly difficult death where the family is divided and hostilities have already commenced. In these circumstances, the priest will be bringing light and grace into deeply troubled situations and needs the protection of the prayers of others.

Increasing numbers of lay people are being called to healing ministry and this need for prayerful support may be even more crucial as, although some formation is available, it is not always on offer where and when it is needed. Prayer together is needed before a healing service and during it by people whose sole task is deep back-up prayer, as well as prayer afterwards with the added possibility of a one-to-one conversation with a skilled priest, deacon, religious or lay person which will help to keep the ministers of healing free to act as conduits of God's grace.

It has been interesting to notice that the two sacraments of healing, Reconciliation and the Sacrament of the Sick, which were both seen as intensely private affairs are moving towards more communal celebrations. There is of course a need for both to be possible as one-to-one encounters but where penitential and healing services are offered they are almost always very well-attended. It is not even that people are just looking for general absolution in the former, because people will still come even if there are long queues for confession. The reason for the preference for communal services is unclear but it may be that there is a sense of people coming together as the broken Body of Christ, aware that no-one there is without sin but that, in solidarity, we can come before God to admit our own weakness and to pray for each other. This is a powerful witness. We are not going on a daytime television programme to wash our dirty linen in public. We do not know what our neighbour is dealing with, but can allow them space to repent and pray for them, knowing that they pray for us. There is, usually, a great sense of prayerfulness and contemplation as people reflect on their own sinfulness and need for God's mercy and love. Such a service also gives a platform to acknowledge corporate sin, those sins that do not belong to an individual but which catch us all up in selfishness and stop us living life to the full. They are also places where people can be anonymous which, for many in the early stages towards healing, can be very important.

The Jubilee Year of Mercy

The Jubilee Year of Mercy of 2015–16 opened up many possibilities, with a clear instruction in the papal bull that it was to be seen as an opportunity to reach out to those who have for so long felt marginalised.

In this Holy Year, we looked forward to the experience of opening our hearts to those living on the outermost fringes of society: fringes which modern society itself creates. How many uncertain and painful situations there are in the world today! How many are the wounds borne by the flesh of those who have no voice because their cry is muffled and drowned out by the indifference of the rich! During this Jubilee, the Church was called even more to heal these wounds, to assuage them with the oil of consolation, to bind them with mercy and cure them with solidarity and vigilant care.[3]

Many initiatives were undertaken around the world with attempts made to help others to see the Church as a field hospital whose first priority is to heal the most obvious wounds first and only later tackle deeper and more complex issues. In this, it is adopting Jesus' own model where He healed first and asked questions later if at all; at least as recorded in the Gospels. Jesus very rarely healed someone who then became part of the group of disciples who followed Him on the road. When, for example, a man liberated from a legion of demons tries to follow Jesus, he is told to return to his village and to share the news of his healing there. (Mk 5: 1–19). It is clear from His dealings with people such as the woman brought before Him who had been caught in adultery, that He was aware of the social and moral issues rumbling below the surface, but His approach was the same: to work through the most obvious problem first

299

which was a group of men preparing to stone a woman to death (Jn 8: 1–11). When a paralysed man is let down through a roof onto the floor before Him, Jesus does not leap into the obvious healing of paralysis but, perhaps, tackles the root cause first—a sin—a memory—a hidden pain that has left him paralysed and unable to move forward (Lk 5: 17–26). In a similar way, healing and penitential services are not the places to deal with deep or traumatic issues, but can offer a setting in which things begin to emerge and the person begins to believe that they can be dealt with by grace of God.

Liturgies of Mercy

During the Year of Mercy, one idea developed by the Diocese of Hexham and Newcastle was that of Liturgies of Mercy. Their purpose was to extend the hands of God's mercy, particularly to those who would not necessarily feel that they had a place in the church or wondered if they would even be welcome if they wanted to come, or perhaps even more challenging, to return after a long time away. The focus of the services was not so much on reconciliation or healing *per se* but on the burdens people carry, be they illness or addiction, their own or of someone they loved; difficult relationships; people in 'irregular' relationships, and so on. Invitations were made available at Sunday Masses for parishioners to take out to people who they thought might benefit from knowing that here was a service specifically for them to come to, just as they were.

There was a deliberate decision not to set it within a Mass or a penitential liturgy. This, in itself, was a challenge for some. Catholic congregations are very familiar with certain forms of service, but few have experienced something quite as informal as these services were planned to be. Each service was tailored to the community in which it was to take place, giving them ownership of the service and hopefully giving them the sense of confidence that they could produce something for themselves in the future.

The role of the welcomers was crucial. Service booklets had been prepared and stones were to be offered to be part of the service later, all of which had to be done efficiently. But the most important part which the welcomers had to play was in ensuring a warm and kind welcome to those for whom just stepping over the threshold of a church had been a major undertaking. One person spoke of having walked around the block four times before plucking up the courage to come in; another admitted to a parishioner of having needed a drink, and asked if they were *really* allowed to be there, and could they *really* go to Confession? This is a reminder that healing ministry is not confined to the more obvious ministers!

The first part of the liturgy was Word-focused, mainly using gospel accounts highlighting Jesus' desire to heal but sometimes with passages from the Old Testament speaking of God's love of His people and reflecting His desire to extend this mercy to each person in the congregation. Parishes had a fairly free choice of readings but it was strongly recommended that they include 'Come to me you who are weary and over-burdened' since this linked with the ritual to follow. This was complemented by a short reflective homily reiterating God's love and mercy and His longing that people should come to Him and allow Him to heal them.

This was followed by a reflection on the stone the individuals had chosen as they arrived. This came to represent the burden they were carrying and it was a profound moment for many as they came forward to place it on an image of the hand of God. Many were visibly moved especially when members of the diocesan Evangelisation Team handed them in return a white mercy stone along with a card with an image of the hand of God being held out to them. The 'mercy stones' were simply small clay stones which had been hand-made and prayed over by volunteers with a small cross embedded in, and the word 'Mercy' written on each. People seemed to sense the prayer in the making of the stones and several asked for a few more to take to those who had not been able to come to the service. This is again a reminder that healing ministry is not confined to the obvious ministers, or even to those physically present at the service.

For many this was enough but the service was extended to include the opportunity for Confession, anointing, spiritual listening and prayer stations at which to pray. A few left at this point, for baby-sitters and buses, but most stayed to enjoy a time of quiet reflection with music or to avail of the opportunities presented to them. The atmosphere of this phase of the service could be described as 'gentle chaos' which again was a little unnerving for some but the movement of people towards priests for Confession or to speak to a listener or simply to visit the prayer stations provided 'cover' for those who might otherwise have felt exposed. Priests were available in confessionals but most were on or around the sanctuary. This might have been off-putting but the comment was made by someone attending that they had seen such love and compassion on the priests' faces and realised that they really wanted to be as Christ to the people who came to them and thus they had themselves felt able to go forward.

The use of anointing evolved as priests discerned that this was something that people needed as part of the encounter. It was gently amusing to see the small jar of blessed oil being passed around the sanctuary as priests recognised the need in the person before them and sought to anoint and bring God's healing to them. One participant reported that the person they had come with had not been to church for over 30 years following family problems. They said that the look on the person's face as they laid down their stone was radiant and that, after going to a priest and receiving anointing, the person seemed transformed.

Listeners with counselling training were available including in some cases deacons with similar backgrounds. Fewer people went to them than anticipated but for those who did, their presence was invaluable. For women particularly the opportunity to speak to another woman was especially helpful. A listener might refer a person to a priest for Confession. Another small detail here is that it was recommended that the priest was named, as in 'If you go to speak to Fr S (*pointed out*), he will be able to offer anointing/absolution'. This highlighted the relationships and mutual trust between the ministers and reassured someone who may not have been near a priest for many years that they would meet compassion rather than the condemnation they may have encountered in the past. The listener's role did not end with passing on the person to a priest, but was extended to praying for God's blessing on the conversation that ensued. Thus both the priest and the person seeking healing and mercy were supported by the prayer of another.

This prayer support may also be one reason why communal services have become more popular. It is in a sense counter-intuitive that people exploring something deep within themselves should be willing to do so in public. Perhaps those television 'confessions' have helped people to be less inhibited but crucially the difference is in the audience. The congregation and ministers at the liturgy of mercy are not there as voyeurs but as participants. Every person there knows that their own life would not stand much scrutiny and so is not there to judge but to receive mercy for themselves. It may even be the case that, as with the woman who anointed Jesus' feet, (Lk 7: 36–50) those who have received the most abundant forgiveness and mercy in their own lives could be among the most powerful intercessors during this part of the service.

When Words Fail

In the Liturgies of Mercy a stone was used as part of a simple ritual. For some people this felt like a cliché, although clichés usually work. Again, for some there was scepticism and a feeling of being taken into something too touchy-feely to be comfortable; others felt it was too closely associated with counselling and therapy situations. However, being one of two hundred people (including the clergy) each reflecting on their stone, recognising in its uniqueness an echo of their own burdens, helped people to see again the value of symbol and ritual.

It is a self-evident fact that billions of words are spoken and written each day in hundreds of different languages. Our liturgies are often full of words and it is true that a word from scripture or a prayer, or a line in a hymn may speak to our condition at any given time. However there comes a moment in many a life when no word in any of the languages of the world can truly express what is going on in the depth of someone's being. As they sit and try to take in a diagnosis, or try to explain why they are stuck in their grief journey, or why they simply cannot forgive someone who has hurt them, words may fail. At such times symbol and ritual have a language that speaks to and from a deep part of ourselves. Science might eventually catch up with their undoubted efficacy, somehow measuring objectively the effects they have on people but, for now, the real-life experience of people from vastly differing cultures and religions is that objects and actions address aspects of the human psyche and spirit that words cannot reach.

In practical terms it is why images, objects and rituals can be so powerful in healing. As well as the stones and the anointing as part of the Liturgies of Mercy, there were prayer stations around the church. These were simply prompts for prayer in keeping with the theme, simple thoughts or activities to engage people more imaginatively or through their senses. They offered an alternative to sitting or kneeling in silent reflection for people who are more kinaesthetic, or who simply felt the need to move around as they plucked up the courage to go to a listener or priest. An example of a station was one using 'stretchy people', a very popular activity where the arms and legs of a small rubbery figure were stretched, representing how we often feel with the pressures and demands of our lives. After a few moments the instructions on the station suggested that the stretchy figure be allowed to come to rest in the palm of a hand, just as God calls each of us to rest in the palm of His hand.

Eventually of course, such experiences and even deeper healing may emerge into words and be confirmed in an ability to speak of them with others whom they can trust and receive from them understanding and compassion and perhaps prayer ministry. Also one might quite often find oneself, against all probability or design, sharing aspects of their experiences and need for healing with someone who needs to hear this story of healing in order to continue to move towards their own.

Summary

Jesus was quite explicit in His teaching of the disciples that healing of the sick was one of the priorities of their mission to the world. In the early years of the Church, it seems that people took this seriously with St Paul listing healers among those with specific ministries and St James giving simple instructions about visiting the sick. Over the centuries, this healing became elevated to the status of a sacrament and continues to be an outward sign of God's grace at work in the world. Many factors, some explored here but others that space does not permit, led to an understanding of this grace being the preserve of clergy to be used only at the point of the danger of death. Improvements in medical care have led to awareness that people can now be very seriously ill but with a reasonable chance of recovery. They may not be in immediate danger as in previous generations but will clearly deal more easily with the illness and its treatment with the added benefit of the healing grace of God. As a nurse-friend said to someone beginning to recover from a serious illness who had been concerned about receiving the Sacrament unworthily, 'You need us to do our jobs and we do, and your family to do theirs and they do, but you also need to allow God to do His!'

A deepening understanding from the world of psychiatry and therapy of the need for inner healing has also reawakened an appreciation of the healing grace of God in dealing with memories and feelings of guilt that inhibit someone becoming the person they were created to be. All these rediscoveries have perhaps led to a renewed sense of being the Body of Christ, each of us broken in any number of ways but united in the solidarity of the broken and risen Body of Christ.

Still seen by many as associated mainly with Charismatic Renewal, there are signs that the wider Church is reclaiming the gift left to her by Jesus. The role of priests is invaluable and precious but deacons and lay people are discovering their own gifts of healing which, used to complement the sacraments, offer a new and more collaborative model for healing ministry.

The Year of Mercy offered an opportunity for the Church to look more widely at the mercy of God. As Pope Francis reminds us, the Sacrament of Reconciliation enables people 'to touch the grandeur of God's mercy with their own hands',[4] but God's healing and mercy extend far beyond the graces of confession and indeed far beyond the Jubilee Year. As Pope Francis quotes his Latin American brothers saying, 'we can (no longer) passively and calmly wait in our church buildings'[5] but need urgently to go beyond their confines. A study[6] of the decline in the Catholic Church throughout the USA and the rising numbers in evangelical churches, concluded that most Catholic parishes were essentially looking inward: church-centred rather than Christ-centred. Some people may be drawn to a church but even more will be drawn to the love and mercy of God as seen incarnate in Jesus Christ. This great mystery reminds us that God's mercy:

> … is not an abstract idea, but a concrete reality with which (God) reveals His love as of that of a father or a mother, moved to the very depths out of love for their child. It is hardly an exaggeration to say that this is a 'visceral' love. It gushes forth from the depths naturally, full of tenderness and compassion, indulgence and mercy.[7]

God yearns to make His people whole and is calling on all His faithful, ordained and lay, to put aside their fears and reservations and to work with Him on this great mission to make His mercy and healing real in a world hungry for both.

Notes

1   *Catechism of the Catholic Church*, 1508, 1521.

2   *Pastoral Care of the Sick—Rights of Anointing and Viaticum* (1983), p. 10.

3   Pope Francis, *Misericordiae Vultus*, 15.

4   *Ibid.*, 17.

5   Pope Francis, *Evangelii Gaudium*, 15.

6   P. Hegy, *Wake up, Lazarus: on Catholic Renewal* (Bloomington In: iUniverse, Inc, 2011), pp. 3–4, 113–164.

7   Pope Francis, *Misericordiae Vultus*, 6.

Appendix 1

Inner Healing—Little by Little

The Story of Ann

Introduction

In order that prayer for inner healing can lead to deep and lasting inner peace and wholeness, it is necessary for much more than the healing of memories by Christ to take place. Part of the reasons for this lies in our early experiences having built up within us damaged patterns of thinking, attitudes, ideas, desires, beliefs, habits and behaviours. In childhood some of the strongholds are God-given defences which enable us to survive what is happening without being overwhelmed by pain. Examples might be self-reliance and denial. However, in later life we realise that these and many other strongholds are no longer working to our advantage but are coming between us and God and inhibiting our deeper relationship with Him and with other people. We find St Paul making reference to these strongholds which form in our unconscious and conscious mind: 'The weapons we use in our fight are not the world's weapons but God's powerful weapons which we use to destroy strongholds' (2 Co 10:4).

Just as the Israelites on their journey from slavery in Egypt to the Promised Land had to destroy many enemies, so we on our spiritual journey of preparation for heaven have to know how to destroy with the victory and authority of Christ, the enemies within us which have kept us enslaved to sin. For most of us this process of inner healing will be a gradual process over a relatively long period of time. 'Do not be afraid of these people, the Lord your God is with you'. He is a great God and one to be feared. Little by little he will drive out these nations as you advance. You will not be able to destroy them all at once. (Dt 7:21–22, Ex 23:29–30).

Healing—a Process

Each person is unique and occasionally God does a great deal of inner healing very quickly as for example in the case of a priest for whom another priest prayed briefly in tongues.[1] Generally however God, whose way is love, needs others who will pause in their own journey to care for and pray for those others they encounter who are badly wounded. When these latter people have suffered very grievously in many ways, and do not find priests and others with sufficient understanding, then their journey towards peace and wholeness can be a very long and painful one. This is the story of one such wonderful person who did not give up despite many setbacks, but for whom there were very many years of deep suffering before she found priests and lay people who begin to bring effective help with the grace of God.

Early Life of Ann

Ann has no distinct memories before the age of eight but she does know she was terrified of her mother. As a child she thought 'you are not nice and I don't like you'. She witnessed her mother's cruelty towards her baby sister and tried to protect her. There were constant physical and verbal fights between her parents and she would try to make things right, doing jobs to please, thinking that would make things better. Ann felt that she herself must have done something very bad for her parents to fight so much. She and the others would frequently be punished with a belt and Ann would say, 'I did it' even when she was not responsible, in the hope it would stop the belting. The husband of a friend began to visit the house while her father was at work. He would be drunk and the children would hide, and the mother would say, sh! She knew not to tell anyone. Ann was often terrified especially one day when this man walked into the bathroom when she was bathing. In these years Ann would talk to Jesus and Our Lady. For her it was as if they were her real parents.

Ann's years at primary school are a blur but there was bullying and she cannot remember playing with other children. At playtime she would often go and sit alone in the church next to the school and talk to Jesus. She was regarded as a dunce particularly by the teachers and the priest, and was bottom of the class. Thankfully things changed when she moved to secondary school, where she was mid-stream even coming first, second, fourth and sixth at some time. The teachers encouraged and praised her. When she was at the school she felt she was a person in her own right without burdens of fear and responsibilities.

Teenage Years

At home she witnessed many things involving her mother's boyfriends, knowing where and when they met. She would be taken on outings and told not to tell anyone. Even as a teenager she and the others had to be in bed by 6–7 pm. She saw her mother's dresses, jewellery, wigs and so on as she would get ready to go dancing with her boyfriend. Years later her father revealed to her that he knew about it but turned a blind eye feeling unable to deal with it.

At about ten, Ann was sexually abused by a man who had a garden plot with strawberries, peas and so on, who groomed her and lured her into the shed/greenhouse. Ann remembers some of the abuse and trying to push him off her before it all went blank. She cannot remember how she got home. She was in her late thirties when the abuse came to light and still cannot remember everything. She does know that she tried to tell her mother at the time but was told to be quiet, and when the man came to the house with garden produce she froze with fear.

When she was thirteen her mother planned to go away on a retreat. Her mother made an excuse not to go so her father went in her place. Ann saw her older siblings taking trunks of her mother's things out of the house. The day her father was due back home she walked to the bus stop and saw her mother and baby sister leave on the bus. The pain in that memory remained very strong. She felt numb, 'Will I ever see my baby sister again?' That night her father returned. She couldn't tell him what had happened because it had become so deeply ingrained not to tell. Ann broke her heart listening to her father crying night after night. After that her mother was never mentioned. No one was allowed to talk or tell anyone. It was as if her mother didn't exist. From an early age it had always been 'never talk to anyone.'

Ann begged her father to keep the family together and he said, 'If we all work together'. This was not how it worked out; her siblings never helped. Ann became her father's housekeeper and his confidante. It was as if she became the parent as her father dumped upon her responsibilities which were far beyond her age, and this role reversal always leaves a deep mark. Her father was very critical of everything she did. She was blamed for every wrong thing which her siblings did. She could do nothing right in her father's eyes or in her siblings' eyes. She became the scapegoat. Her father never listened to her needs but gave constant lectures.

Ann would beg for help as the responsibilities were too much to bear, only to be told, 'You're alright, take a tonic and you'll be fine'. Eventually she became resigned to just getting on with it. She had come to feel that she was a non-person, nobody's child, that she had no rights. She came to the conclusion that she deserved it all because she must be a terrible child. 'Maybe one day someone will notice me.'

Her uncle sexually abused her and her sister. Then at fourteen a teenager sexually assaulted her but she was able to break free and ran home. She said she had fallen over as she was a mess but needed to remain strong for the sake of her younger siblings. She was petrified with no one to talk to and scared to go out.

Ann had no decent clothes and didn't know how to deal with personal hygiene. Her life was just home, chores and school. She felt stupid, useless and that she knew nothing. She left school so as to work at home unpaid to look after the family. Eventually she plucked up courage to get a night job and then a full-time job, but still had to look after her father and siblings. She began to witness others of her age having freedom to socialise, but if occasionally she went out she was made to feel guilty if all the jobs were not done. She begged for help but none was given. She felt that she died inside, with constant fights, refusal of help, unnoticed, ignored. She gave up, feeling there was no point to it all, but then a doctor lectured her which was what she needed, as she decided to pick herself up and keep going, 'I can do this'. She was attacked by two of her mum's men friends and by a family friend.

Marriage

When she began courting she came under pressure and criticism if she had a day out because the chores were not done. No one else would do them. When she planned to marry they piled on emotional blackmail, 'How will we cope? I'm not going to do these jobs, who will look after us if you leave?' She almost had a breakdown and even after she married she continued with her responsibilities to look after her father.

At first her marriage appeared normal. However it became clear that he was a controlling bully. They planned to have a child but after the birth he turned to drink. It was only later that she learned that before they met he had been a drinker, boy racer, a gambler and in debt. He accused her of having affairs, told her 'the brat' was hers and that she and the child could live off the family allowance. He would ransack the house for money, pin her against the wall, verbally abusive straight into her face and then punch the wall next to her face. She was terrified and couldn't sleep. He threatened to take the child away. Ann would sit in the child's bedroom crying, desperate for help. She would put the child in a pushchair and walk the streets, frightened to go home. She begged the bank manager for money and asked the pub landlord to stop accepting his cheques to no avail. When she went for help she got the following responses:

Police: It's a domestic.

Priest: Go back to your husband.

Social Services: Sell your belongings.

Family: Your child needs a father.

Doctor: you are depressed.

At times her husband would disappear for days or weeks and she never knew when to expect him back. Then he would sexually assault her in degrading ways. He claimed to have bugged the phone and booby-trapped the car. He would ring her father and verbally abuse him and say 'Come and get your ** daughter and your grandchild'. Ann's family would tell her not to be so soft with him. She blamed herself, feeling 'I'm not a good wife or mother, I'm good for nothing.' Eventually her husband put her and the child out of the house with just what they wore. When the police came to escort her back to get some belongings, her husband laughed and joked with them. She felt totally rejected.

For eight months she lived with her father earning her own and the child's keep. Her child began to be blamed and criticised; history repeating itself. Ann was accused of wrongly handling the divorce, and sat in the box room with two bin bags of possessions, crying, and desperate, hurt, alone, abandoned and frightened. Her ex-husband continued to be abusive and harassing. She didn't get social security payments because her ex-husband claimed falsely that he was paying her. He convinced magistrates, judges, police, friends and a priest who didn't believe her. Even the police welfare officer tried to kiss her when he visited her father's house, so she had to stop him coming. Her own siblings ganged up on her with her ex-husband.

Following Divorce

Fortunately she became involved in BE, Beginning Experience (see Chapter 11), at a local retreat centre. She began to receive help and encouragement to keep going and protect herself and her child. But she still lived in fear of the child being abducted by the father. The council gave her a house which was a wreck and she had no money or furniture. When her child said, 'Can we sleep tonight?' that gave her the strength to keep going. It took another two years to claim attachment of earnings from her ex-husband, who continued to barge in drunk, abusive, hostile. She was not given police protection because it was just a domestic. The husband of a friend made unwanted advances. The school gave little support. The family continued to criticise her. A fellow parishioner said that she had no right to receive Communion.

When Ann became self-employed, her ex-husband took her to court claiming that she had higher earnings. These cases which stretched over a long time, were soul-destroying as he destroyed her character. She was forced to change her phone number over a dozen times, to keep the doors locked and her child could not play out freely. At ten her child was bullied and belittled by a teacher, coming close to a nervous breakdown. Ann felt let down by the head teacher and the priest, Change of school improved the child's happiness but there was lasting damage, because the child, now grown up, had lost faith in teachers, people, priests and God.

Ann was receiving help and support through BE, with a prayer partner praying for her. She began to experience the beginning of the spiritual healing for which she had yearned for years. She met priests and lay people talking about childhood traumas and telling her that she had done nothing wrong. She was moved at the loving warmth which she received from priests and lay people ministering to her using their God given gifts. At a church mission a priest recommended a spiritual director and more of the blocked past was revealed through prayer with laying on of hands and Ann began to feel the beginnings of wonderful healing. Ann was introduced to a lady who continued the healing through listening and praying, and she was able to join her prayer group, but with the problem that she could ill afford to travel to the meeting place.

Grandchild—a Mirror to the Past

Then Ann learned that a grandchild was on the way which led to many years of struggle and suffering trying to protect and care for her grandchild. It has involved three tribunals, and when the relationship with the parents and grandparents had broken down, Ann's family pulled away from her telling her she had no rights and showing hostility. She became in her words 'a wreck desperately seeking healing', and yet in the midst of this she began a prayer group which was very powerful with praise of God and people praying with one another. She had to go through stages when the court placed the grandchild with the mother who was mentally disturbed, so Ann had a hysterical grandchild clinging to her, begging in desperation to be allowed to live with her rather than go back to the mother. There was a five-year battle of a dirty, hungry, exhausted, frightened, neglected grandchild who would not go upstairs, hysterical if doors were shut, the child crying for hours before going home under court order. Ann, who could ill afford to do so, refurbished the grandchild's home, thinking that the mother was receiving help. She paid the debts but the child's mother turned nasty. Ann cried day and night seeing the desperate, pleading eyes of her grandchild, knowing that the child was left home alone at five years of age, locked in the bedroom or left to find food.

Ann would hug her grandchild and speak about Jesus. The child began to ask Jesus to protect Ann because of threats made against her by the child's mother. He said, 'I talk a lot to Jesus and tell Him to look after you, I won't let them hurt you Gran.' Thus history was repeating itself as Ann had spoken with Jesus as a child.

Ann's own child (the grandchild's father) remarried and sent her a solicitor's letter accusing her of keeping the grandchild away. Ann was devastated and went to sort things out only to be told to leave. The pain, hurt, loss, fear and anguish of not seeing any of them for months were unbearable. The grandchild has been neglected by parents, supplied with drink, abandoned while the child's mother went on holiday or nights out from the age of eleven.

Ann found it very difficult to open up to priests because of all her past experiences. When she did make the attempt they often did not know how to help and referred her to others. She now realises that this was because she did not then know how to reveal and express her emotions and that some priests have had no experience or training in how to help in family traumas, abuse, divorce, substance misuse, racism etc. It is not easy for anyone to become proficient in helping in any area of human distress purely through head knowledge. It is only when one has increasing personal contact with those in deep suffering as some priests do all too frequently, that really effective help and healing results in empathic listening and prayer.

Experience of working with people in difficulties of many kinds, teaches us that we do not need to have immediate solutions. Jesus was brilliant at giving individuals His whole attention (for example in Mk 7:31–37). In healing the deaf man 'He took him aside in private, away from the crowds.' Learning from Jesus, the first requirement in helping is to receive individuals with respect, compassion and seriousness. We share a common humanity and we all appreciate the kind of attentiveness that signals that we are valued. Being willing and unafraid to listen is a hallmark of those who minister in the name of Jesus. How we receive people is crucial. It may well have taken great courage for the troubled person to come in the first place and he or she will pick up immediately the non-verbal signals of acceptance or reluctance. A priest once offered the thought that perhaps to have been the receiver of the full attention of Jesus was so liberating that the Lord didn't need to do anything else. The received wisdom of groups like the Samaritans demonstrates the sacredness of being good listeners. Gentle, non-judgemental and non-directive listening is not accusing but in fact honours the person seeking help and creates the trust to enable them to return. Only God knows the full story. We place ourselves in His hands to feel the way for the next step.

The ability to reflect on the differences between those who have listened or ministered to each of us-and those who have not, may help to show the importance of taking the time to be there for another wounded pilgrim on life's journey. To acknowledge our own need for help can be a rich resource to enable us in our turn to help others.

Ann was often told by people and priests such things as, 'You are hanging on to things of the past, you should be better now. You are doing it wrong which is why you are not healed'. There have been many books which Ann read suggesting that there should be a quick fix. It raised questions or statements in Ann's mind such as 'How could I be fully healed when my childhood is still surfacing?' 'The abuse is buried so deeply I might never fully know about it'. As outlined in Chapter 14, Ann has only recently become aware that some parts of her seem to have split off to protect her from being aware of the full severity of her pain. Her subconscious mind has also tended to say, 'You deserved it; you are unworthy'. She has realised that she was held back till recently by saying as a child 'I'm alright, I won't show my feelings to anyone. I'll get by'. Ann was also held back for a long time after prayer ministry by people she felt were genuinely concerned to help, by being plagued by such thoughts as 'I'm stupid, I'm full of self-pity, I wonder what they really think of me'.

Present Day

Now at last Ann is becoming more free to love and accept herself and to praise God through many kinds of prayer ministry and help which has enabled her to reveal her past and to release to Christ on the cross, burdens of anger, pain, guilt, poor self-worth and so on. She has found help from prayers and support at the retreat centre, a parish priest, intergenerational healing Masses, healing services, prayer groups and ministry from others. She writes that, 'without Jesus and Mary walking with me and all these people using their gifts in ministry, I would still be a crippled, fearful shell of myself. I want to share this so that many more will know and receive the Lord's gift of healing'.

We Need to Learn from Ann's Experiences

The healing of deep roots requires much listening and discernment. Having been hurt so many times and in so many ways and not having anyone in her childhood who would listen and try to understand her pain and her needs, Ann buried her distress and hurts. Her personality was strong enough to avoid her crumbling under it all, and she learned to get by on her own without revealing the depths of the pain within her. In fact, she remembers saying to herself, 'I will never let others see just how I feel'. When eventually she began to seek some help she subconsciously displayed some bravado to the people and priests she turned to, so that they were misled. They did not become aware of the depths of her hurts and needs. One priest said, 'Why are you not crying?' He and others gravely underestimated the depths of pain and despair; it is only relatively recently that she has had the gift of tears about some of the hurts. Those to whom she went were not able to see past the image which through bitter pains she had learned to present. They did not understand that she was just looking for people who would listen and pray with love and sensitivity. She was not looking for experts. Since the healing of deep roots of hurts was not taking place, a number of Christians blamed her for going back over old ground and accused her of wanting to hold on to wounds and pain rather than move on.

'Through His Wounds We are Healed.' (Is 53:5)

Thus, over the years, many of Ann's tentative attempts to seek help did not bring about deeper lasting peace and healing, but instead left her mind churning away, feeling guilty that she was doing things wrong as she was being accused. Each failed attempt to get lasting help meant that it took longer and longer before she could make a further attempt to seek help. Her thoughts would be a jumble of confusion, poor self-worth and guilt, constantly blaming herself for holding on to hurts and not moving on. Ann used the phrase, 'It was like being tumbled about inside a washing machine'; of course it was not being washed clean but going round and round with all the dirty water sloshing about in her mind. When Jesus draws out our pain through His wounds into His suffering on the cross and gives us the grace of forgiveness, He cleanses us with the living waters of the Holy Spirit in a very gentle process.

Growth of Trust and Openness

It says in Psalm 32:3–4, 'All the time I kept silent my bones were wasting away with groans, day in, day out; day and night your hand lay heavy upon me; my heart grew parched as stubble in summer drought'.

Thus if we begin to speak out as Ann eventually did and try to reveal to other Christians more of the inner pain and all we meet is insensitivity, unawareness, helplessness to assist or even condemnatory comments, then we are driven back for a while into our silence. Now however it is worse than the original silence had been before the cracks in our defences started to appear. Each knock back from a failed or limited attempt to get help can set up fresh barriers. These drove Ann back into guilt and feeling that people were only trying to help out of sympathy and pity. This reactivated old memories of childhood with people making untrue accusatory statements to her. These had become deeply ingrained in her mind. Early on in the process these false statements were entirely in the subconscious mind, but even after Ann became aware of them, it was still a battle for her to recognise them as untruths and to become free from them through prayer and speaking the truth to herself, particularly to the child within herself. Thankfully today, Ann is emerging more and more into the light and truth of being the wonderful creation of God which she is. The Lord has greatly blessed and gifted her and is using her in many ways to help others.

Notes

1   A. Guile, *Journey into Wholeness: Prayer for Inner Healing—An Essential Ministry of the Church* (Leominster: Gracewing, 2013), pp. 46–47.

Appendix 2

The Testimony of a Cenacolo Brother

We have so much in Common

When I was asked to write this little testimony of my life and what I got from my time with community Cenacolo I was glad, glad to have the opportunity to share a little of myself, and glad to have the opportunity to reinforce this important passage in my life. However, as I reflected on the key events in my walk, I realized that I could never truly convey their importance, their depth or their true essence as I lived it. For it was and is my experience and mine alone. Nevertheless, I believe that we all have many shared human experiences, and I believe that whoever reads this will in his or her own way understand. What do a 57-year-old Asian heroin addict and a 23-year-old Spanish seminarian have in common? At first glance it would seem nothing, or not a whole lot! But once I got to know them both on a deeper level, it turned out that they had a whole lot more in common than what separated them! And me! The human person experiences fears, hopes, failures, victories, the need to be loved, and the fear of loneliness. One thing I learned in the community is that we are all much more alike than we are different, we are all children, we are all human. And, thanks to my fall, and thanks to the community, today I feel more awake, more alive, and more truly human than ever before.

My Early Life

It all started about 29 years ago in Poland, where I was born to a hard-working mother and father, with an older brother and sister. When I was only one my father left for work in Canada, as did others who had the chance. He worked very hard, and sacrificed much. For three years he worked and saved in Canada as his wife and three children waited in Poland. Eventually he bought a house, and in 1989, when the Berlin Wall fell, and the borders opened, we joined him in the 'Promised Land'. Here began a new struggle. Mostly for my parents and siblings, as I was only four, and don't remember the whole thing, but I felt the residual effects later in my life. My mum, who was a respected engineer in Poland, was unable to find work. Her degrees were not accepted in Canada, and she didn't speak English. So she worked nights at a coffee shop, and days stocking shelves at a bargain store. My brother who was eight and my sister who was twelve were bullied at school for being different, strangely dressed, speaking no English. They often came home crying, but my overworked and stressed parents were rarely home, and lacked the strength, and the ability to comfort them. There was a total communication breakdown, not that it was all that great before (so I have heard).

You see, my father is a good man. He never yelled, never raised his hand against any of us, he worked very hard to put a roof over our heads, and food on the table. What he lacked was the ability to show affection, to communicate. He was like this, because his father was like that, and his father was like that, because his father was like that, and so things go, father to son, father to son. Thus I became, a hardworking, kind man, who was incapable of effectively sharing affection or communicating.

Early Experiences of Drugs and Alcohol

When I was thirteen years old, I smoked my first joint. Honestly, it was completely out of boredom. We lived in a suburb, where there was nothing to do, and as I didn't play sports, and I was not particularly popular, not at all actually. I had nothing to do by myself. I found some weed, and called a friend, and we got high, and I was no longer bored, I found my hobby. After that day I quickly began to smoke weed every day. I began to make friends smoking weed, it became my identity. I had finally found something I was good at, somewhere I belonged. From morning till night I would smoke. I got a job washing dishes at a bar to support my habit, and there I made more friends, and began to drink. The drinking helped me to open up, be more fun, less shy, and that felt good. At the age of thirteen, the doorway to adulthood when I should have been developing important life skills, suffering with puberty, hormones and all that other good stuff that shapes a young adult and prepares him for life I was zonked out. You see, I didn't like to suffer, and I discovered I didn't have to. All it took was a hit from the bong, a drink of vodka, and poof! The problem was gone! But little did I know it wasn't gone. The problems didn't disappear, they would crawl behind me, slowly they would creep up, but I was faster, and I could just keep avoiding problems, and if I just kept going they would not catch up. So I kept going, and it really didn't seem like a big deal at the time. If I was feeling sad, I knew how to adjust that, shy, no problem, angry, anxious, lonely, whatever the suffering and discomfort, I knew the escape route.

Deeper Addiction and Depression

At seventeen I went to college, and after being dumped by my high school sweetheart, I fell into depression. There were such strong feelings, such strong pain, I was way over my head, I needed something stronger, and I found cocaine, and that's how I dealt with it, the same way I dealt with everything, run away, anything not to feel. Anyway, things went on this way. My drinking and drug use slowly but surely escalated, I began to escape physically from places, even moving across the country at the drop of a hat once. In the middle of the night I just got on a plane and flew across the country without telling anyone, just up and left. Those years and years of problems I had avoided were close behind, and I was getting tired. The more I drank to run away, the more the problems piled up, and the more I had to drink to stay ahead, and like this I went along, this is the downward spiral.

Crying out to God

I was no longer drinking and taking drugs socially, I stayed at home, too embarrassed to be seen. I would black out on average four times a week, with no memory of entire days. I feared what hid in those blackouts, so I drank more. One night, I remember clearly, it was 3am, I was out of drugs, and there was not enough liquor to knock me out. I began to feel and I cried, and cried, and cried. I felt so desperate, so absolutely hopeless, disgusted by who I had become. I began to pray. I screamed in my heart, I screamed so loud it must have shook heaven, because I know inside myself, that that prayer was heard, that desperate prayer began a new path for me.

So you probably think that things got better after that night? No, not right away anyway, first they got worse, within two weeks I lost my job, my apartment, and was in the hospital with alcohol poisoning, and this was the answer to my prayer, I hit bottom, the last things that held me were gone. I remember being in the hospital bed, my mother crying, and for the first time I felt a taste of freedom, freedom from that mask I was wearing, saying that everything was alright. The mask was off and for the first time I was being seen for what I truly was, a mess, a desperate mess. So now that the cat was out of the bag. After a week in detox, I began to search for a rehab. Looking online I was shocked to see the prices! On average $200 a day! My parents were ready to sell the house to pay. Thankfully we found Cenacolo, a free program, and the best part, it was in Florida!

Entering Cenacolo in Florida

I called the local contact for my area and went for working days on a 3-day orientation, and a couple of weeks after that, I packed my bags and entered. It was quite a shock. I left Canada 28 November 2012. I left in a blizzard and a couple of hours later I got off the plane to be greeted by palm trees and the Florida sun! I felt pretty silly in my winter coat. When I arrived at the house I was given a Guardian Angel, a guy who had been in the community for a while, to help me during my first month. The job of a Guardian Angel is slowly to incorporate a new guy into community life. The community is built on fraternal correction, so everyone tells everyone what they see in them and this would no doubt be overwhelming for someone new, so for the first month, only the Guardian Angel is allowed to correct the new guy, and there are lots to correct!

The community life is far from outside life. Everything is governed by rules. I was now in a new world, one with no drugs, no alcohol, no TV, no news, no smoking, no Internet, no phones, no radio, no money, no girls, no girls, no girls!! But anything was better than where I was. I was willing to do anything to be free, so I went along. When I entered I didn't feel much of anything, I was still in a haze, mostly numb. I could feel only shadows of feelings, but with each passing day they became stronger, clearer. The first feelings were the negative ones. I remember cleaning the bathroom mirror. I hated mirrors, I tried to not look at my reflection; when I saw myself I became sad, angry, disgusted. My body ached from the long days of work, and I couldn't sleep. Through all of this however there was a silver lining. A tiny satisfaction deep inside me, I glimmer of hope was being born. I was fighting, I was getting my butt kicked, but I was fighting, and I wasn't alone. The days went on, each hour a lifetime, the days felt like months. Each day I became a little stronger, my body adjusted, I began to sleep. Oh sweet sleep, how long I have not been able to sleep without getting drunk.

Learning Hard Lessons which built up Fortitude

I was put to work in the garden. The only problem, the garden was currently a forest. So first we had to clear the woods. It was full of snakes, and giant orange spiders with black legs, and all kinds of foreign things. The huge Florida sun overhead burning my pale Canadian skin. There was a small bulldozer. I was sure that's how we would clear the woods which would be the logical thing to do! No, we went in with shovels, machetes and axes and cleared them by hand. Then we took out the roots, by hand, then we turned the soil, by hand, hulled away the wood and you guessed it, by hand. We put up a fence, built a shed, and finally, we could start to garden! So we made rows, seed by seed we planted all sorts of things. To water we had to fill a trash can on a little cart and pull it over, about 200m, four trips a day, then water, by hand.

After a while, the first plants began to sprout! I felt so satisfied! All that work, all that suffering, and finally, there was something to show for it! Each day we watered them, and they grew and I was glad. And then one night, came a frost and killed all the plants! My heart fell. But, we didn't give up! We cleaned the dead plants, one by one we re-seeded, and we watered, and they grew, and I was glad. Then one night the temperature fell and there was another frost and again it killed everything! Once again, we cleaned up the dead plants. One by one we re-seeded, watered, and once again they grew and grew and grew. I was so proud, we didn't give up, and now the plants were over a foot tall, and there was no more frost!

Then one day it began to rain, and it rained, and rained and rained. For three days it poured down non-stop. After it finally stopped, we went out to see the garden. The nearby pond burst its banks and flooded the whole garden. The plants were a foot tall and the water was a foot and an inch deep. The pond fish were swimming through the tomato plants! The water went down, the land dried, we cleaned up, re-seeded, watered, and then, well I don't know because I was transferred to France! Hehe! I tell this story because it taught me a valuable lesson in fortitude. I am very proud of that barren garden, not because it was beautiful, or produced, but because we didn't give up. My time in the community provided a wealth of such lessons. Mother Elvira always said that the community is not a rehabilitation, it is a School of Life. I have discovered that these lessons sank into me in a deep way because I lived them and felt them on my own skin. All the lectures in the world would not have taught me as much as that garden.

The Move to Cenacolo in Lourdes

I arrived in Lourdes after six months of community. It is a beautiful house on a hillside under the Pyrenees. This was a very difficult time for me in the beginning. The house was much larger from my last one, the languages were French and Italian, neither of which I spoke. I quickly felt out of place, lonely, and far from home. I felt trapped, and I began to feel that I was cured, that I no longer needed to stay in the community. After two months in France I couldn't take it anymore. I asked for my things so I could leave. I called my parents to advise them, and ask them to get me a ticket home.

To make a long story short, they would not help me to leave. At first when I heard their response I was in shock. I didn't feel much of anything, I couldn't understand. And then, all at once, like a ton of bricks fell on my head, I was flooded with emotions. I was gripped with an all-encompassing anger, towards them for not helping me escape, at myself for getting into this mess, at the community, at God. I could have left, I had a visa with $5000, and that was enough to get back to Canada on my own, or start a life in Europe. I can't explain why I didn't leave that day, I was so angry, and so fed up, and escape was so close. The Holy Spirit began to speak inside of me. I felt the truth that I did not want to see. I knew that if I left then I would go straight to a bar, I would fall harder than before. I decided to stay. Anger and spite became my fuel. I told myself that I would stay until I was strong enough to leave on my own, that I would never so much as look at my parents ever again, that I would become a happy and successful man and never forgive them. It's strange, if you would have asked me before that day, I would have told you that I had a good relationship with my parents, but the truth was that it was superficial. There were many wounds, and unsaid things that had settled in the bottom of my soul. Like a pond with clean water, into which a stone is thrown. The stone hits the bottom and all that sediment is kicked up. That is what that moment did to me. All the unforgiven things of the past came up all at once.

The Darkest Period of my Life—Unwillingness to Forgive my Parents

What followed was probably the darkest period of my life. Although I had very hard and dark times before community, I was never forced to live them truly, there was always an escape. But not this time! For three months I lived and breathed anger, I had trouble sleeping, eating, every time I closed my eyes, I saw myself hurting my parents. And this was all perpetuated by the fact that I couldn't speak to anyone about it. Even the priests that came for us to confess spoke only Italian or French. After all these months of constant pain, I couldn't take it anymore. One night I went to the chapel. I knelt in front of the Holy Sacrament and I reluctantly prayed. I prayed that He would lift this anger from me because I could not carry it any more. I still wasn't going to forgive my parents; I just didn't want to suffer with it any more.

The community teaches that it is important to lose the face or to say what you think, so this is what I felt I should do. After lights out I would go to the chapel to try and write a letter to my parents to tell them what I was living. I wrote my first long letter, read it, and threw it out. Re-wrote, read, threw it out; re-wrote, read, threw it out. I did this a bunch of times until I realized that I couldn't explain what I was living in a substantial way; the only way for them to understand would be for them to be there.

Working with my Father—Leading to Reconciliation

From this was born the desire that my father might come to do an experience and live alongside us for a while. I finally settled on a letter, it was just a couple of lines, asking my dad if he would come for an experience. He accepted and returned to France with us and stayed for ten days. I was working in the stables at the time, and the deal was that he would be alongside me the whole time. So that meant 4:30 am off to milk the cows! Then wash up, 6 am rosary, 7 am breakfast, then back to work, harvesting hay (by hand) under the hot sun and herding the cows, 12 noon lunch, praying, back to work till 6 pm, prayer, dinner, and then finally bed. Rinse and repeat. It was really something to experience how this hard work and disciplined routine brought us together. This suffering together in my experience created a much stronger and deeper bond then say, a weekend on the beach. We were reliant on one another to pull this weight. One day while we were working together I began to tell him what I felt towards him: the betrayal, the anger, the confusion. Thanks to my time in the community I was now for the first time capable of communicating what I was living. I had been talking for a while and realized that he wasn't saying anything. I turned around to look if he was listening. He was standing there, making a weird face, one I had never seen on my dad. Then I realized, he was holding in tears. He came up to me and wrapped his arms around me, and cried. Inside of me, I felt the anger melt away, all the hate, the spite, the expectations, everything, just melted away. And then I began to cry. And we just stood there, hugging and crying. For the first time I saw my father as a poor, wounded child, just like me. This was arguably the most important moment of my adult life! All the suffering, all the pain, everything I had been through was worth it for that one moment. I still find it amazing how God will turn the worst darkness, into the most splendid light if I only let Him.

After this powerful experience with my father, I was fuelled up to continue my walk. That was the first tangible fruit I had received from my walk. Something real, and outside of myself had changed, my life was changing and so was that of my family, and I wanted more.

Reconciliation with my Mother

Later I was transferred to Italy, where my mother came and, also did an experience. This was also an important moment in my walk. A curious thing occurred that I saw clearly through my relationship with mum. In the past our relationship was often superficial. The energy it took me to keep secrets from her, and to present myself only as the person I thought she wanted to see, distorted everything. Now that I was in the community, all of my masks were off, my poverties which I was very open about were on the table, and I had nothing to hide. I simply appeared as the person I was, including many unattractive things. What I found is that it was at this point that a much deeper and more rewarding relationship was created between us. I showed my fragility at risk of being hurt, and was accepted with greater love. This in turn prompted my mum to be more open with me, she also took off some masks, and for the first time I saw her fragility. Before me was a young, scared child, just doing her best, with regrets, fears, broken dreams, and hopes. This was a part of her I had never seen, and the reality of it allowed me to love her much more deeply. I was able to stop my expectations of what she should have done, or should be like, and lovingly accept her how she truly is. This was a big moment for us.

The Blessings of Real Humanity in Cenacolo Community

There is so much to say about what I lived in my time in community, but I think I can sum it all up with the word humanity. There was such a richness of human interaction, the good the bad and the ugly. I was able to accept others as they are, with all their poverties, with much empathy and understanding. This led ultimately to me being able to finally accept myself for who I truly am, and that led to increased inner peace. I think that is the key to my healing. Not that things are without struggle or easier now, because they are not, they are real, and that is beautiful! Today I can say that I am thankful for my story, and I am so thankful to community for being the platform through which the Lord could touch my life in such a beautiful way. I will finish with a quote from Community Cenacolo's foundress, Mother Elvira:

> In the darkest night it is possible to find light again. Even in the darkest sadness, joy can be rekindled. Even in the bitterest loneliness, a friend's love can pierce a hardened heart. Yes, we want to be witnesses of this hope. We want to announce to this world that the secret of rebirth is to open our hearts to that marvellous Father who waits for each of us as His most precious child.

Lightning Source UK Ltd.
Milton Keynes UK
UKOW01f2154020817
306562UK00003B/14/P